Filippo Pedrocco

TITIAN

SCALA/RIVERSIDE

CONTENTS

The illustrations for this volume come from the SCALA ARCHIVE, which specializes in large-format colour transparencies of visual arts from all over the world. Over 50,000 different subjects are accessible to users by means of computerized systems which facilitate the rapid completion of even the most complex iconographical research.

© Copyright 1993 by SCALA, Istituto Fotografico Editoriale, S.p.A., Antella (Florence)
Layout: Ilaria Casalino
Translation: Susan Madocks
Photographs: SCALA (M. Falsini, M. Sarri) except for nos. 6, 7, 13, 22, 41, 42, 64, 66, 86, 93, 94 (by courtesy of the National Gallery, London); nos. 12, 23, 83, 84 (Duke of Sutherland Collection, on loan to the National Gallery of Scotland); no. 17 (A. Guerra); nos. 20, 21, 56, 69, 70, 71, 77 (Prado, Madrid); no. 28 (Gemäldegalerie, Dresden); nos. 59, 62, 78 (by courtesy of the National Gallery of Art, Washington); no. 74 (Gemäldegalerie, Kassel); no. 85 (by courtesy of the Isabella Stewart Gardner Museum, Boston); no 88 (Fotografía cedida y autorizada por el Patrimonio Nacional, El Escorial); nos. 90, 102 (Izobrazitelnoye Iskusstvo); nos. 27, 92, 104 (Kunsthistorisches Museum, Vienna); no. 96 (The Saint Louis Art Museum); no. 98 (by courtesy of the Fitzwilliam Museum, Cambridge); no. 103 (Museum Boymans-van Beuningen, Rotterdam)
Photocomposition: "m & m" Fotocomposizione, Florence
Colour separations: RAF, Florence
Produced by SCALA
Printed in Italy by Amilcare Pizzi S.p.A.-arti grafiche Cinisello Balsamo (Milan), 1993

1. Birth of Adonis, detail
Padua, Museo Civico

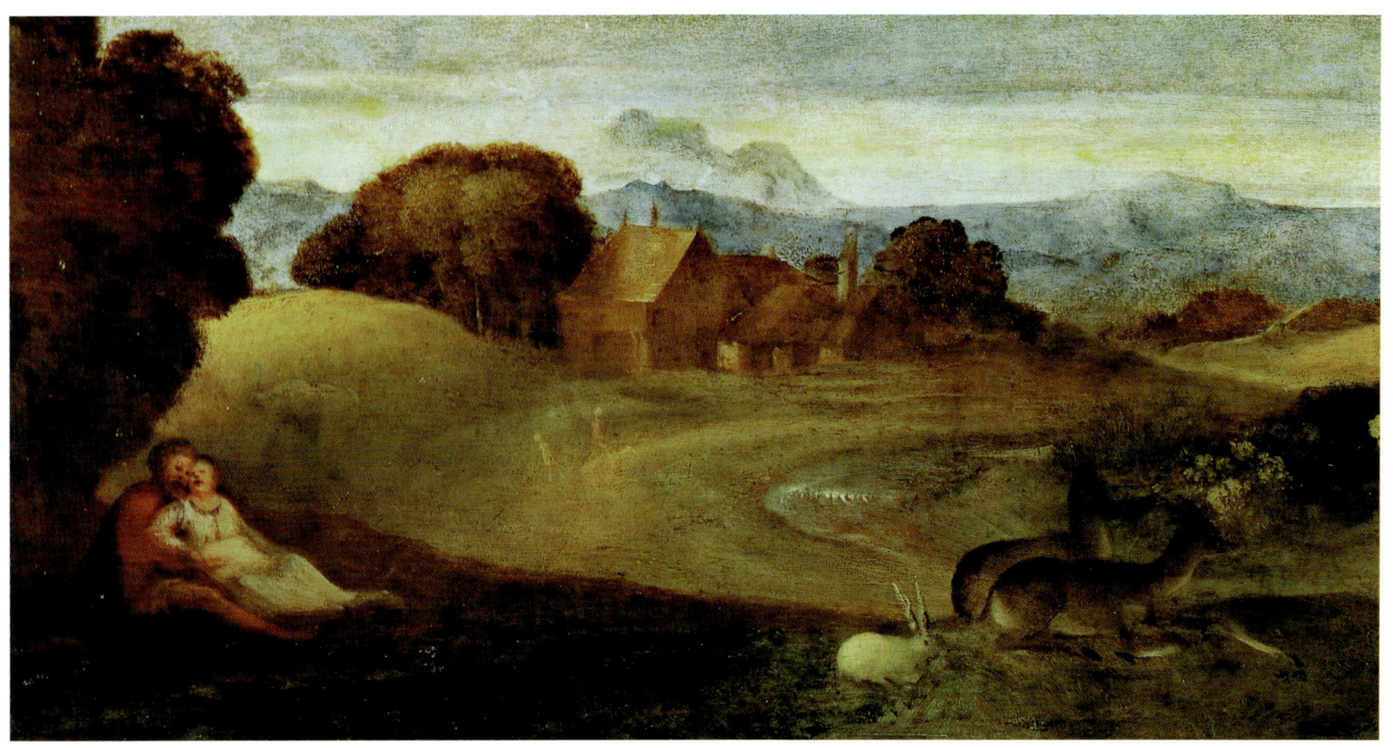

The Early Years

Tiziano Vecellio was born at Pieve di Cadore into a family of ancient roots and distinguished traditions. No document records the precise date of his birth which has long been the subject of much critical debate: the problem is not insignificant since it involves the piecing together of the chronology of Titian's early works. A document in the register of deaths of the parish of San Canciano in Venice, where the painter ended his days on the 27 August 1576, states that he "died at the age of a hundred and three" ("morto de anni cento e tre") thus leading a body of critics to deduce that he was born in 1473. This theory that Titian was over a hundred years old at his death seems to find confirmation in a letter of 1 August 1571 to Philip II in which the painter laments the fact that he was then ninety five years old.

This reconstruction is at odds with the written testimony of some of his contemporaries. In the second edition of the *Lives of the Artists*, published in 1568. Vasari maintains that Titian was 76 years old at the time of their meeting in Venice in 1566. Dolce, writing in 1557, states that when Titian was working on the frescoes of the Fondaco dei Tedeschi between 1508 and 1509 "he was only just twenty". So, on the basis of these accounts, Titian was born sometime between 1488 and 1490.

The third theory is based on the presumed dating of an early work, the votive altarpiece, now in Antwerp, depicting *Pope Alexander VI Presenting Jacopo Pesaro to Saint Peter*. This was painted to celebrate the defeat of the Turks at Santa Maura on 30 August 1502: the victorious papal fleet was led by Jacopo Pesaro while his cousin Benedetto commanded the allied Venetian fleet. Some critics believe the altarpiece should be dated close to the event with which it is so explicitly linked; this means fixing Titian's birth date in the first half of the 1480's since he must have been at least twenty when he painted the altarpiece.

Out of the three hypotheses the second one still seems the most likely. In fact, leaving aside the information supplied by Titian's contemporaries, which certainly came from the painter himself, it should be pointed out that if Titian really was born in 1473 his earliest works would have been produced unusually late in his life — when he was over thirty years old. On the other hand the proposed dating of 1503-1506 for the Antwerp altarpiece is by no means certain. In fact it should be given a later dating, placing it just before the altarpiece now in the sacristy of the church of the Salute and datable to 1510, with which it has notable stylistic similarities.

The contemporary sources agree that Titian was a particularly precocious artist. Little more than a child when he arrived in Venice, he and his brother Francesco entered the workshop of Sebastiano Zuccato, father of the San Marco mosaicists Valerio and Francesco. Titian then passed into the workshop of Gentile and Giovanni Bellini, the leading artists of the day. Here he met the rising stars of Venetian painting, Sebastiano del Piombo and Giorgione. It was above all with the latter that Titian had the most contact. So much so that in 1508 and 1509 both young painters worked, although probably not simultaneously, on the decoration of the facade of the recently constructed Fondaco dei Tedeschi. Giorgione was given the main facade on the Grand Canal while the younger Titian got the side giving onto the street — the 'calle del Buso'.

Very little has survived of this imposing decorative scheme which was celebrated with enthusiasm by contemporaries. The ruined figure of a *Nude* by Giorgione and five fragments by Titian's hand are preserved in the Galleria Franchetti of the Ca' d'Oro in Venice. By comparing for example Titian's so-called *Judith* or *Justice* with the Giorgione *Nude* it is easy to pinpoint the essential differences which divide the two artists at this stage. Titian is dynamic and severely vigorous in his depiction of the powerful female figure caught in the act of trampling on a bleeding head; the drawing is incisive and the colour realistic. Giorgione, on the other hand, immerses himself in a stylized elegance, adopting a self-consciously artificial colour scheme

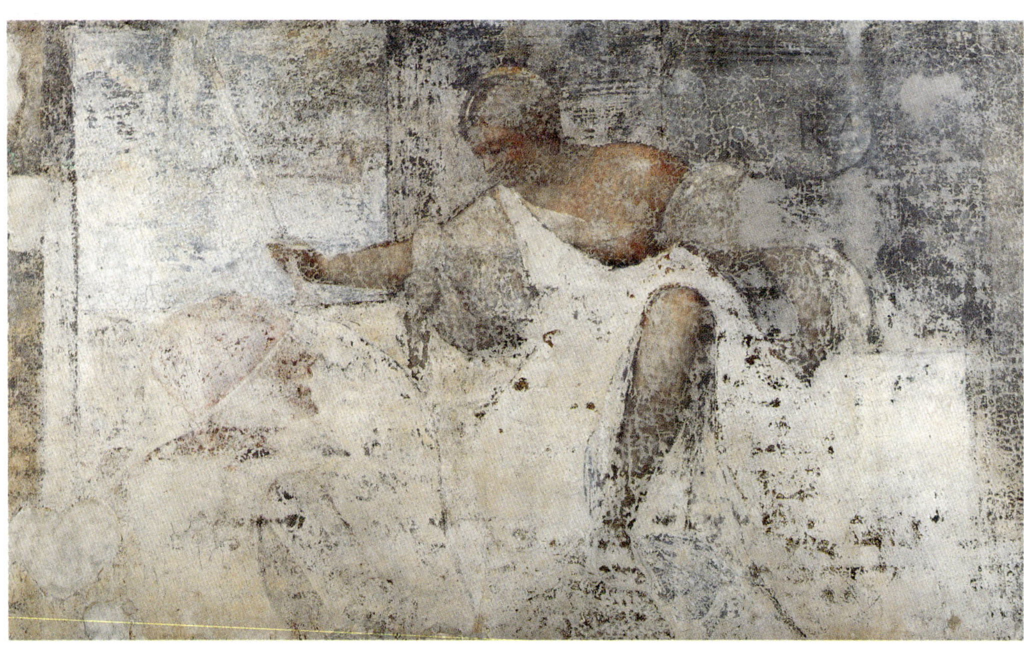

2. *Judith (1508/1509)*
212x345 cm
Venice, Ca' d'Oro

3. *The Legend of Polydorus (c. 1508)*
35x162 cm
Padua, Museo Civico

4. *Birth of Adonis (c. 1508)*
35x162 cm
Padua, Museo Civico

5. *Orpheus and Eurydice (c. 1508)*
39x53 cm
Bergamo, Accademia Carrara

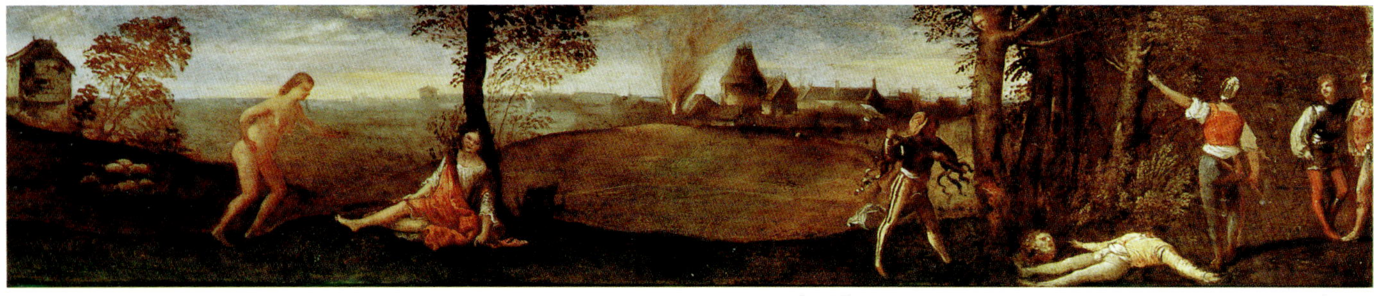

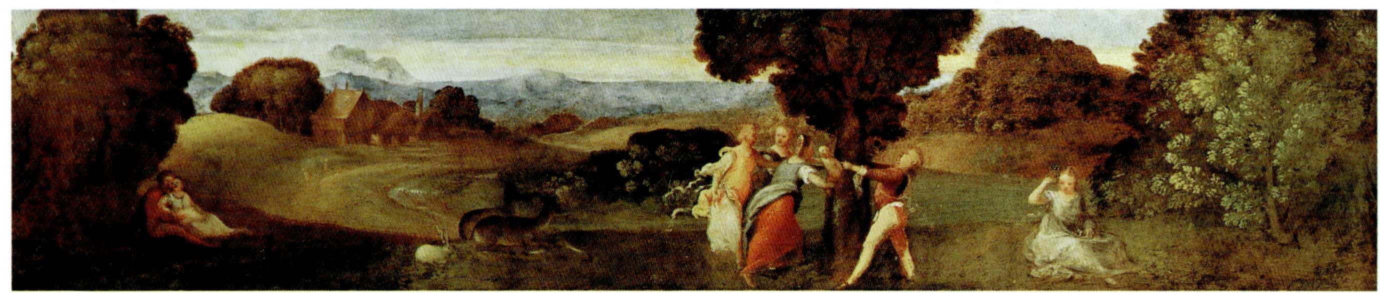

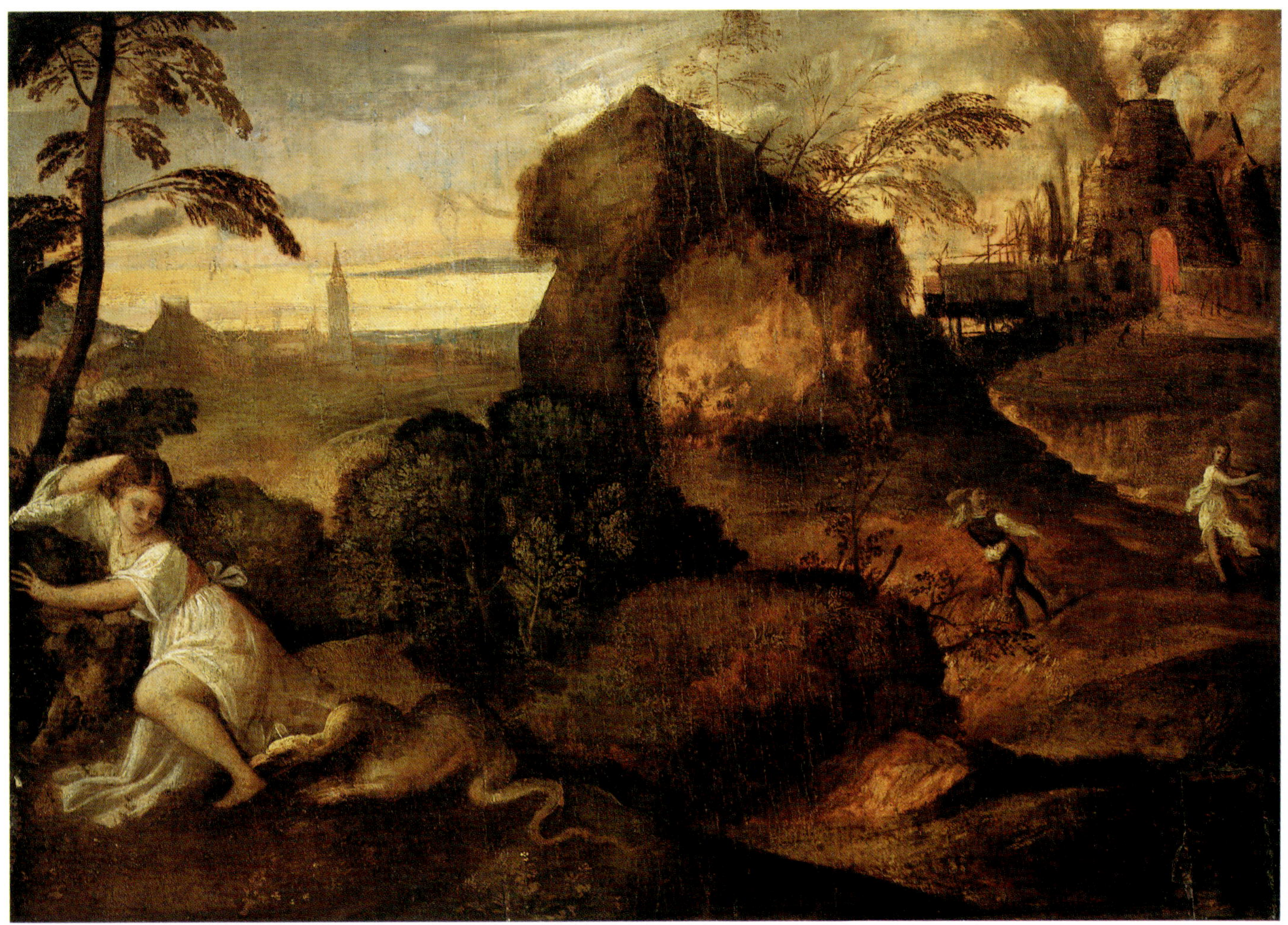

— that "tinta sanguigna e fiammeggiante" ("blood-red and blazing hue") commented on by Anton Maria Zanetti in 1760. Generally speaking Titian's Fondaco frescoes are more nordic than classical in spirit; possibly the intent was to exalt the civic and military virtues of the Venetians in the face of any possible enemy and in particular against the German army of the Emperor. Indeed, the end of 1508 and the beginning of 1509 was a particularly difficult period for Venice, with storm clouds gathering on the horizon as a result of the terrible danger constituted by the League of Cambrai. It is evident in this and in other early paintings of Titian that he was interested in the works of the numerous northern artists then in Venice. Prominent among these was, of course, the figure of Albrecht Dürer who was present in the Venetian area for the first time in 1494-95 and then again in 1505-06 when he was invited by the German merchants of the Fondaco to paint the *Madonna of the Rose Garlands* for the vicarial church of San Bartolomeo. There is no doubt that the very young Titian was part of that band of local painters who (as Dürer himself recounted in a letter to his friend Pirckheimer in 1506) tormented Dürer during his days in Venice, pursuing him right up to the door of his studio in their efforts to divest him of drawings and ideas. Titian's interest in the northern world is also documented by Vasari, who recalls how as a young man the painter had extended his hospitality to a number of German artists so that he could learn from them the secrets of landscape painting, and that the young Titian also used to study animals "from life". Vasari mentions this in reference to Titian's painting of the *Flight into Egypt* commissioned by Andrea Loredan; this is identifiable with the canvas now in St Petersburg. But many other paintings dating from the very earliest years of Titian's activity reflect this deep interest in the realistic depiction of the natural world; for example the 'cassone' (wedding-chest) panels from the Padua Museum, the *Landscape with Endymion* of the Barnes Collection in Merion and the *Orpheus and Eurydice* in Bergamo. The portraits from this period are also strongly realistic. Of remarkably fine quality are two portraits in the National Gallery, London; the *Portrait of a Man* (early critics erroneously identified it as a portrait of Ariosto; it is perhaps a likeness of Titian's earliest patron — a member of the noble Barbarigo family) and a portrait of a woman

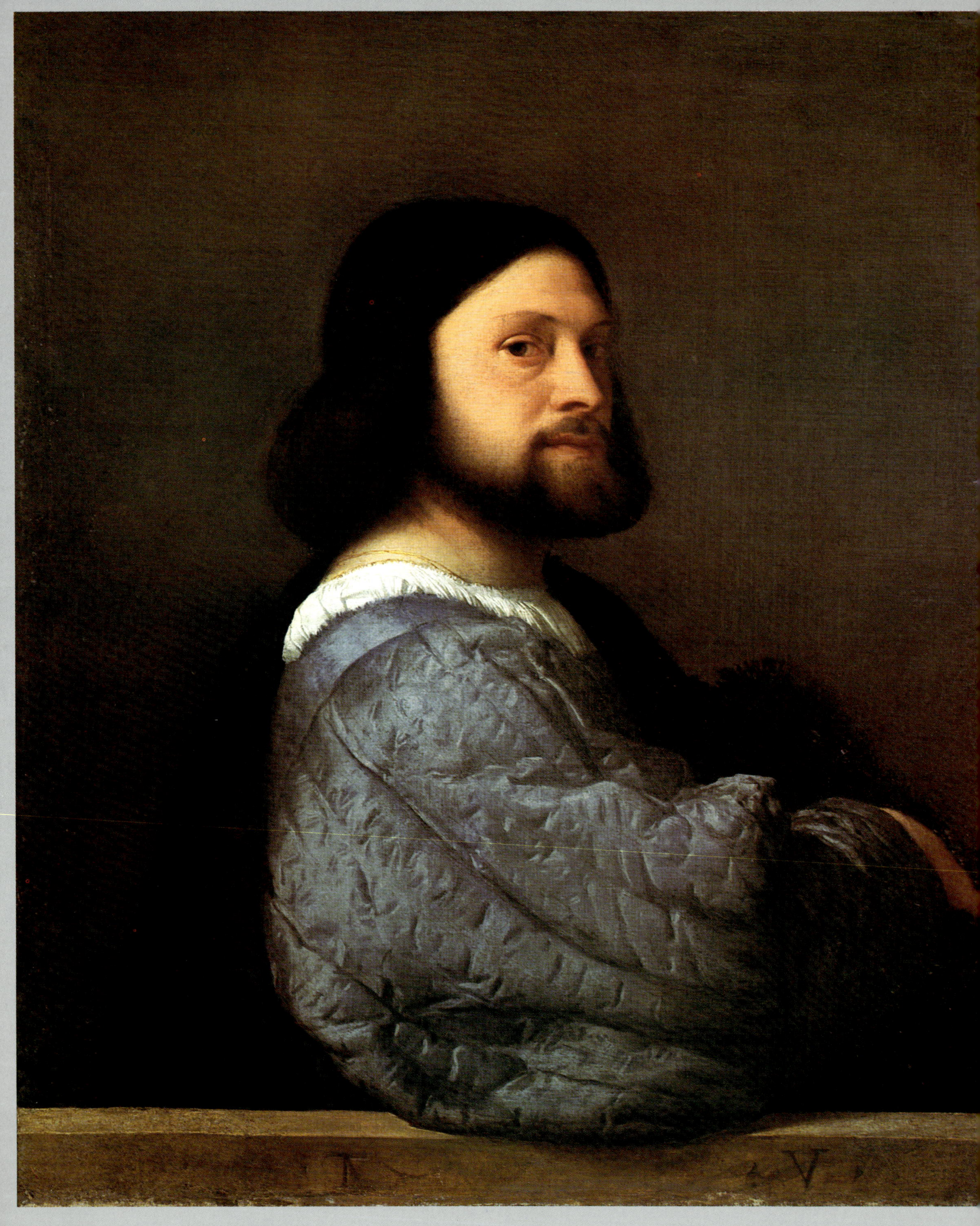

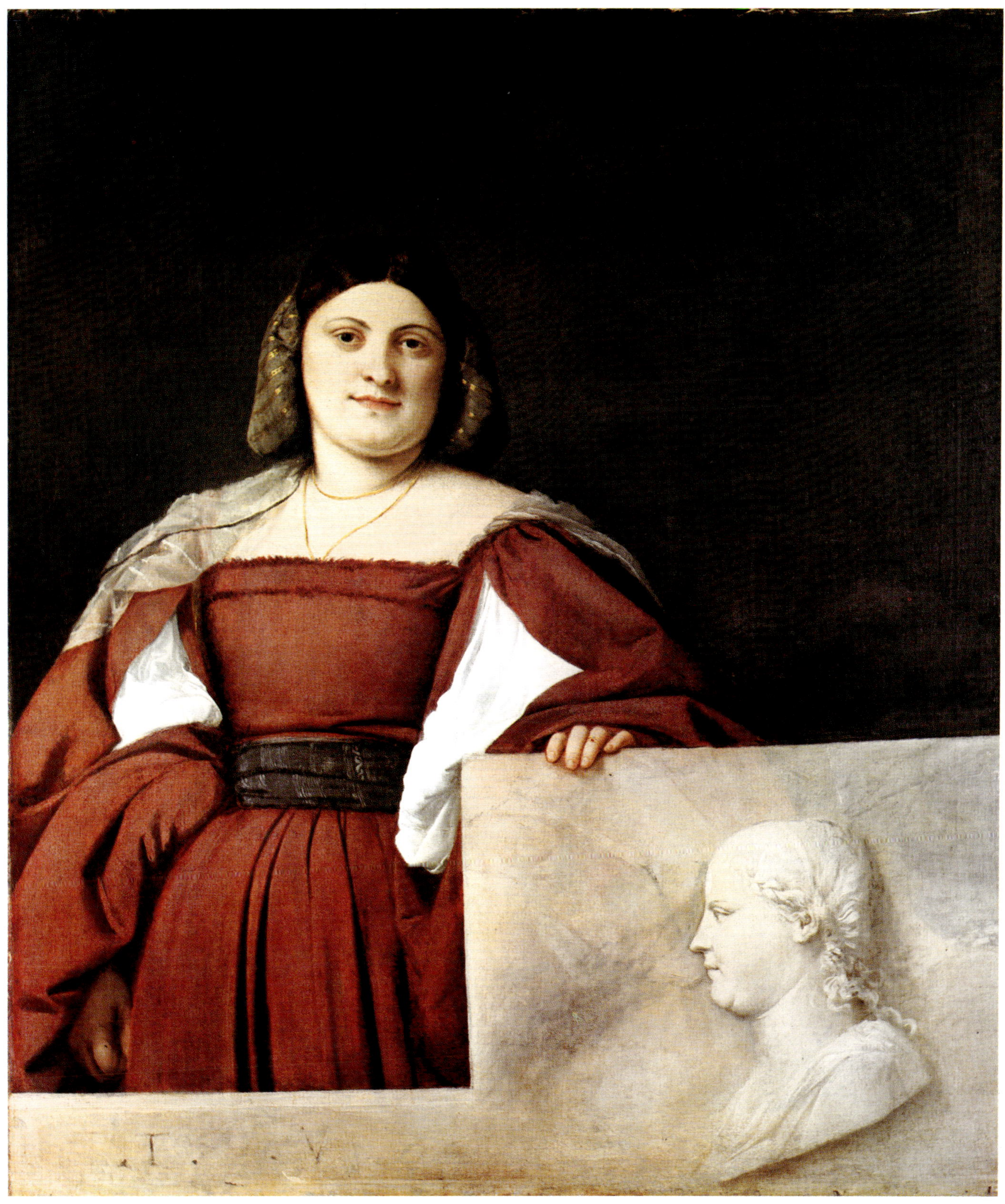

6. *Portrait of a Man (1508/1510)*
81x66 cm
London, National Gallery

7. *Portrait of a Woman called 'La Schiavona'*
(1508/1510)
117x97 cm
London, National Gallery

known as *La Schiavona*. With unrestrained skill Titian poses these personalities in such a way as to make the most of a novel compositional idea; the figures stand out in bold relief against the plain background and the colour emphasises the unusual lighting, revealing the mood of the sitters as well as capturing their physical presence.

"He saw and understood the idea of painting perfectly"

In these portraits Titian paints in a new, straightforward style which challenges the sentimentality of Giorgione. This departure from the latter's style is, however, less evident in Titian's religious paintings. Among his youthful works a good example is the altarpiece for the church of Santo Spirito in Isola (now in the sacristy of the church of the Salute) painted to celebrate the end of the tragic plague which had struck the city in 1510. Here the four saints who are traditionally invoked for protection from the plague — Saints Cosmas and Damian to the left, Roch and Sebastian to the right — are placed in pairs on each side of the altar where Saint Mark, patron saint of Venice, is seated. A new stylistic direction is evident in the way Titian paints the four standing saints. They have a classical nobility of form and a hieratic air which points to the influence of Bellini. On the other hand, the saints on the left — certainly portraits — are given a very realistic sense of individuality which is in strong contrast to the almost Giorgionesque reserve of the figures to the right. The Santo Spirito altarpiece seems to assume a significant position in Titian's artistic development; it comes at that moment when, following the death of the thirty-three year old Giorgione in the autumn of 1510, Titian reflects on his example. This reflection results in works of the very highest quality of style and poetical feeling: the *Interrupted Concert* (Pitti Palace) the *Fête Champêtre* (Louvre), the London *Noli Me Tangere* and the *Three Ages of Man* in Edinburgh. It is not surprising that these works have been the subject of scholarly debate concerning their attribution to either one of the two artists.

The Pitti *Concert* is centred on three figures who emerge strongly from the dark background: a singer, a harpsichord player and a Dominican friar who holds a viola da gamba. The less imposing figure of the singer is placed a little further back in the composition, while that of the musician (who looks over his shoulder without interrupting his playing) and the friar dominate the painting with their expressive poses and vigorous three-dimensionality — qualities common to Titian's portraits such as the so-called *Ariosto* in London.

The Louvre *Fête Champêtre* is even more reminiscent of Giorgione's style. Here the pastoral subject matter imposes a certain restaint on the emergence of those stylistic and psychological qualities which characterize the early work of Titian. It now seems indisputable that this painting is by Titian's hand, although it is so replete with Giorgionesque elements (the interplay of light and colour and the complex composition, for example) that any doubts in the past as to its attribution were more than justifiable. On the other hand, the typically Titianesque qualities of the canvas lie in the tense handling of colour and drawing, the vitality of the scene, the resonance of the colour which seems to be almost saturated with light and the studied sensuality of the figures, with the two magnificent female nudes who are much more provocative and physical than, for example, Giorgione's Dresden *Venus*.

In the Edinburgh *Three Ages of Man* the young

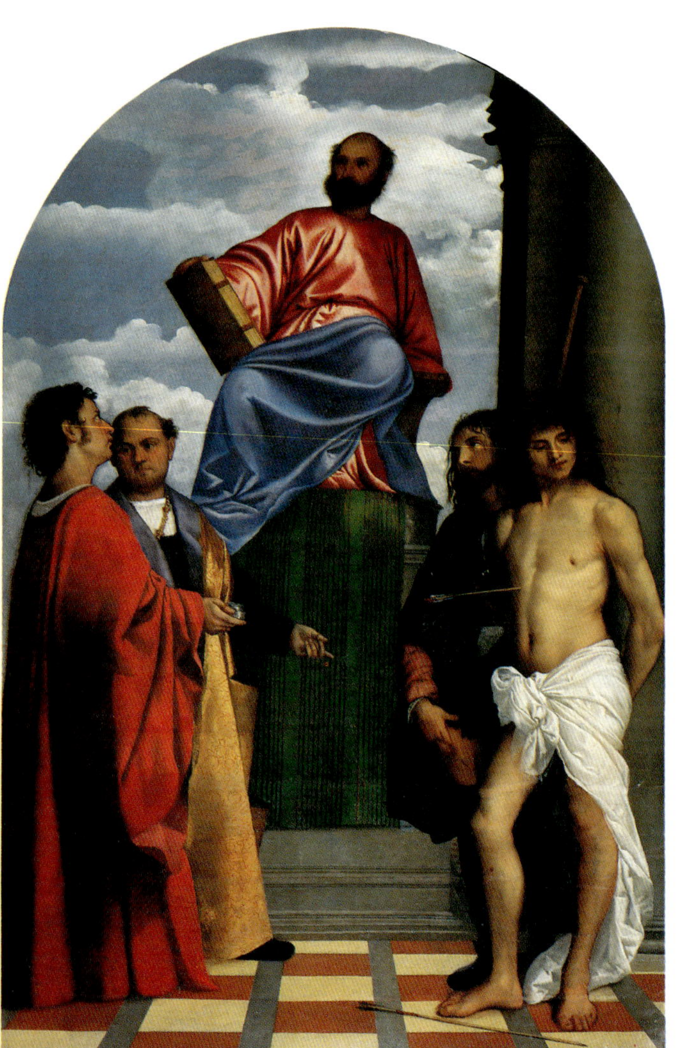

8, 9. St Mark Enthroned with Saints (1510)
230x149 cm
Venice, Church of Santa Maria della Salute

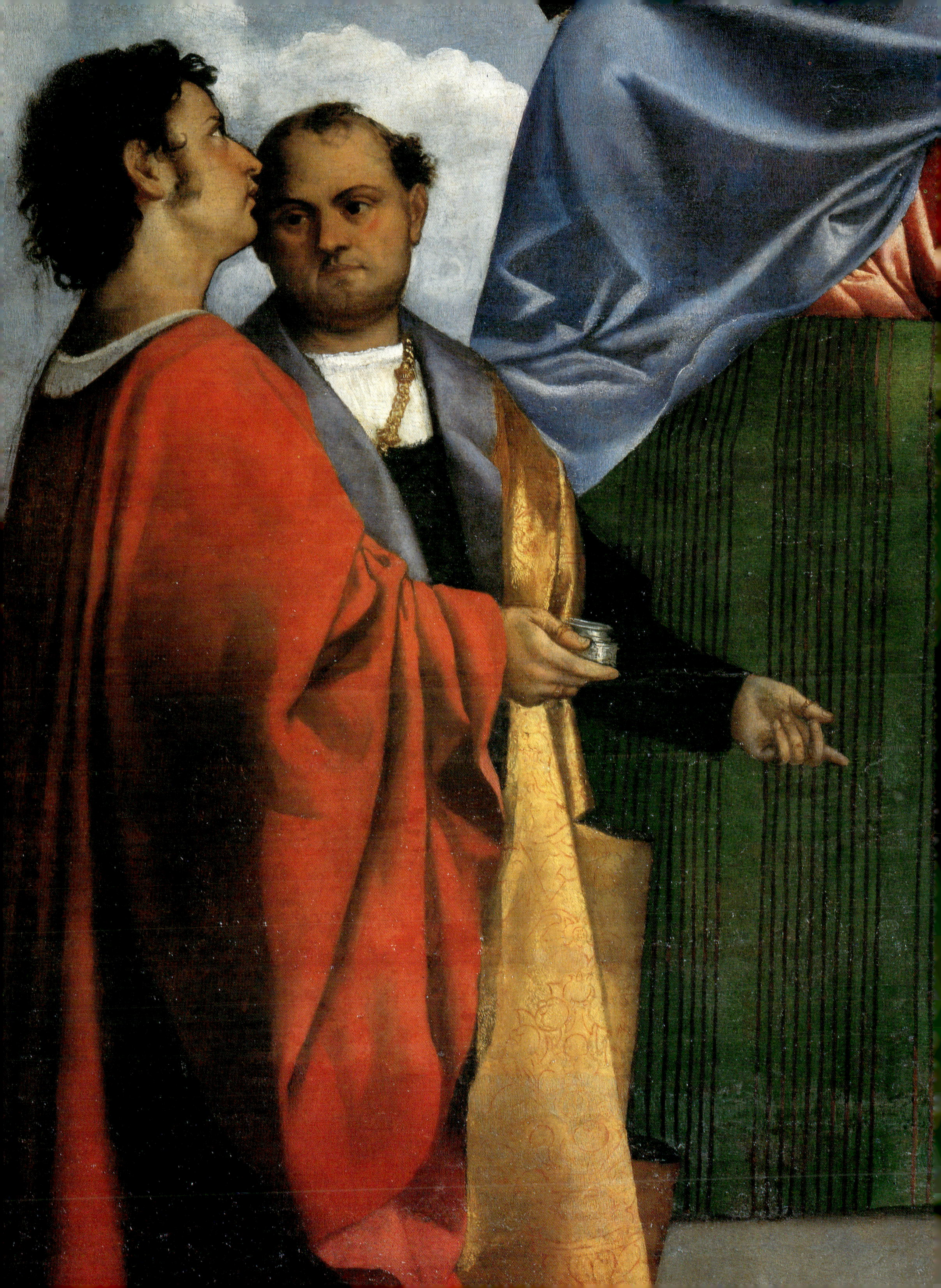

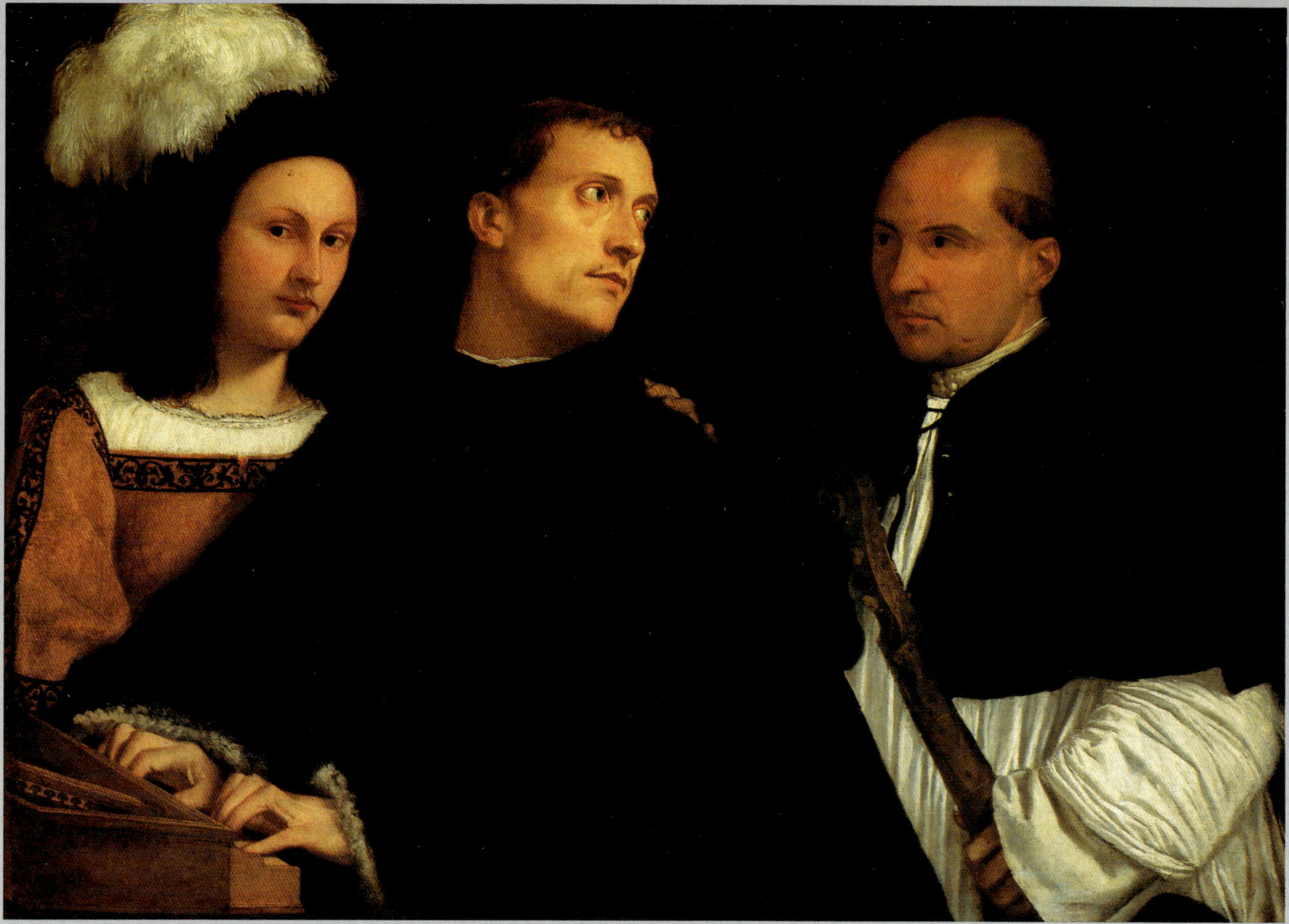

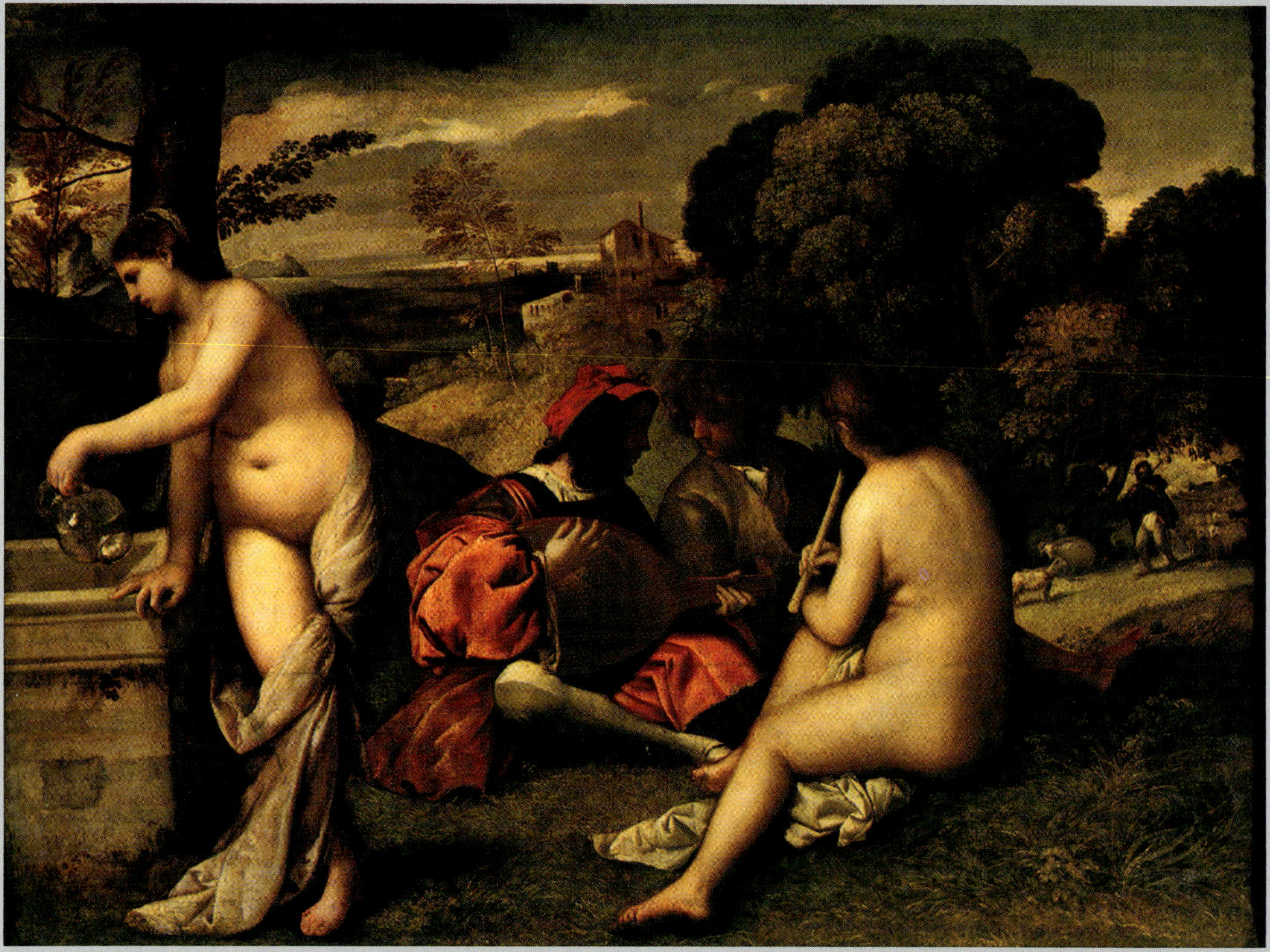

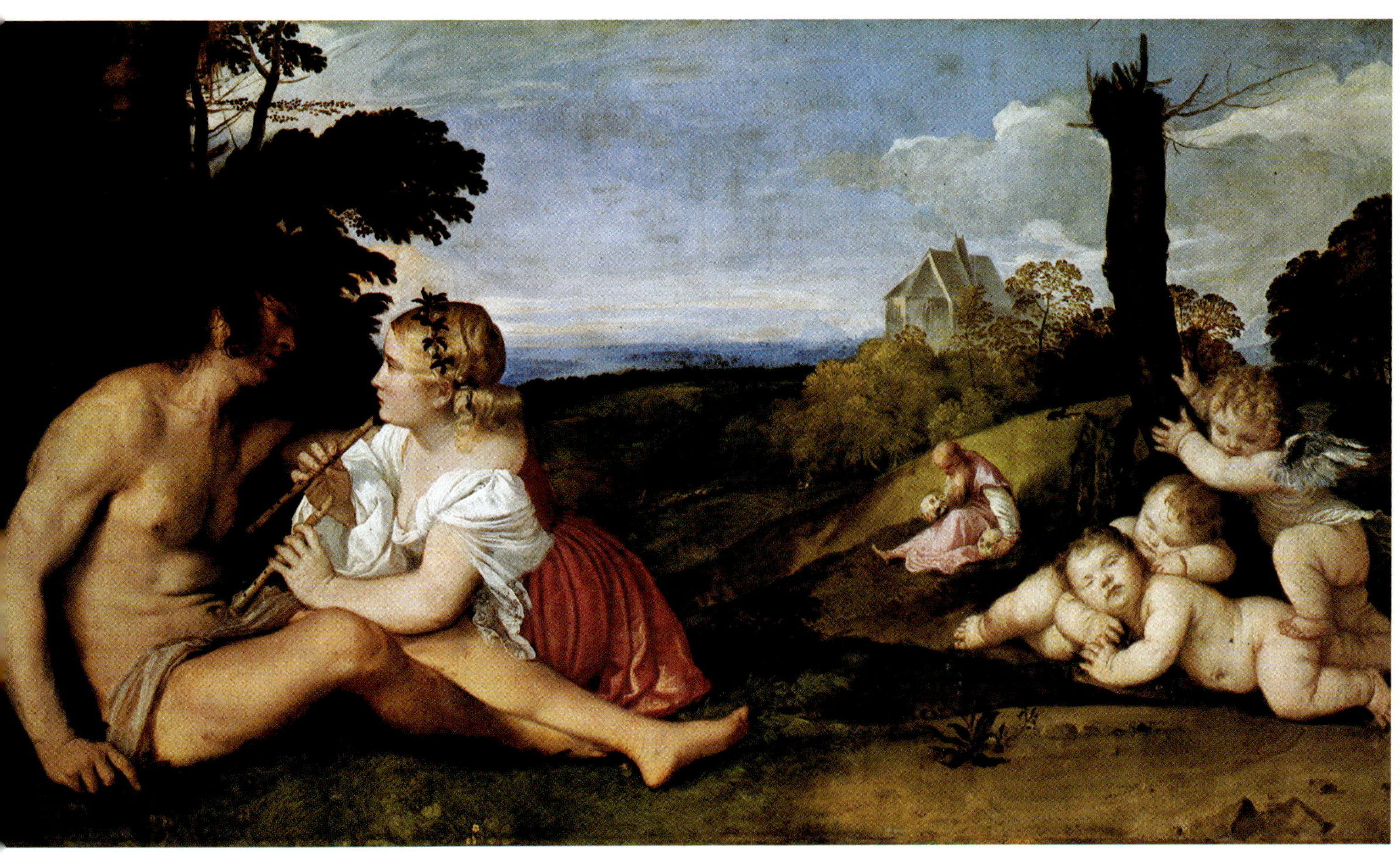

10. *The Interrupted Concert (1511/1512)*
86.5x123.5 cm
Florence, Galleria Palatina, Pitti Palace

11. *Fête Champêtre (1511/1512)*
105x136.5 cm
Paris, Louvre

12. *The Three Ages of Man (1511/1512)*
90x151 cm
Edinburgh, National Gallery of Scotland (on loan from the Duke of Sutherland Collection)

Titian again reaches the heights of poetic feeling. It has been rightly noted that: "the teaching of the old masters is transported beyond any idealized concept of beauty'or intimist dream, in favour of a feeling of *joie de vivre*. This is created through the way in which the generous forms, painted in large areas of colour, and the splendour of the sumptuous hues are offset by the recession into space through alternating areas of luminosity and atmospheric half-shadows". It is precisely in Titian's use of full-bodied colour, made more incisive by the light which gives lustre to the brilliance of the tones, that Titian is so unmistakably different from Giorgione, even when he is imitating Giorgionesque themes.

These three paintings are linked not only stylistically but also thematically; they illustrate the concept of musical harmony as a reflection of cosmic harmony. In the *Noli Mc Tangere* Titian abandons the esoteric themes of the learned humanist circles to return to religious subjects, although Giorgionesque elements are still very evident. For example the group of houses overlooked by old city walls to the right of the painting derives unchanged from the background of Giorgione's Dresden *Venus*.

The frescoes carried out by Titian in 1511 for the Scuola del Santo in Padua also bear the imprint of Giorgione's influence. In addition to the finished frescoes — the *Miracle of the Newborn Child* on the north west wall, the *Healing of the Wrathful Son* and the *Miracle of the Jealous Husband* both on the north east wall — Titian planned a fourth scene, although he only got as far as the remarkable under-drawing, discovered in 1969. The subject of this fresco is unclear; it perhaps illustrates one of those numerous miracles performed posthumously by Saint Anthony. The finished frescoes show Titian painting in a straightforward, expressive style typical of the didactic tradition of Fran-

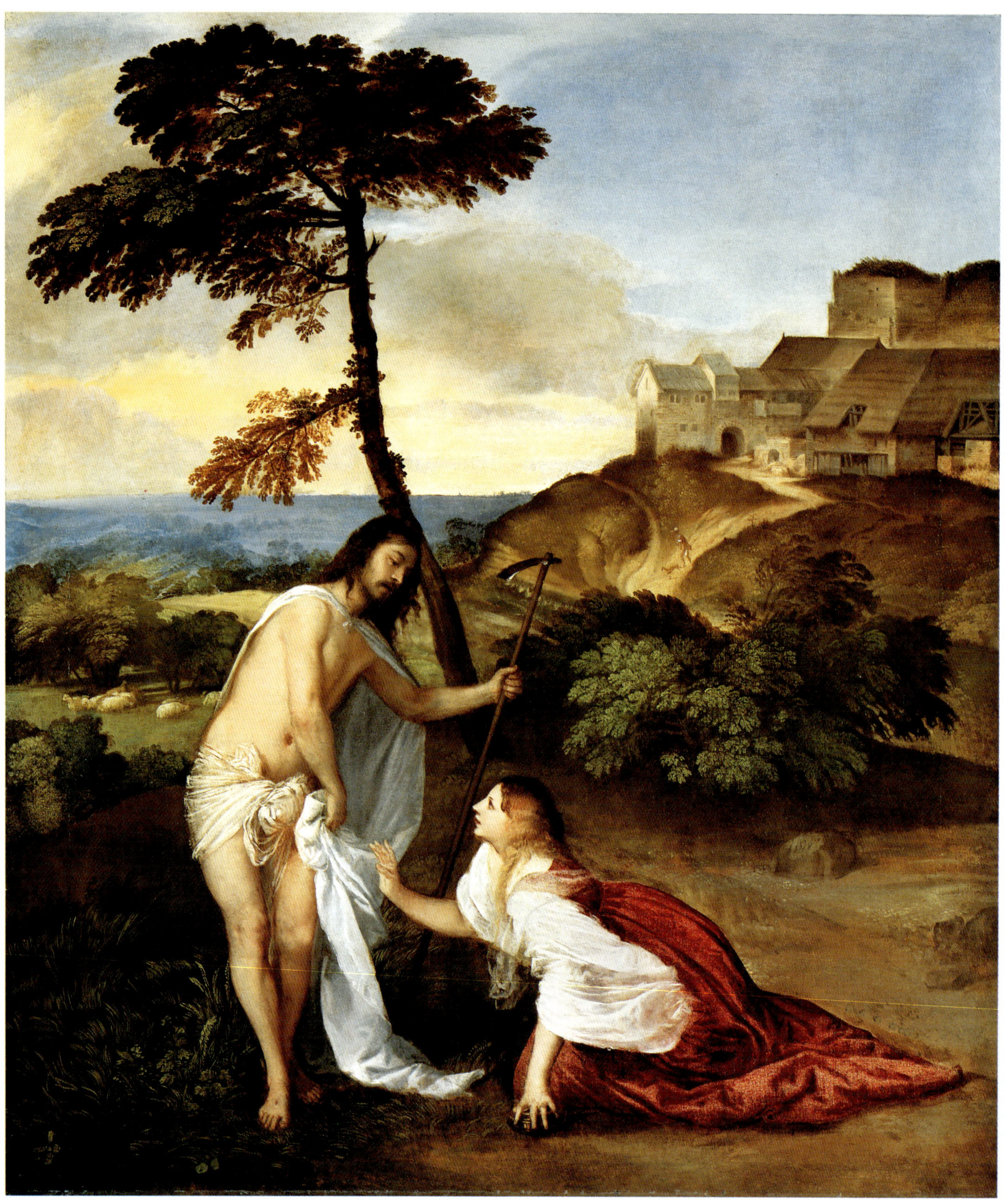

ciscan narrative painting, which favoured depiction of the miracles of Saint Anthony in a clear and un-complicated manner which would be easily under-stood by the masses. Yet there is a grandiosity in Titian's narrative powers which enables him to project the tragic message of the stories and the dra-matic intensity of the emotions of the participants.

It is frequently acknowledged that the succession of terrible events which marked the end of the first decade of the century weighed heavily on the poet-ic quality of Titian's work in this period. The cul-mination came in 1509 at Agnadello, where the Venetian Republic suffered a heavy military set-back at the hands of the troops of the League of

13. *Noli Me Tangere (1511/1512)*
109x91 cm
London, National Gallery

14. *The Miracle of the Newborn Child*
320x315 cm
Padua, Scuola del Santo

15. *The Healing of the Wrathful Son*
(1511)
327x220 cm
Padua, Scuola del Santo

16. *The Miracle of the Jealous Husband*
(1511)
327x123
Padua, Scuola del Santo

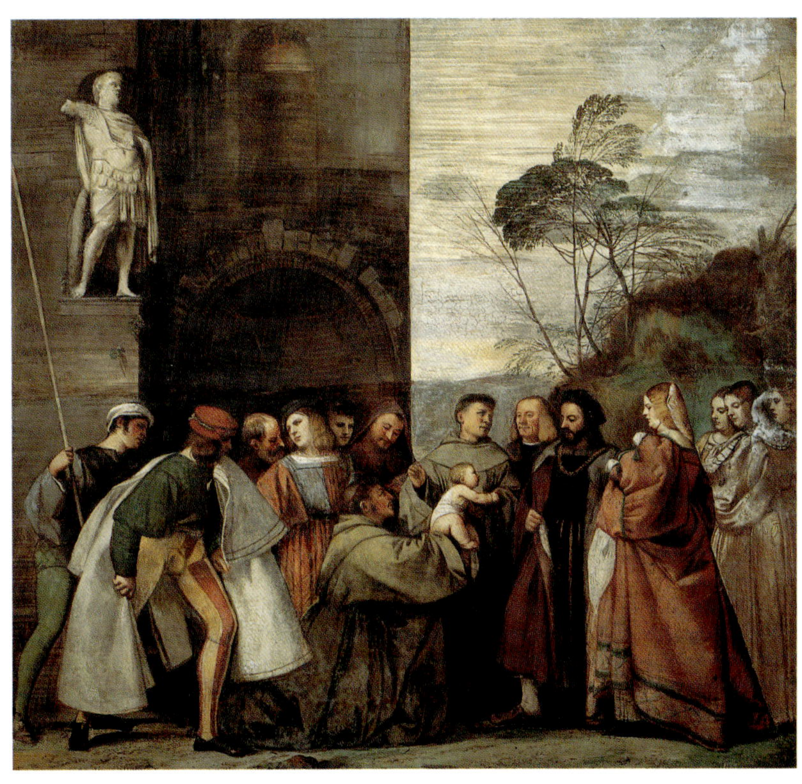

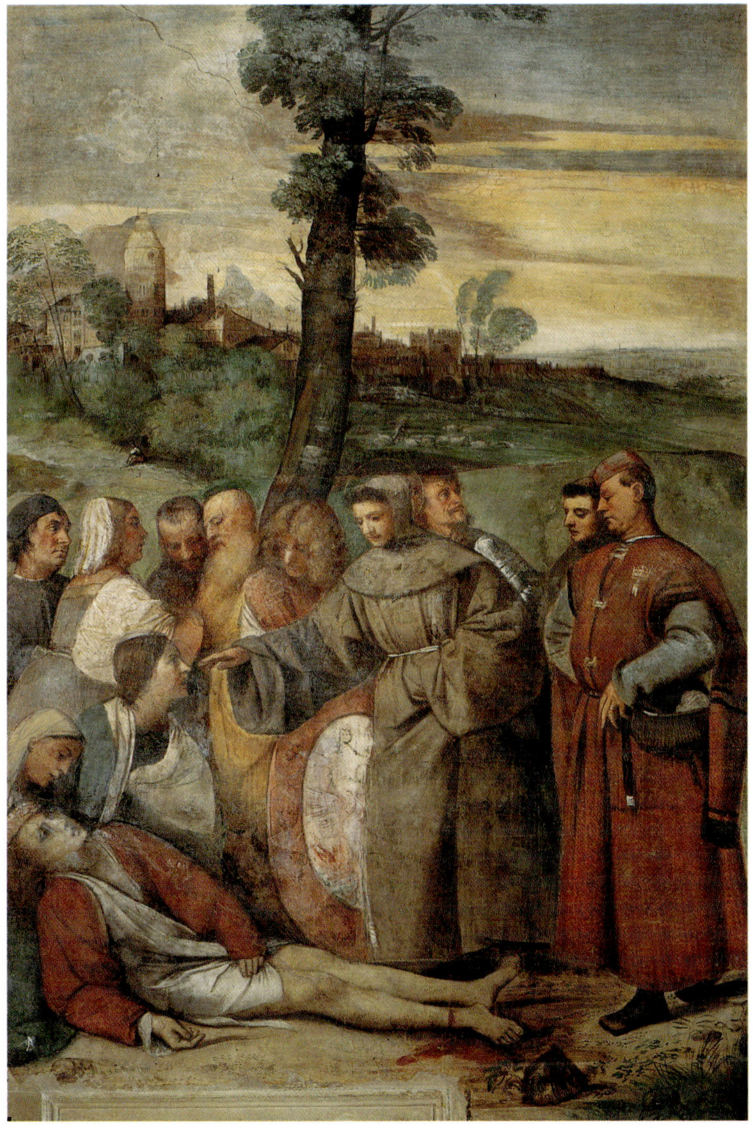

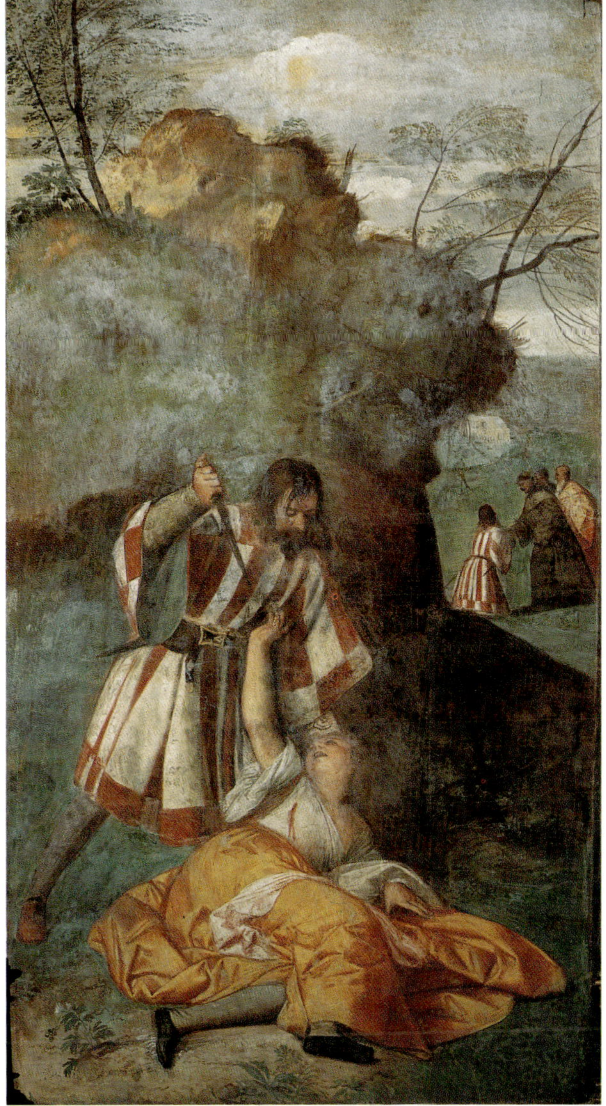

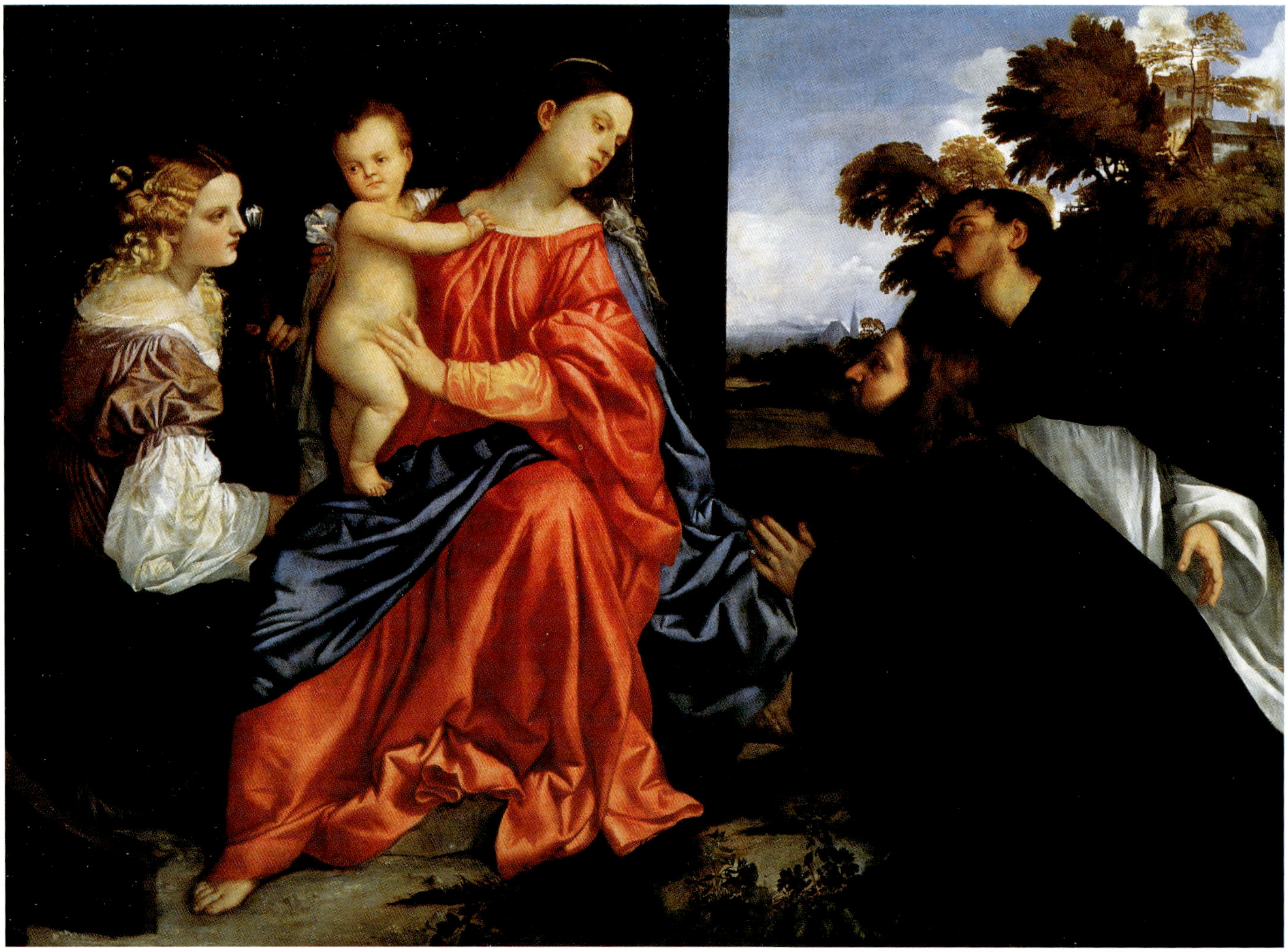

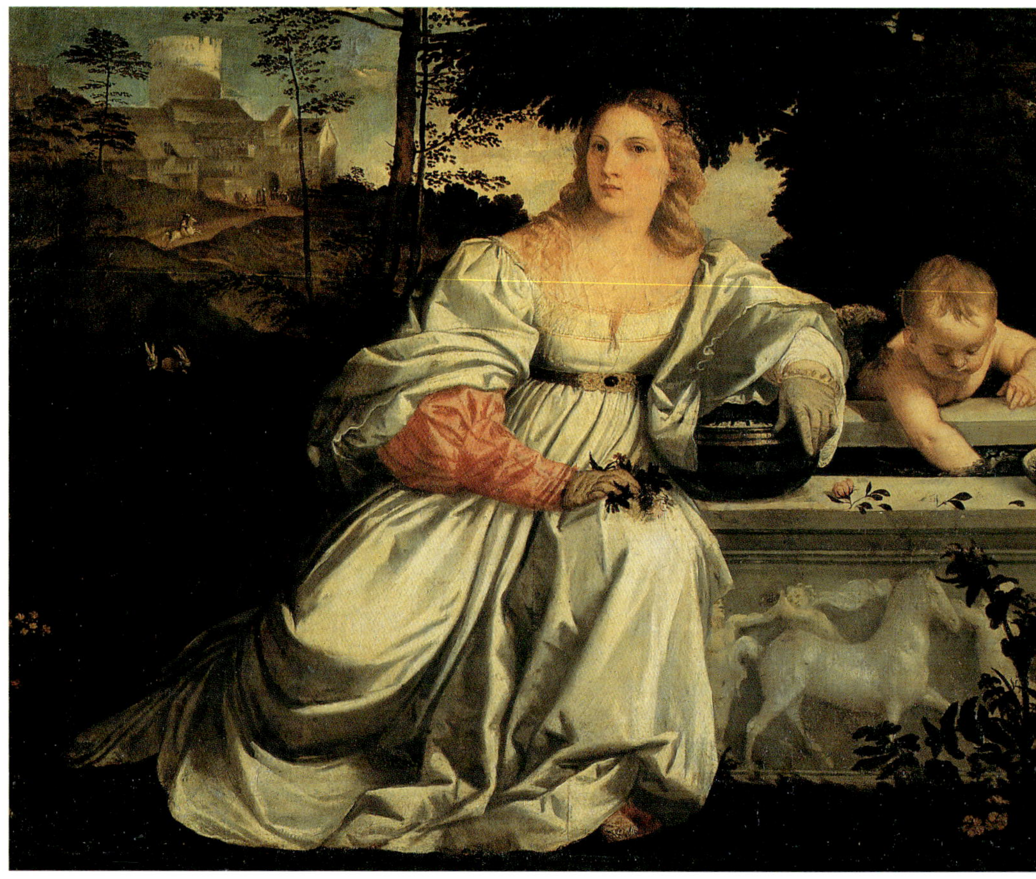

17. Sacra Conversazione
(1512/1514)
138x185 cm
Mamiano (Parma)
Magnani Rocca Collection

Cambrai and the safety of Venice herself was threatened when the Imperial forces established a bridgehead on the threshold of the lagoon. Nevertheless Titian demonstrates his ability to react decisively to this painful nightmare by developing a new humanism of heroic character in his art. From it emerges his faith in man and in his dominion over the world. This is forcefully expressed in Titian's numerous portraits where the psychological introspection of the personalities is complemented by their wonderfully plastic quality. This can also be seen in the many *Sacra Conversazione* paintings from this period, such as the grandiose altarpiece, datable between 1512 and 1514, in the Magnani Rocca Collection at Mamiano. The donor, who is perhaps a certain Domenico Balbi, is portrayed with extraordinary psychological insight. Of particular interest are the monumental figures of the Virgin Mary and Saint Catherine, who dominate the foreground in sure possession of the space they occupy, presenting themselves confidently to the viewer. Another masterpiece from these years displays the same style although the subject matter is quite different: the *Sacred and Profane Love* in the Borghese Gallery, Rome which was painted in 1514 on the occasion of the marriage of the ducal chancellor Nicolò Aurelio to Laura Bagarotto-Aurelio's coat of arms appears in the bas-relief which decorates the sarcophagus-shaped fountain, on which are seated the twin Venus figures symbolizing celestial Love (the nude figure) and earthly Love (the clothed one); the complex allegorical subject matter reflects the sophisticated tastes of the cultured patron. The painting must also be considered as something of a milestone in Titian's career as an artist. The reference to the antique past in the allegorical bas-relief decorating the sarcophagus can be seen as a piece of self-conscious classicism which serves to underline the meaning of the subject matter. But the superb vitality of the artist bursts forth in the two female figures who are symbolically counterpoised, but at the same time so in harmony with each other that they express that *joie de vivre*, that delight in the senses and in the events of human life that was to become characteristic of the Venetian Renaissance.

In this period Titian often uses the female image to supply his wealthy patrons with paintings which subtly allude to earthly love. This is the case with the *Flora* in the Uffizi Gallery; this is not a portrait but an allegorical figure of *Flora Meretrix*, protagonist of the most popular and licentious ancient Roman festivals.

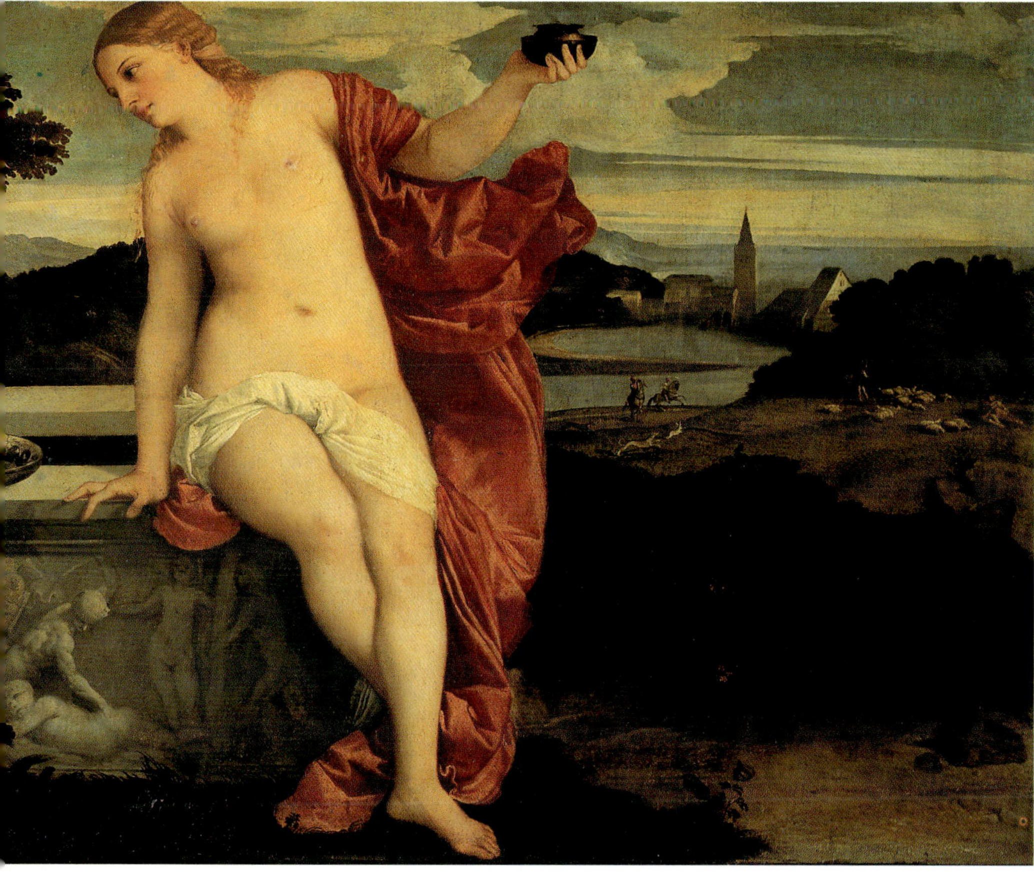

18. Sacred and Profane Love (1514)
118x279 cm
Rome, Borghese Gallery

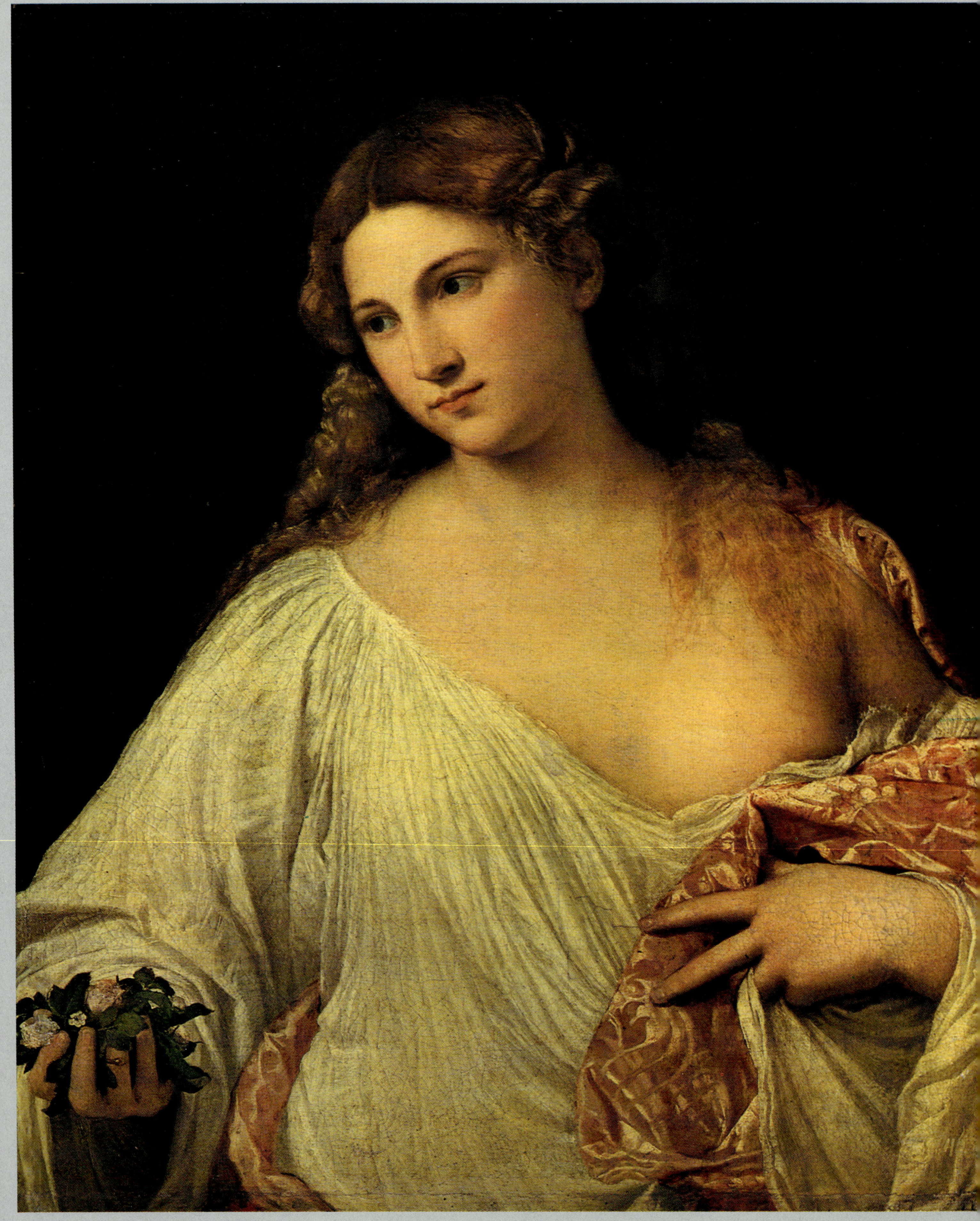

"The people began to be astonished by the new 'maniera'"

Titian's fame was now at its peak: in 1513 he had been invited by Pope Leo X, through the mediation of Cardinal Bembo, to move to the papal court, but he had turned down this tempting proposition in order to offer his services to the Venetian Republic, declaring his desire to succeed the elderly Giovanni Bellini in the 'Senseria' or Agency of the Fondaco dei Tedeschi. In practice the artist who held this office was tacitly recognized as the official painter of the Venetian state. In the meantime he confidently offered to demonstrate his exceptional skills by painting, in the Grand Council Chamber of the Doge's palace, the *Battle of Cadore* "which is most difficult and until this moment no man has wanted to burden himself with such an undertaking". The office of the 'Senseria' was not assigned to him until 1517, following the death of Giovanni Bellini, and work on the canvas of the *Battle* was so long drawn out that it was not completed until 1538. By then Titian was long established as the most important artist in Venice.

At the same time Titian began to make himself known to 'foreign' courts. In 1516, for example, he made contact with Alfonso I d'Este, Duke of Ferrara for whom he was to work for a decade on pictures destined for the Alabaster Chamber. Between 1516 and 1518 he executed the *Worship of Venus* now in the Prado, then, between 1523 and 1524, the *Bacchanal of the Andrians*, also in the Prado and, finally, the *Bacchus and Ariadne* now in London. In these Dionysian themes (which should also include the Edinburgh *Venus Anadyomene*) Titian combines a richness of colouristic expression with a great formal elegance. These are the elements which characterize this whole so-called "classic" phase in Titian's development and which is dominated by the supreme masterpiece of the Frari *Assumption of the Virgin*.

Titian worked on this huge altarpiece for more than two years from 1516 to 1518. It has to be seen as another milestone in Titian's career establishing him as a more universal artist who drew inspira-

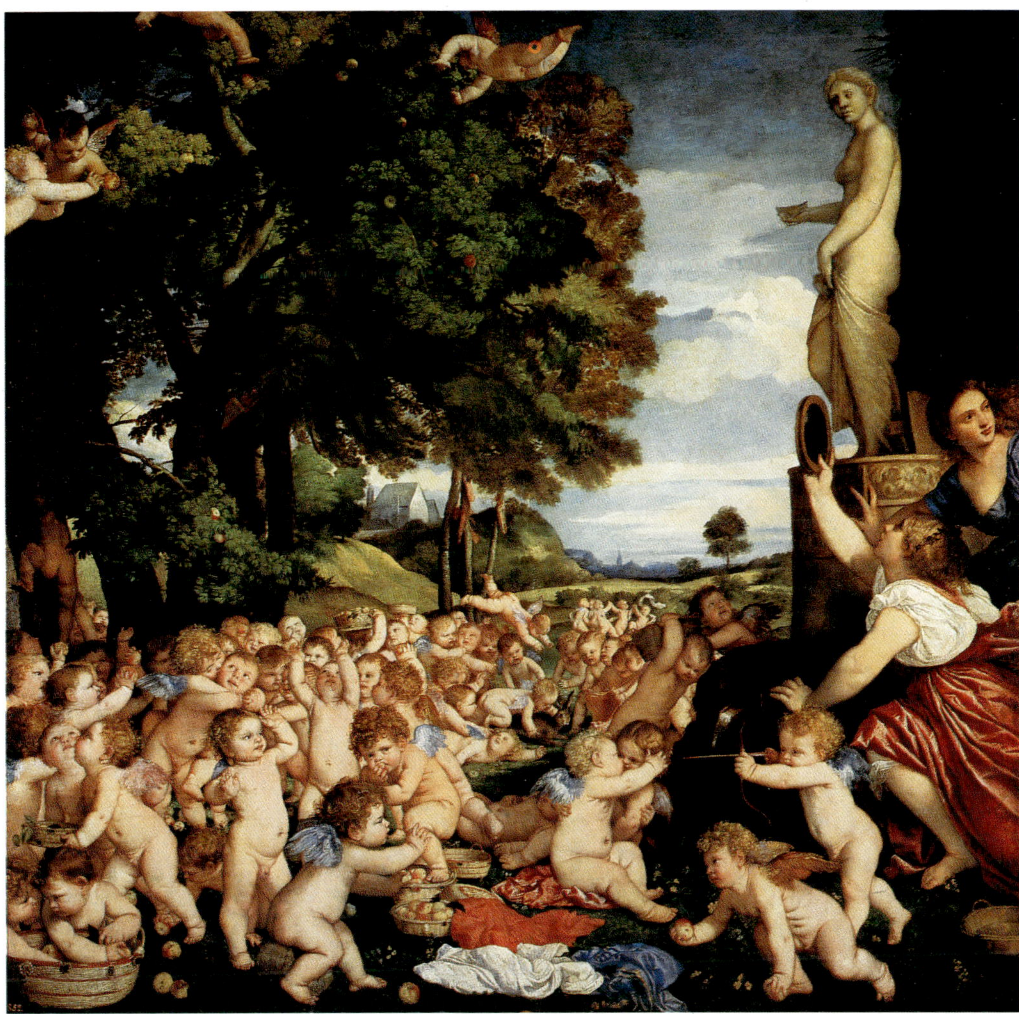

19. Flora (c. 1515)
80x63 cm
Florence, Uffizi

20. The Worship of
Venus (1516/1518)
172x175 cm
Madrid, Prado

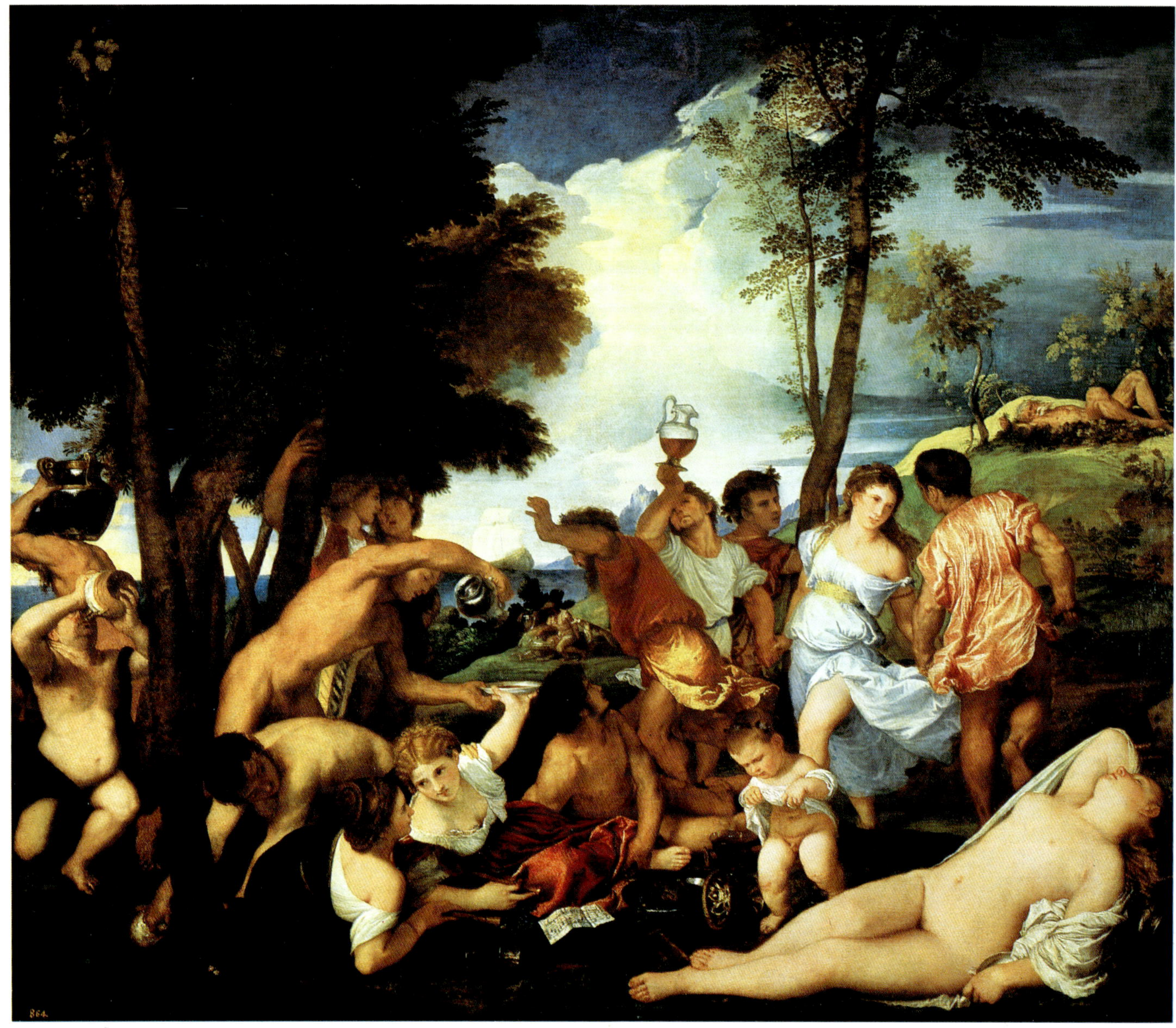

tion from outside the confines of Venice. Indeed the powerful figures of the Apostles reflect the influence of Michelangelo, whereas the painting demonstrates clear iconographical similarities with the works of Raphael. Above all, what emerges most strongly in the *Assumption* is Titian's desire to break definitively with the traditions of Venetian painting in order to arrive at a synthesis of dramatic force and dynamic tension which will become from this moment on the most obvious characteristic of his work.

Particularly representative of this phase are the *Tribute Money* in Dresden, painted for Alfonso d'Este and the *Madonna of the Cherries* in Vienna, where the somewhat old-fashioned composition, derived from models such as Dürer's *Madonna of the Siskin* (1506), is enlivened by the rich luminosity of the colour and by the majestic three-dimensionality of the forms.

21. Bacchanal of the Andrians (1523/1524)
175x193 cm
Madrid, Prado

22. Bacchus and Ariadne (1523/1524)
175x190 cm
London, National Gallery

In 1520 Titian put his signature to the altarpiece for the church of San Francesco at Ancona (now in the Civic Museum), commissioned by Luigi Gozzi, depicting the *Madonna in Glory with the Christ Child and Saints Francis and Alvise with the Donor.* While the influence of Raphael's *Madonna of Foligno* is evident in the composition, the vitality of the figures is entirely Titianesque. These same characteristics emerge even more strongly in another religious masterpiece from this period, the *Polyptych*

of the Resurrection in the church of Santi Nazaro
e Celso in Brescia. It was painted between 1520
and 1522 for Altobello Averoldi, papal legate to
Venice. New Mannerist tendencies are apparent
here, possibly transmitted to Titian through the
work of Pordenone, and these elements subtly con-
tribute to the dramatic intensity of the work. In both
those works the landscape backgrounds are of the
very highest quality, with recognizable views of
Venice and Brescia.

The first half of the 1520's saw the production
of a great many portraits, some of which are truly
great works of art. Among these is the presumed
portrait of *Vincenzo Mosti* in the Pitti Palace,
remarkable for its harmonious colour scheme and
for the freedom of the brushstrokes which enliven
the details of the clothes and the face. The sitter's
features are highlighted and accentuated through
a device typical of Titian's portraiture, a touch of
light colour at the neck — in this case the irides-
cent white of the refined shirt collar. Another
masterpiece is the superb *Man with a Glove* in the
Louvre; here the severe self-confidence exhibited
in so many of Titian's portraits for once gives way
to an appealingly melancholy figure. In the portrait of *Federigo Gonzaga* in the Prado, Titian in-
dulges in the chromatic interplay of the variegated
blue of the duke's doublet with the white of the
faithful dog, portrayed together with his master.

As if to consolidate Titian's artistic supremacy in
Venice, the 1520's saw the production of two
masterpieces for the major monastic churches of

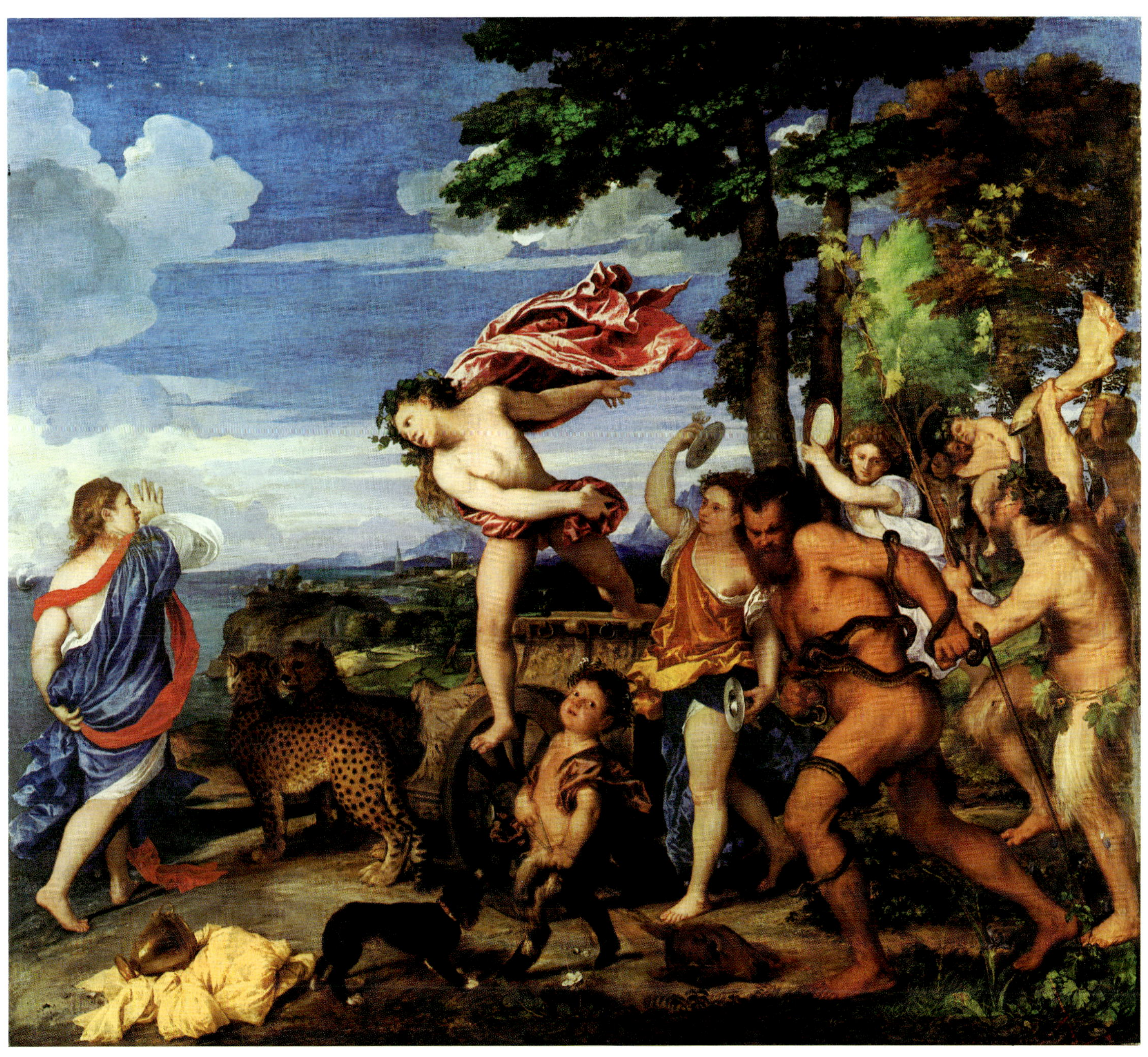

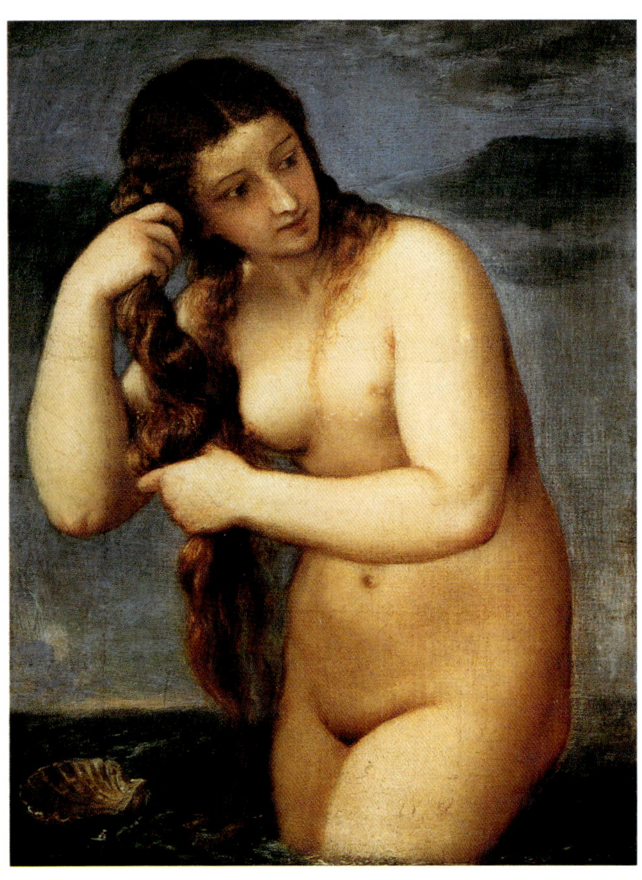

the city — Santa Maria Gloriosa dei Frari and Santi Giovanni e Paolo — where the great personalities of the Republic were buried. The *Pesaro Altarpiece*, placed above the altar of the Immaculate Conception in the Frari church, was commissioned in 1519 but Titian took seven years to complete it. The traditional scheme of the *Sacra Conversazione* with the Madonna and Child, saints and donors, is completely transformed and the altarpiece becomes an excuse for a magnificent group portrait of members of the Pesaro family. They are depicted with unparalleled realism in a bright, sunny light which transforms the clothes and the standards into a fanfare of colour.

The *Martyrdom of St Peter Martyr* must have been as revolutionary as the *Pesaro Altarpiece*. Delivered on 27 April 1530 to the friars of the church of Santi Giovanni e Paolo, it was unfortunately destroyed by the fire which devastated the Chapel of the Rosary — where, by a tragic twist of fate, the altarpiece had been moved for restoration — on 16 August 1867. All that remains are enthusiastic contemporary accounts of the work (Vasari described it as: "by far the most finished,

23. Venus Anadyomene (1519/1525)
76x57.3 cm
Edinburgh, National Gallery of Scotland (on loan from the Duke of Sutherland Collection)

24, 25. Assumption of the Virgin (1516/1518)
690x360 cm
Venice, Santa Maria Gloriosa dei Frari

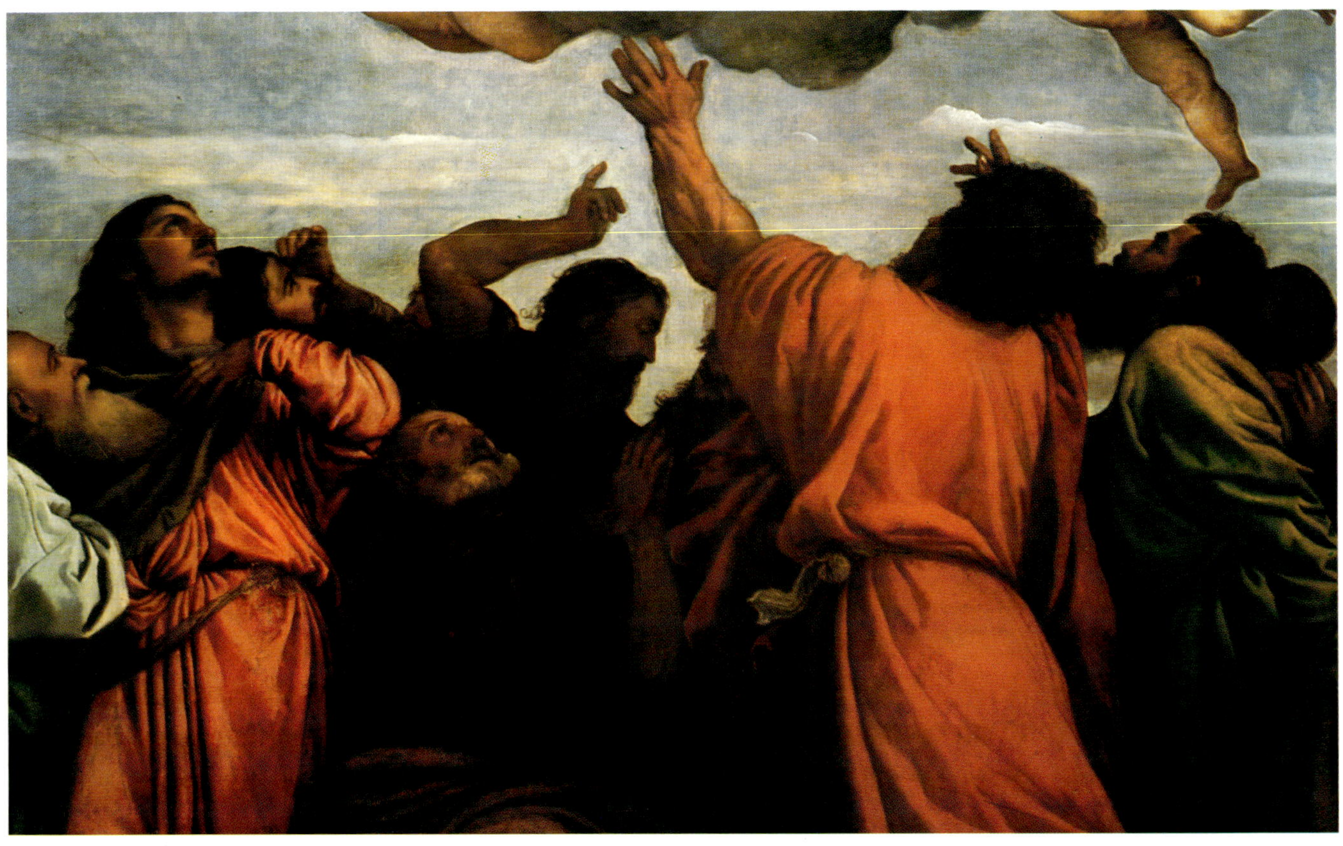

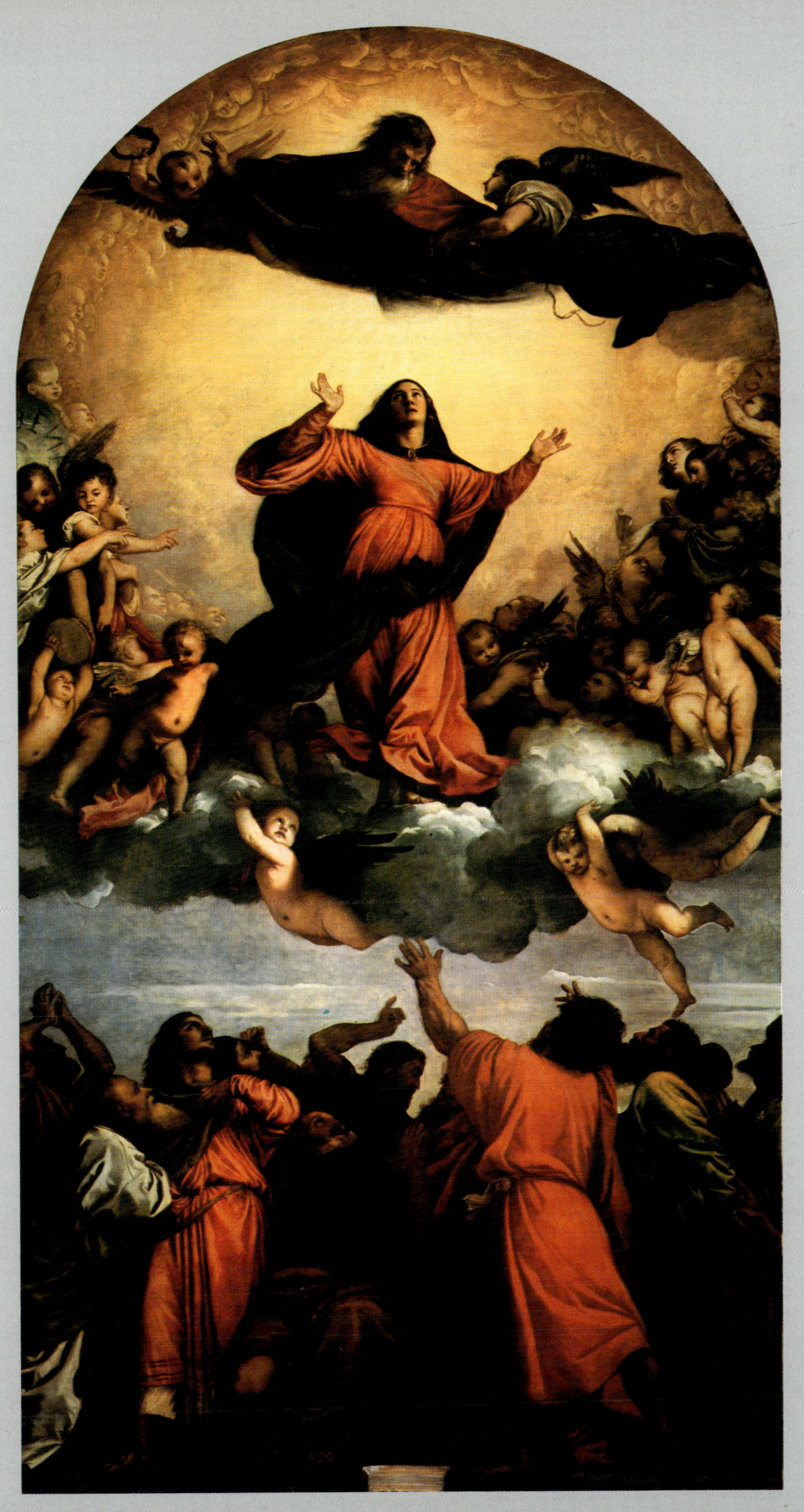

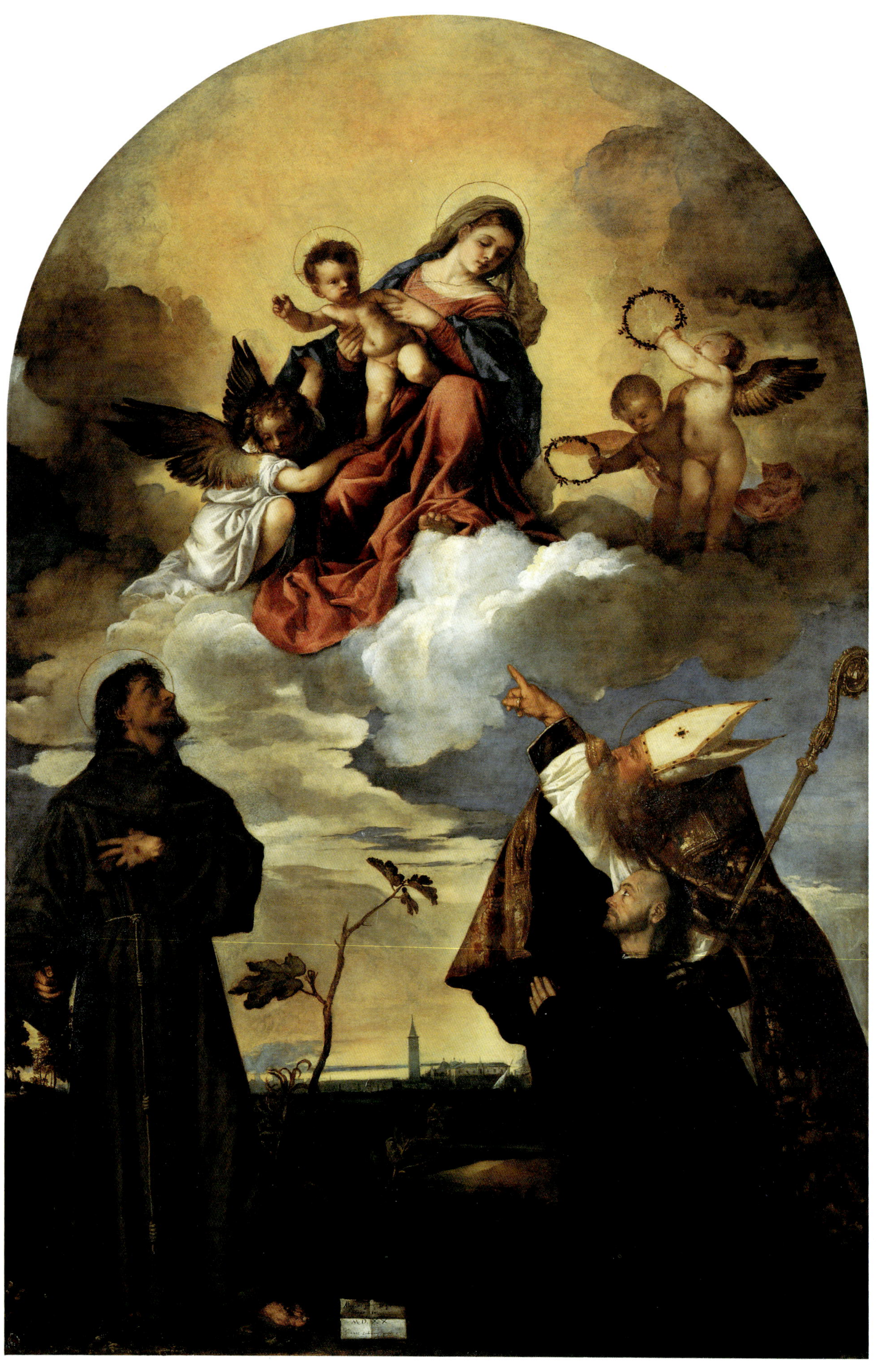

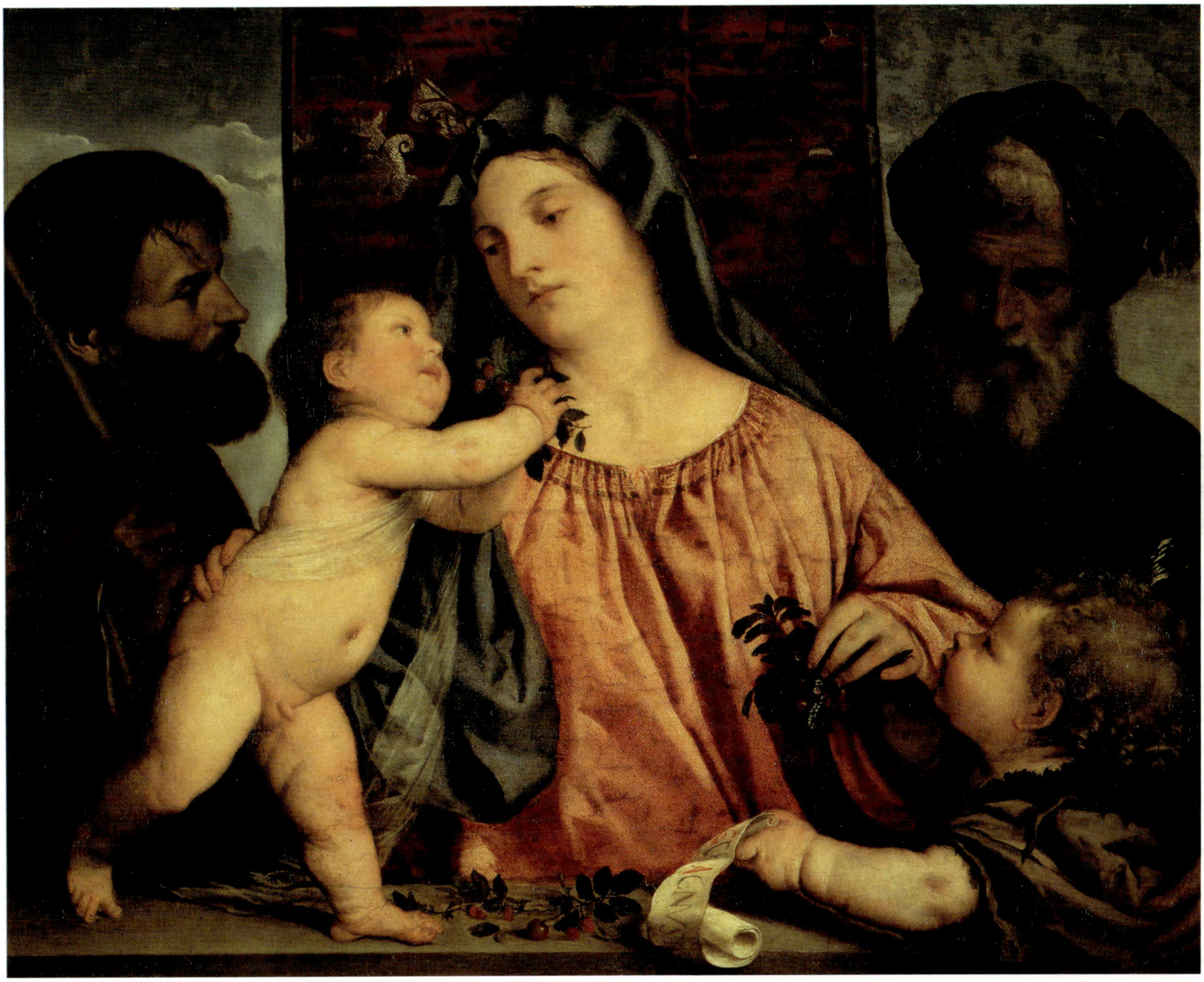

26. *Madonna in Glory with the Christ Child and Saints*
Francis and Aluise with the Donor (1520)
312x215 cm
Ancona, Museo Civico

27. *Madonna of the Cherries (1517/1518)*
81x99.5 cm
Vienna, Kunsthistorisches Museum

28. *The Tribute Money (1516/1518)*
75x56 cm
Dresden, Gemäldegalerie

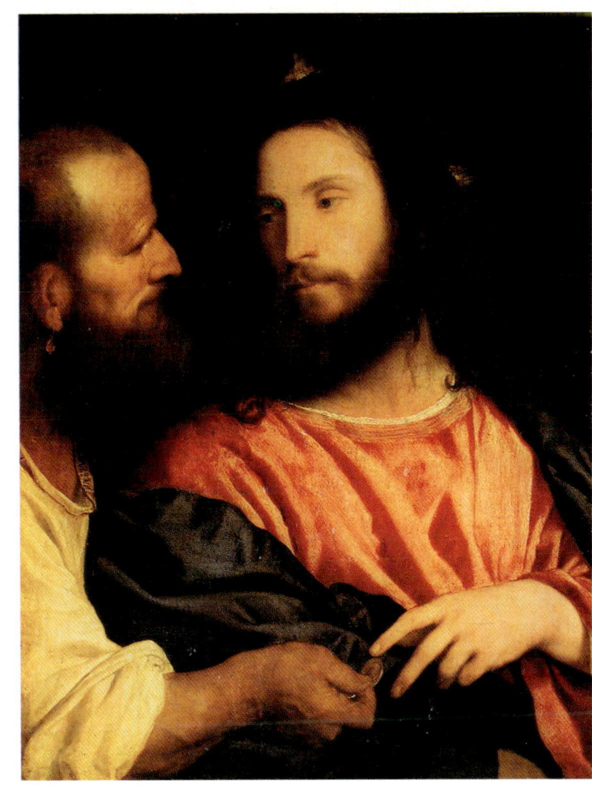

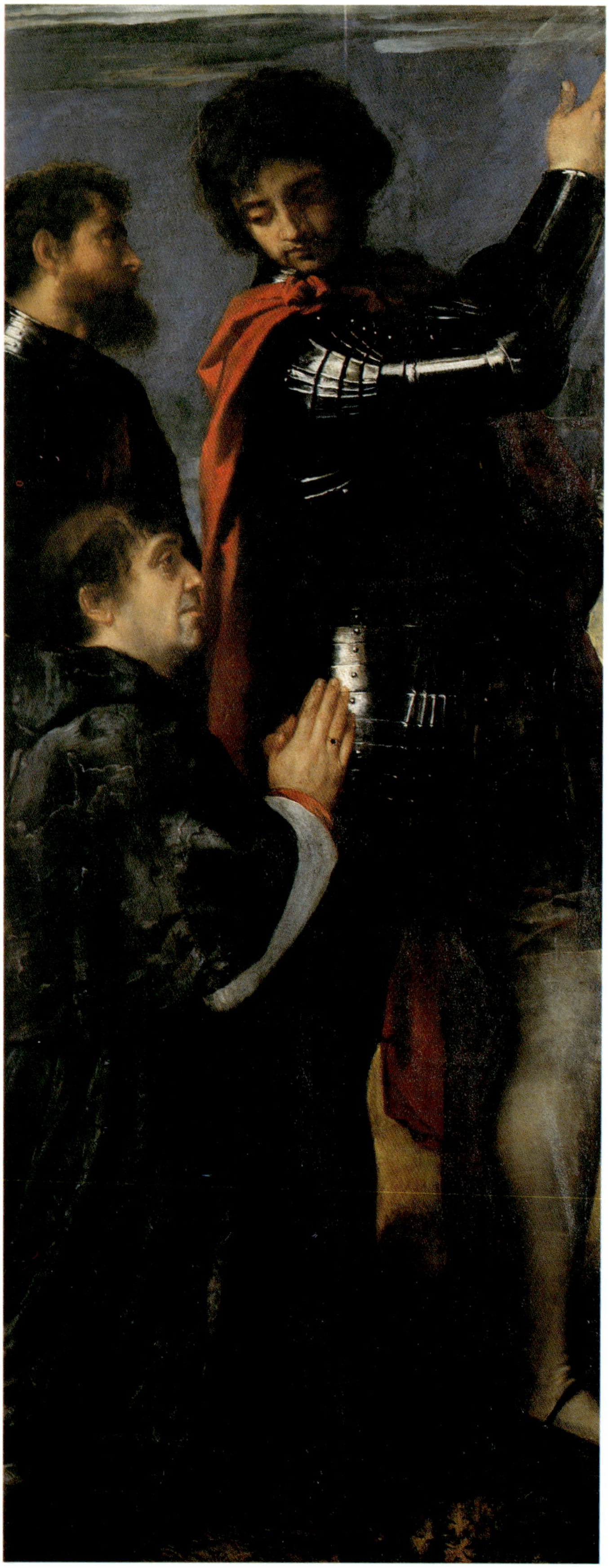

29. *Polyptych of the Resurrection*
detail of Saints Nazaro and Celso with the donor
Altobello Averoldi

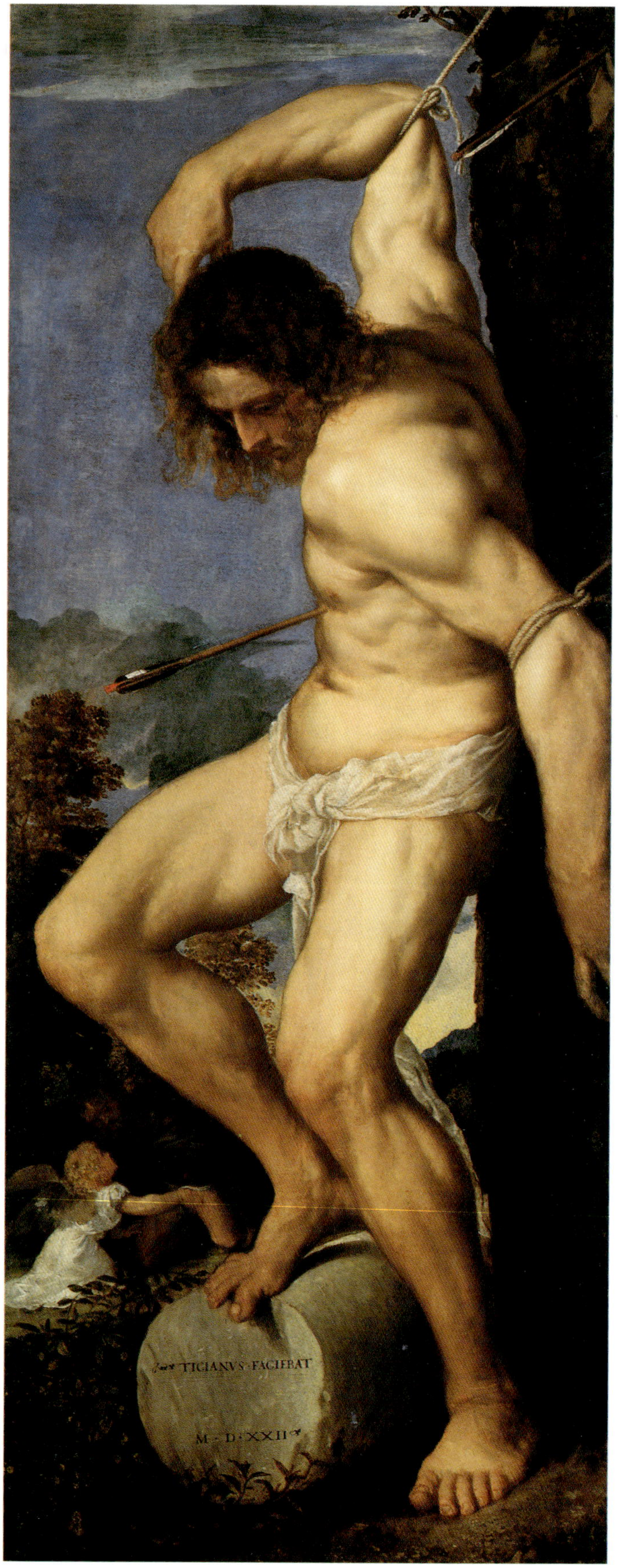

30. *Polyptych of the Resurrection*
detail of St Sebastian

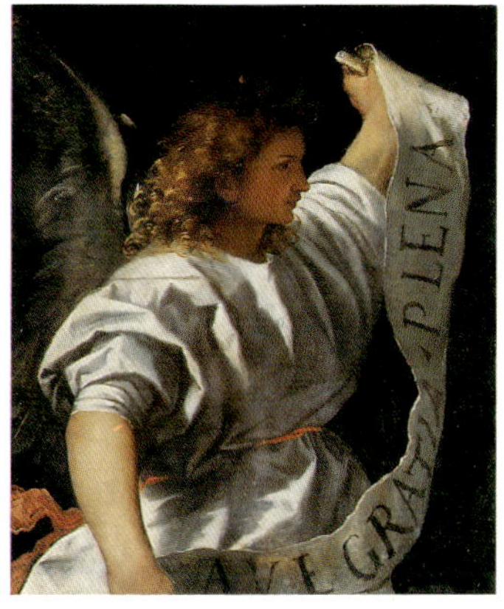
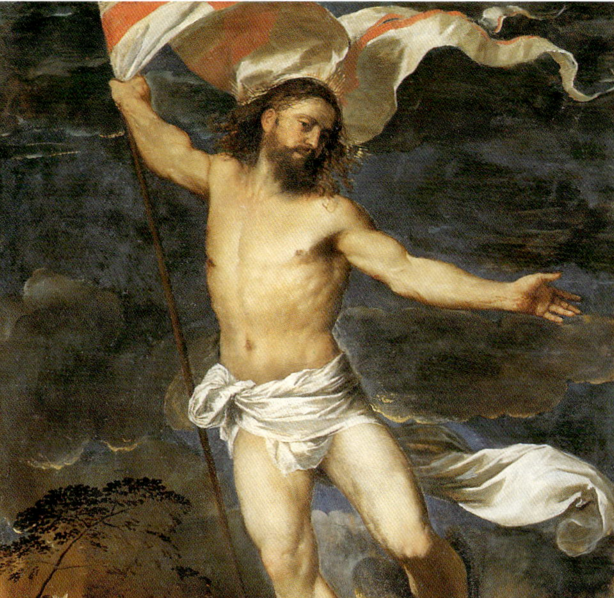
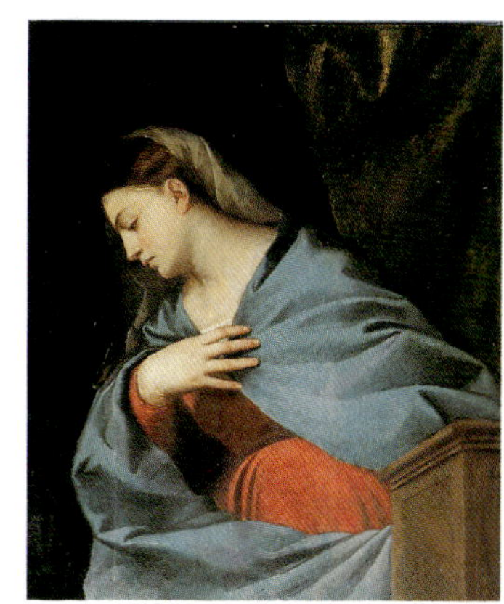
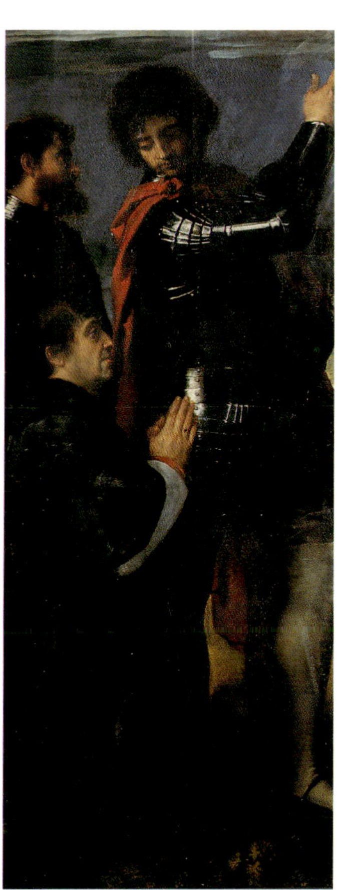
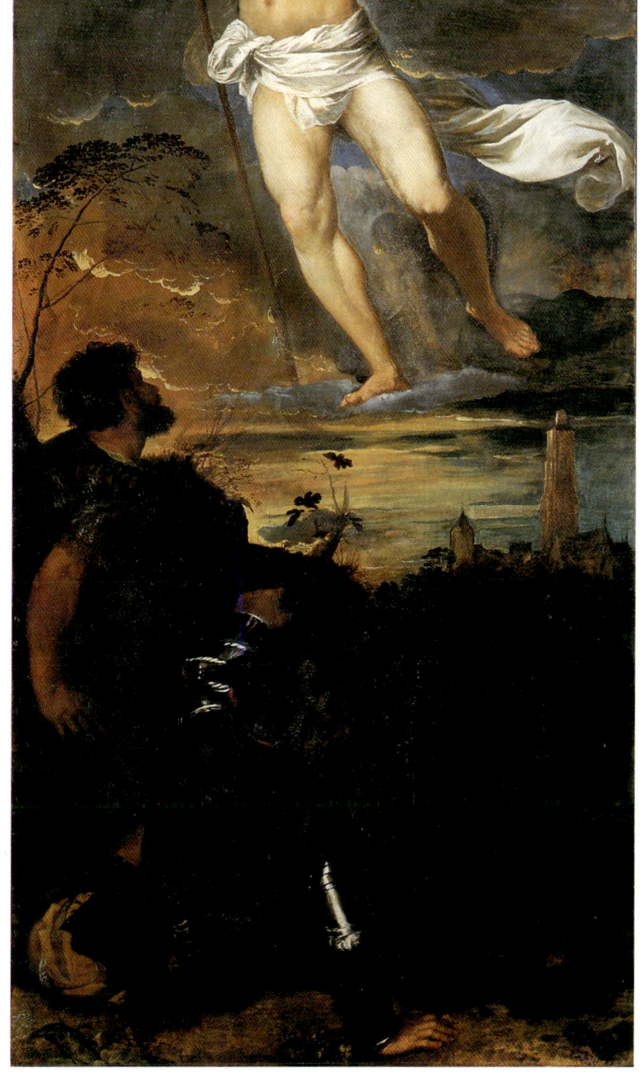
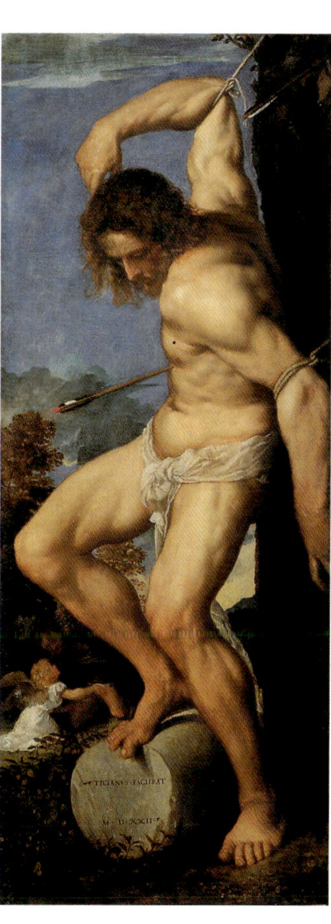

31. Polyptych of the Resurrection (1522)
Brescia, Church of Santi Nazaro e Celso

the most celebrated, the greatest and the best conceived and executed of all the pictures painted so far by Titian") and a few copies such as the one now on the altar, thought to be by Loth. From these it is possible to imagine the extraordinary dynamism of Titian's composition, with the action set on the edge of a great dark wood which provides a gloomy backdrop to the scene of slaughter. It is perhaps possible to discern some compositional similarities between the *Saint Peter* altarpiece and the deeply moving painting of the Louvre *Entombment of Christ*, datable towards the end of the 1530's. Here too, all the intensely dramatic figures are placed

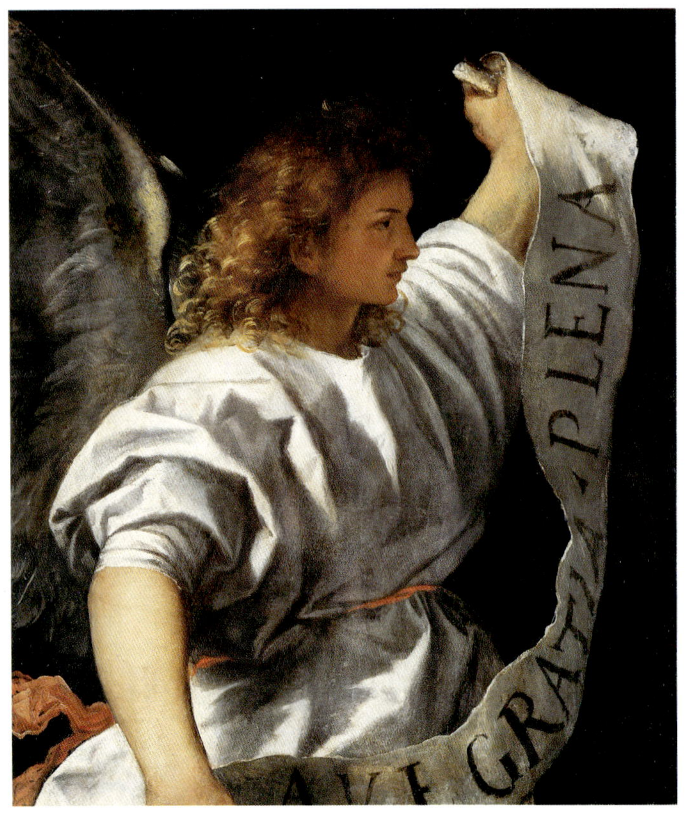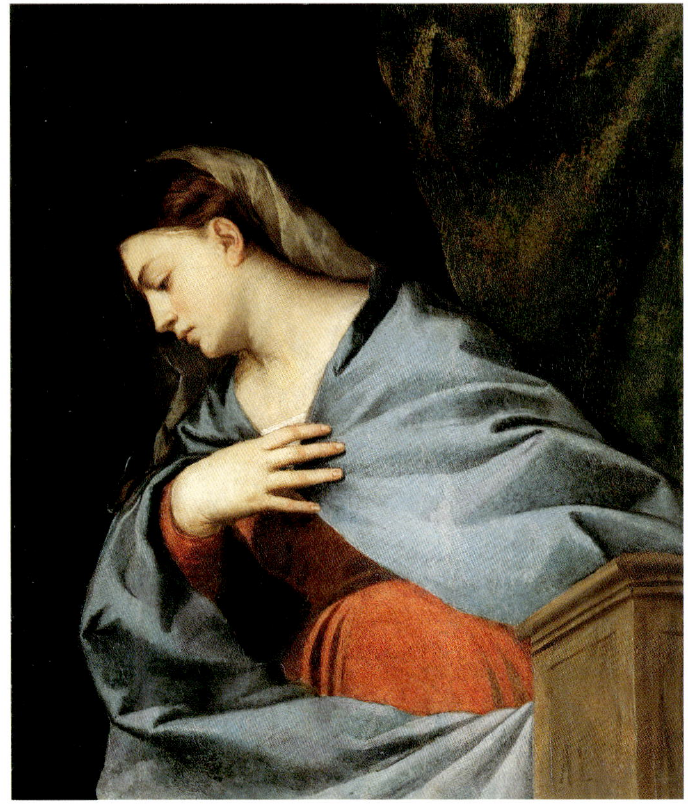

*32, 33. Polyptych of the Resurrection
details of the Angel of the Annunciation and of the
Virgin Annunciate*

*34. St Christopher (1523)
300x179 cm
Venice, Doges' Palace*

well to the foreground, juxtaposed against the
wooded background. Points of similarity are also
evident in the London *Madonna and Child with
the Young Saint John the Baptist and Saint Catherine*, painted in 1530 possibly for the Duke of Mantua, and the *Adoration of the Shepherds*, a
charming night scene painted between 1532 and
1533 for Francesco Maria della Rovere.

By now Titian's working life was marked by fran-
tic activity. In 1523 he had made contact with Federico Gonzaga in Venice and in 1529 Titian repaid
the visit by going to Mantua; the new Doge, Andrea Gritti, claimed from Titian, in his capacity as
official painter of the Republic, the portraits his position obliged him to paint, the projected *Battle of
Cadore* and a "votive painting". The latter was not
delivered until October 1531 and was to be destroyed in a fire of 1574. In the meantime another
important turning point in Titian's career took place
in Parma in 1529; here, through the good offices
of Federico Gonzaga, he met his future patron —

the Emperor Charles V. At their second meeting, which took place at Bologna in 1533, Charles V enobled Titian with the title of Count Palatine and made him a Knight of the Golden Spur; it was also on that occasion that Titian painted the portrait of the ruler now in the Prado.

In Venice Titian had become friends with Pietro Aretino and Jacopo Sansovino (who had both arrived in the city in 1527 following the Sack of Rome) thus forming the triad that was to dominate Venetian cultural life for many years. Titian's new position as Imperial painter brought with it an enormous quantity of privileges and, above all, a renown unattainable for any other artist. Therefore it is no surprise that in 1532 Titian is featured in Ariosto's *Orlando furioso* alongside the very greatest of modern artists, Raphael and Michelangelo, and

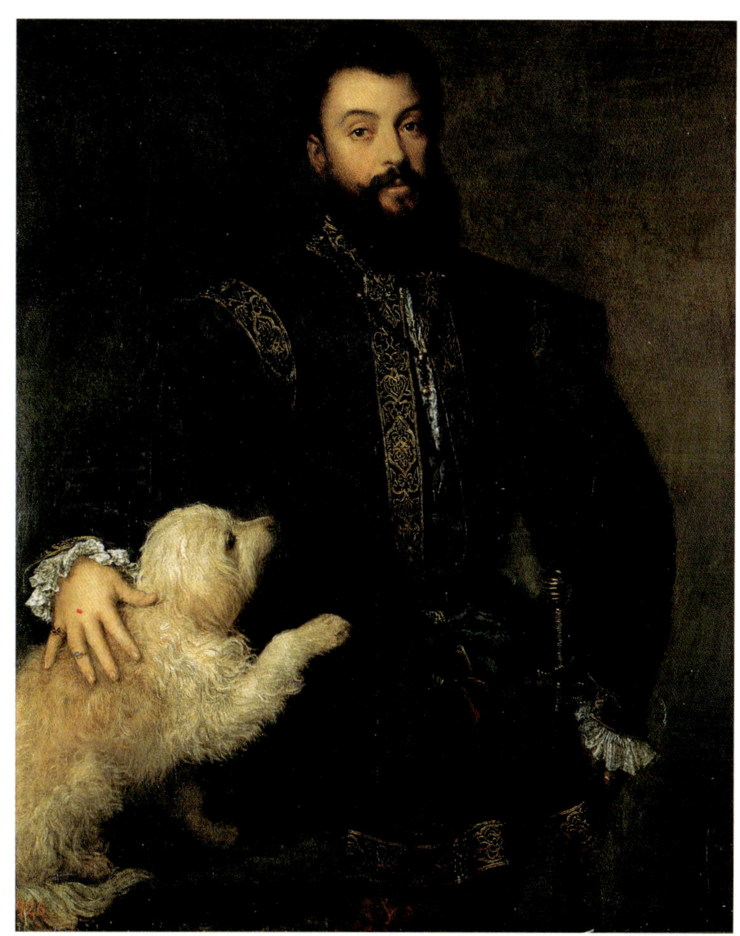

35. Portrait of Federico Gonzaga ((1523/1526)
125x99 cm
Madrid, Prado

36. Man with a Glove (1520/1525)
100x89 cm
Paris, Louvre

37. Portrait of Vincenzo Mosti (1520/1525)
85x66 cm
Florence, Galleria Palatina, Pitti Palace

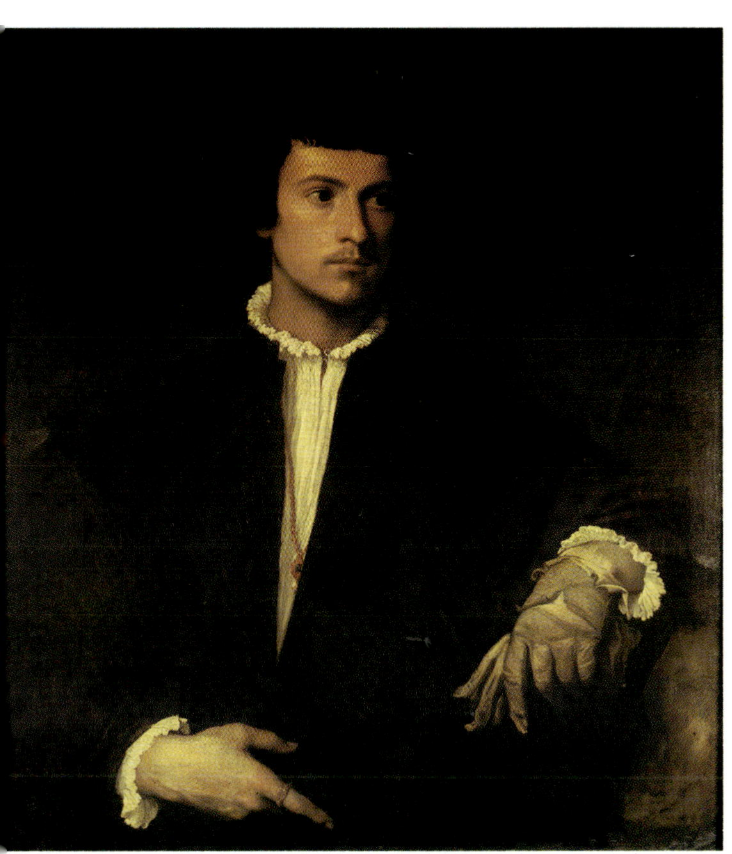

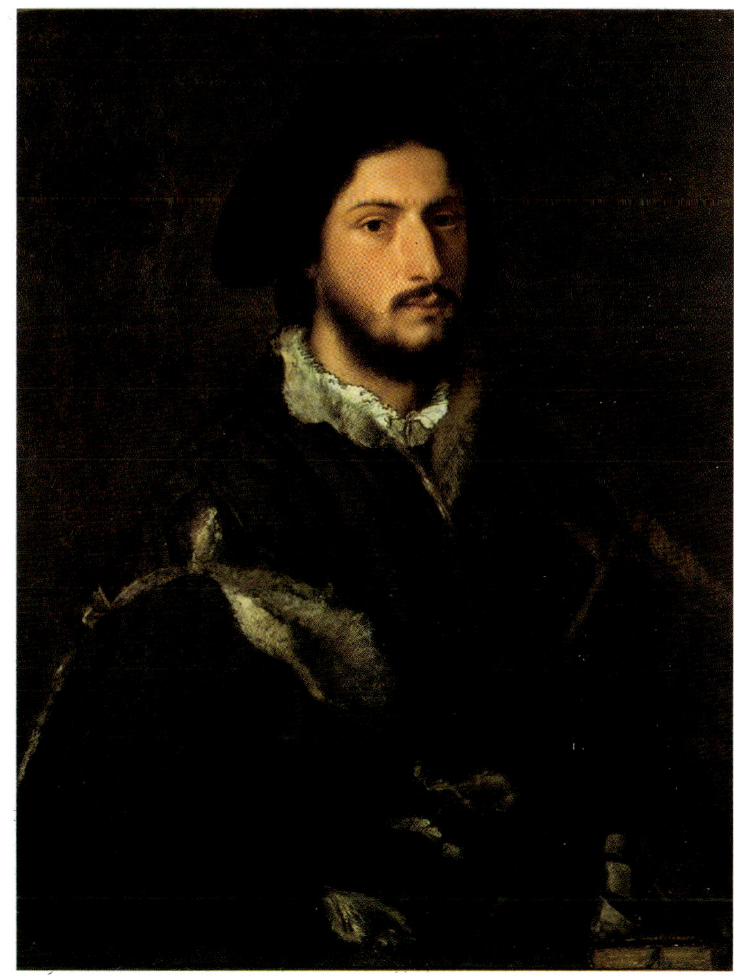

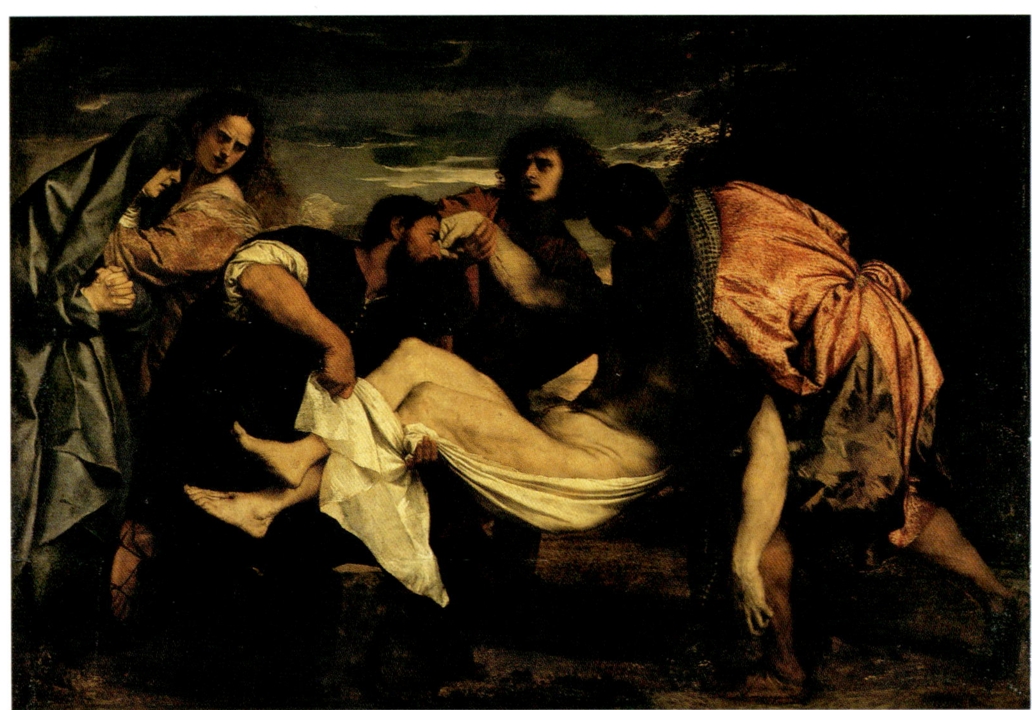

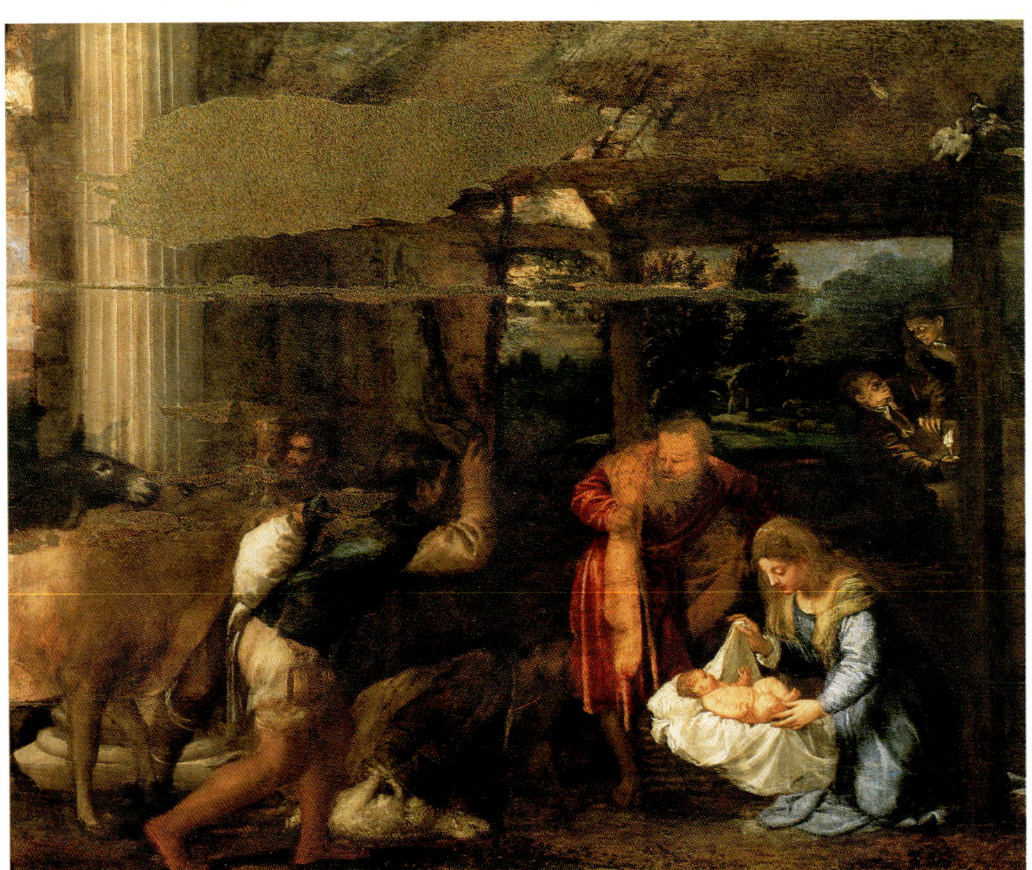

that all the Italian princely courts vied with each other to obtain works by his hand. For Francesco Maria della Rovere, Duke of Urbino (whose majestic portrait Titian painted together with that of his wife Eleonora Gonzaga) he produced at the beginning of the 1530's that triumph of sensual beauty — the *Mary Magdalene* now in the Pitti Palace and the mysterious *Bella* also in the Pitti. In 1538 Titian painted for the duke's heir, Guidobaldo, the so-called *Venus of Urbino* perhaps the most seductive of Titian's images of women. If the pose of this Venus brings to mind that of Giorgione's Dresden *Venus* (which the young Titian had completed after Giorgione's death) the intent of the painting is quite different. Titian's Venus has nothing to do with Giorgione's idealised image of female beau-

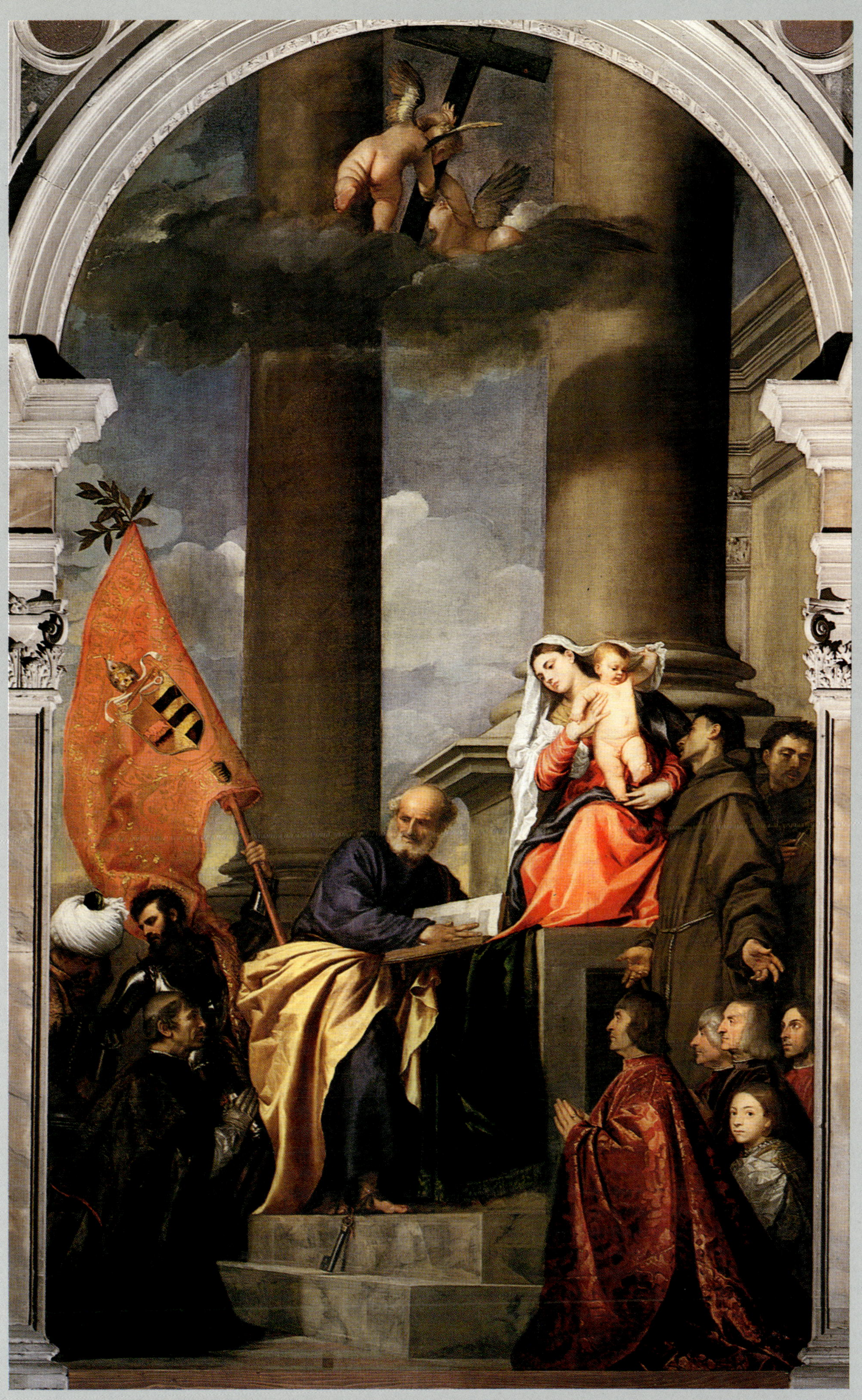

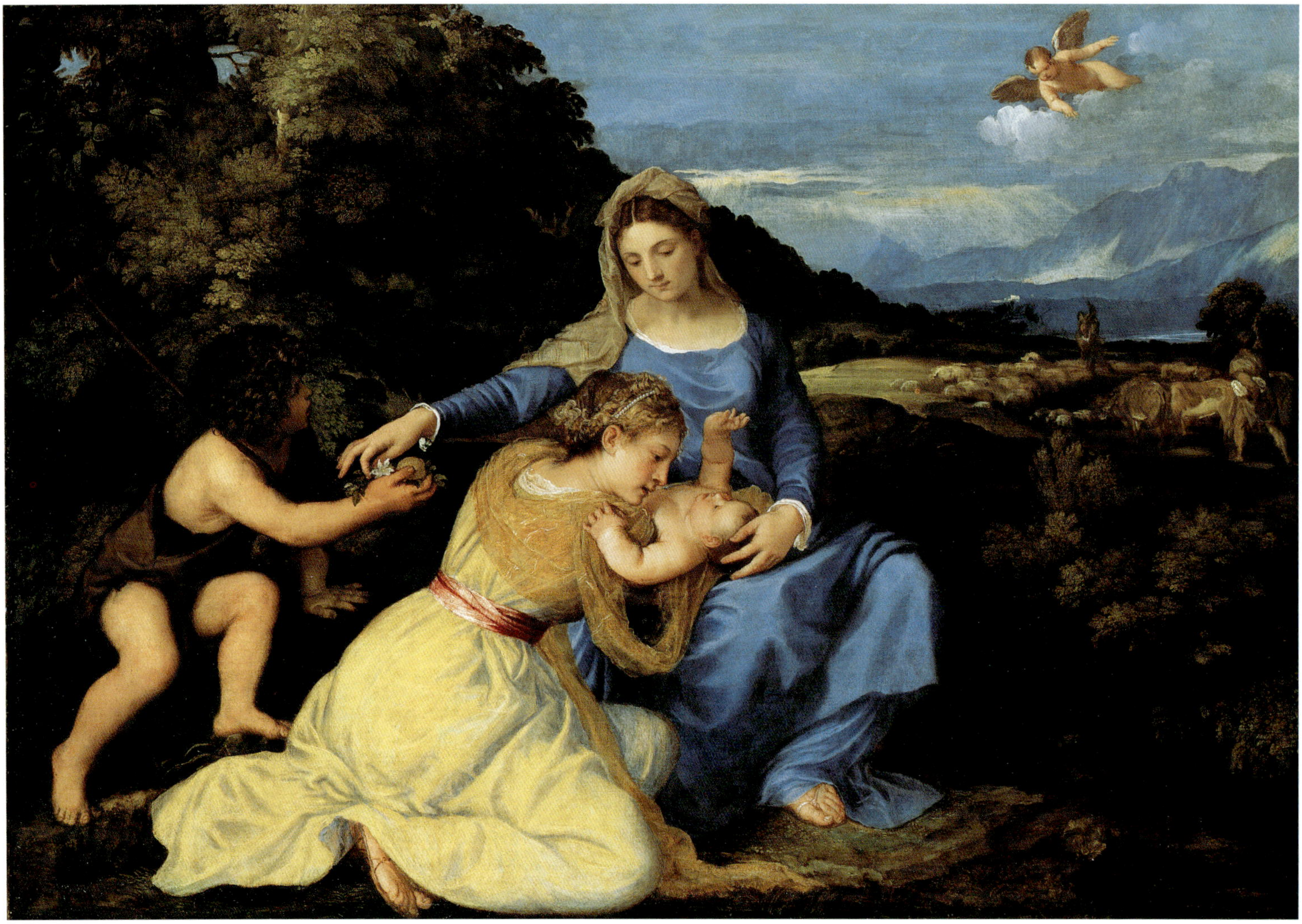

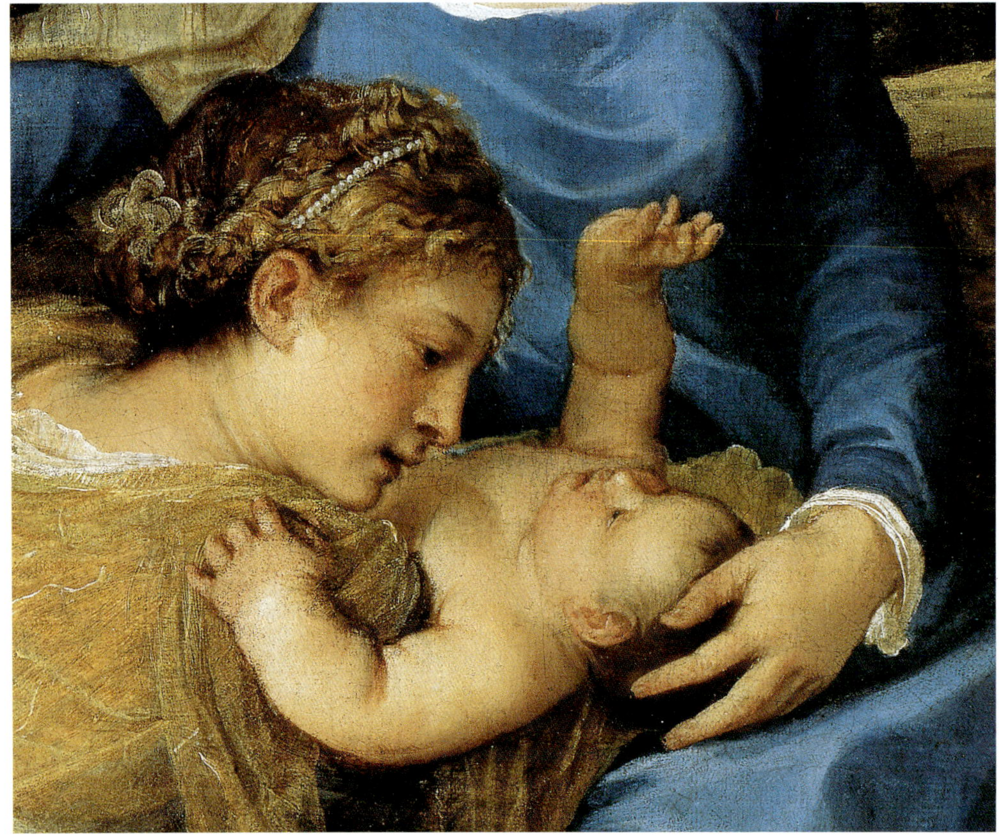

41, 42. *Madonna and Child with the Young Saint John the Baptist and Saint Catherine* (1530)
101x142 cm
London, National Gallery

43. *Portrait of Ippolito dei Medici* (1532/1534)
139x107 cm
Florence, Galleria Palatina, Pitti Palace

44. *Portrait of Charles V* (1533)
192x111 cm
Madrid, Prado

45. *Portrait of Francesco Maria della Rovere* (1538)
114x100 cm
Florence, Uffizi

46. *Portrait of Eleonora Gonzaga della Rovere* (1538)
112x102 cm
Florence, Uffizi

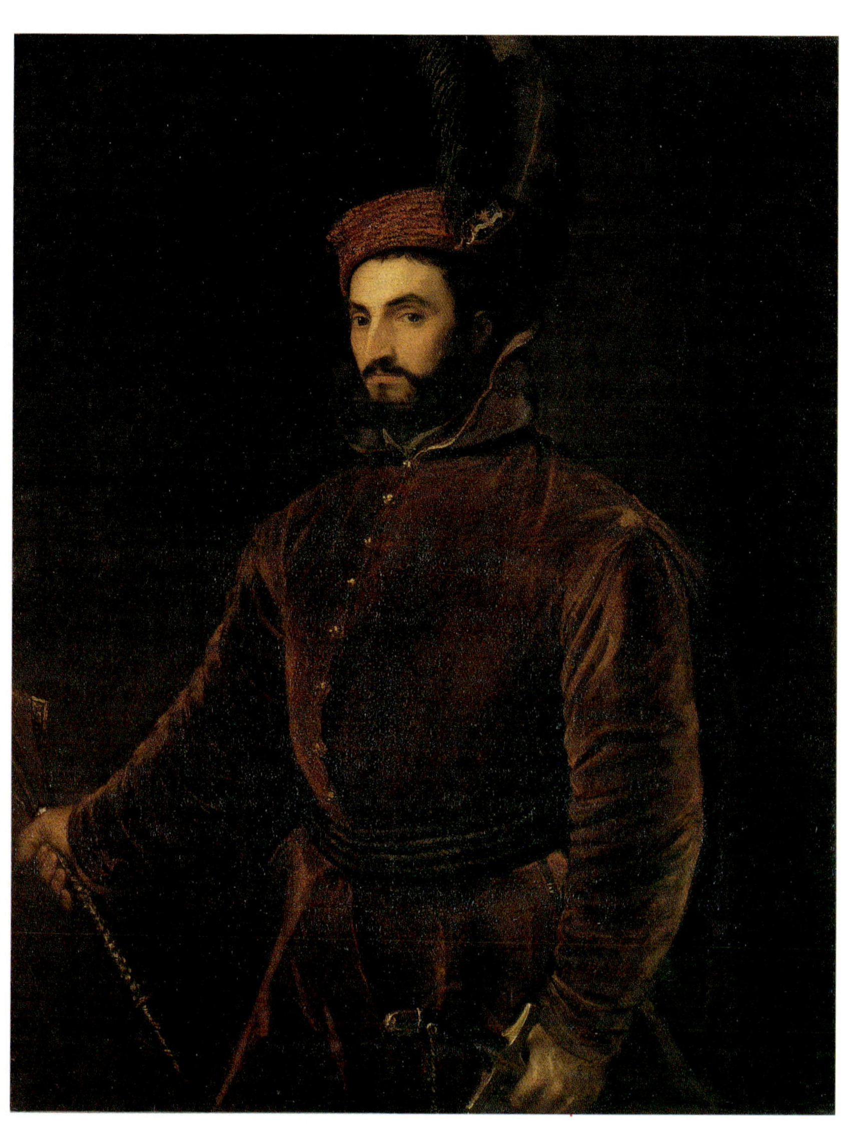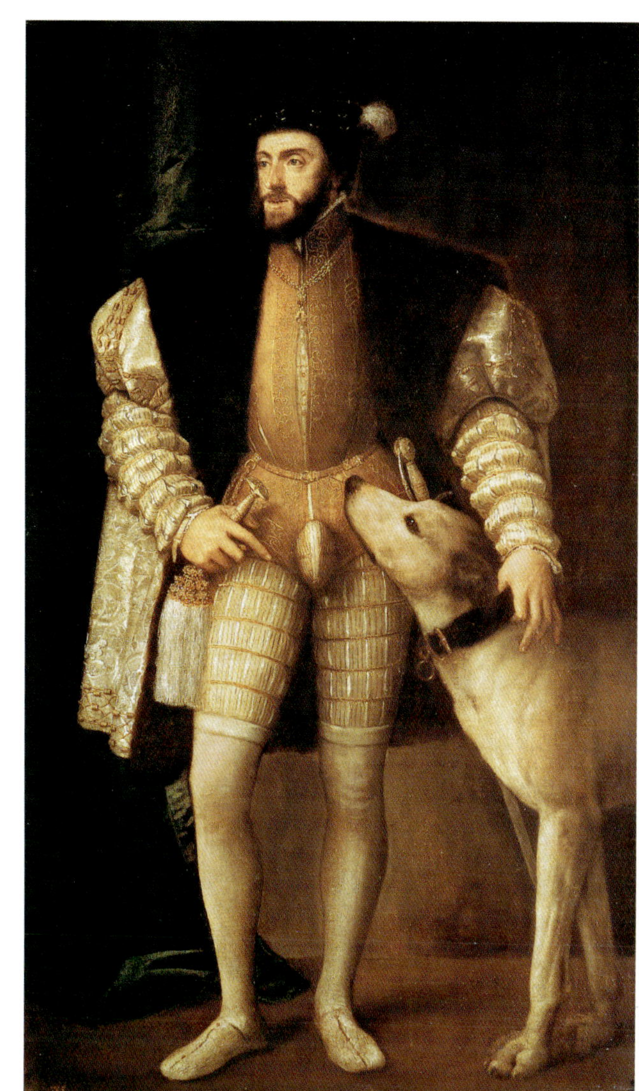

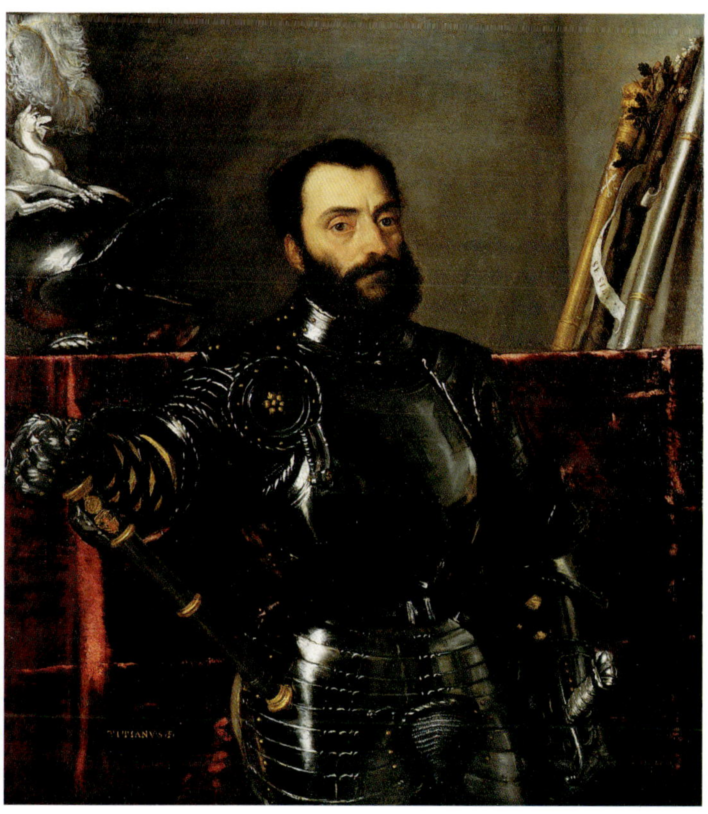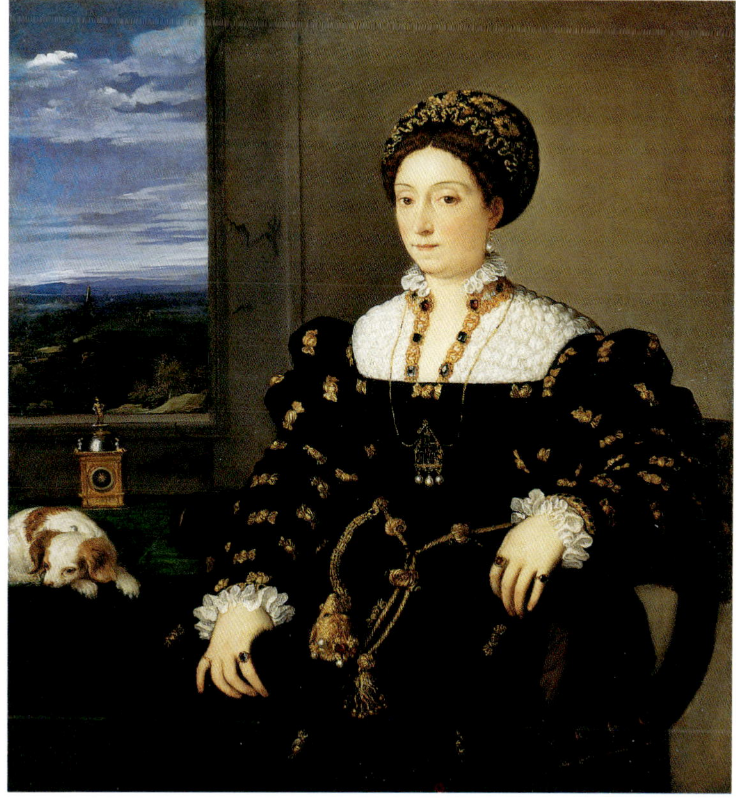

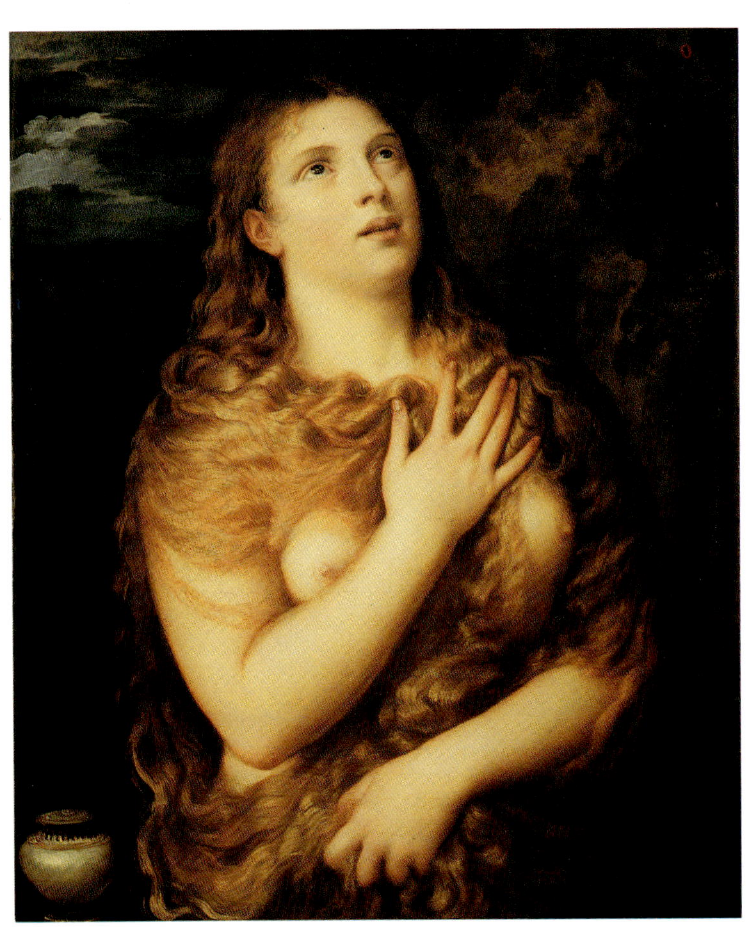

47. Mary Magdalene (c. 1533)
84x69.2 cm
Florence, Galleria Palatina, Pitti Palace

48, 50. Venus of Urbino (1538)
119x165 cm
Florence, Uffizi

49. La Bella (1536)
89x75.5 cm
Florence, Galleria Palatina, Pitti Palace

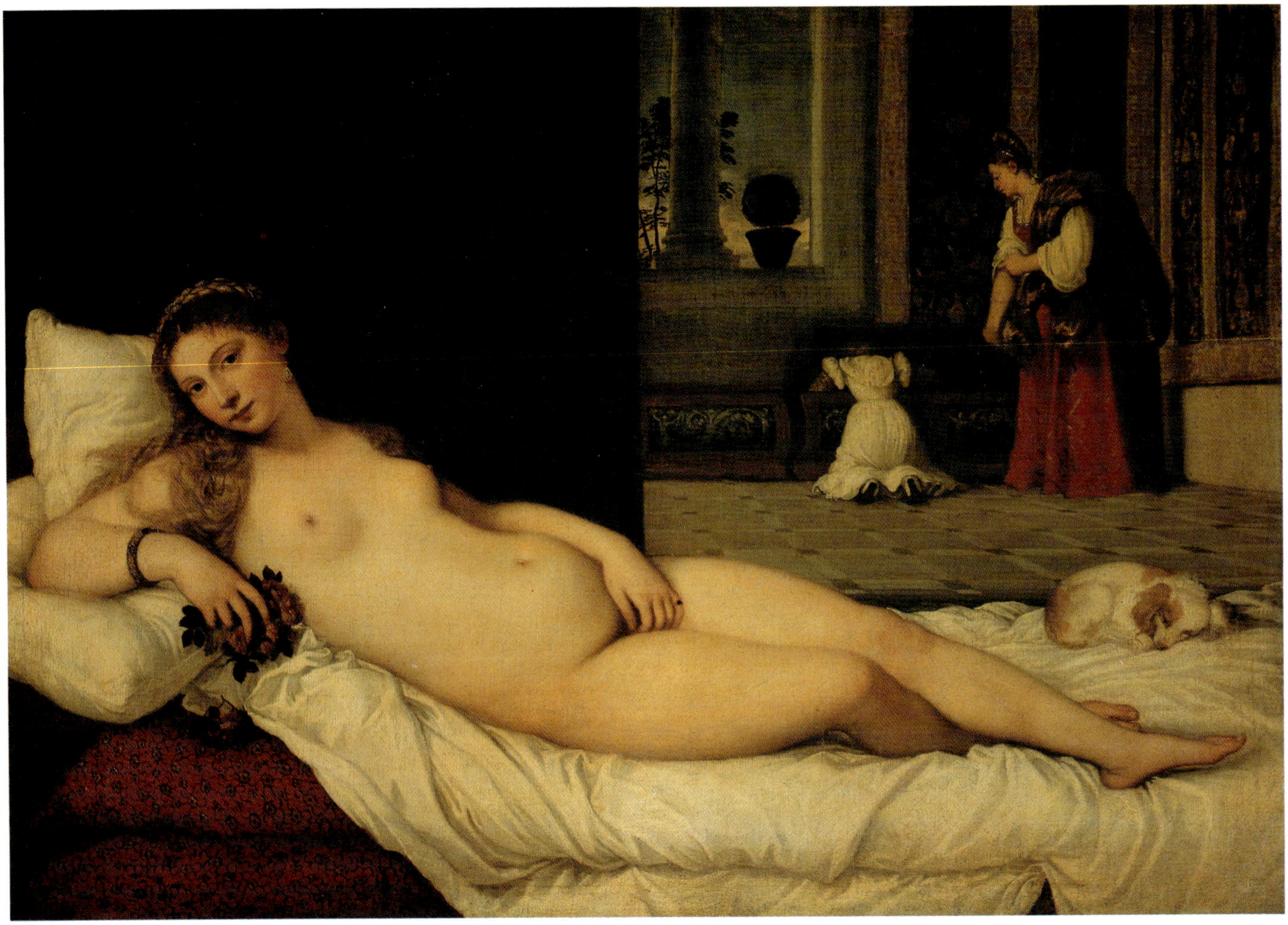

ty; she is presented to us quite simply as the goddess of carnal love — a courtesan in her boudoir.

The year 1538 was another decisive one for Titian. Resisting the blandishments of the Spanish emissaries who were intent on luring him to Madrid, he decided once again to remain in Venice, where he finally completed the *Battle of Cadore* which he had begun back in 1513. This huge canvas was also destroyed in the fire of 20 December 1577 and all that remains are a few preparatory drawings and a copy in the Uffizi Gallery. From these and from the written testimony of those who saw the work *in situ*, it is clear that Titian had in mind the battle frescoes planned by Leonardo and Michelangelo for the Palazzo Vecchio in Florence. He brought to his canvas a scene of passionate commotion and heroic turmoil emphasised by the energetic dynamism of the figures. The lost *Annunciation* of 1537 (carried out for the Murano convent of Santa Maria degli Angeli but rejected by them) must have displayed similar characteristics; it is known today only through an engraving by Caraglio.

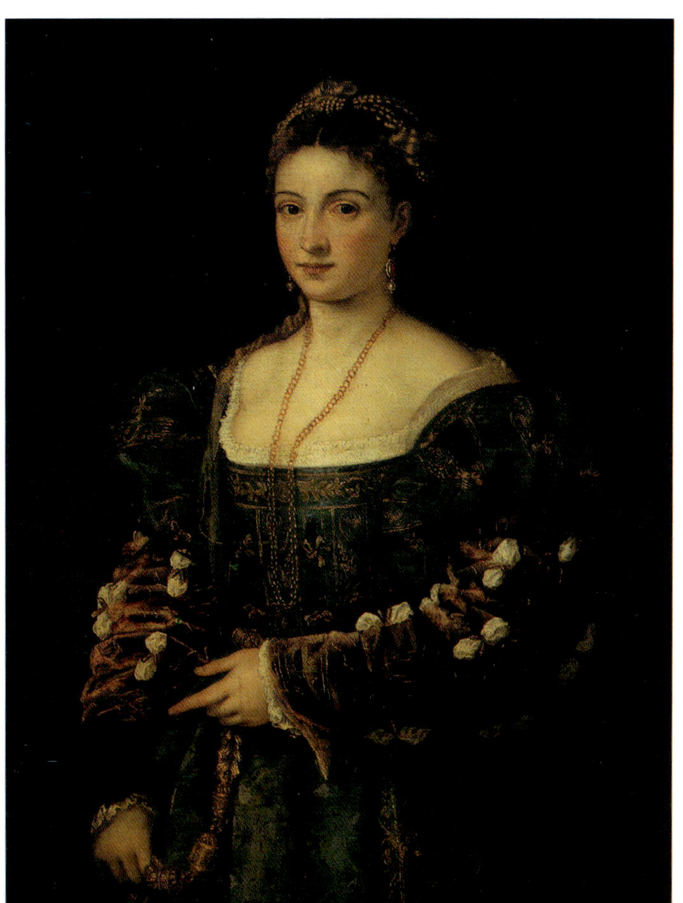

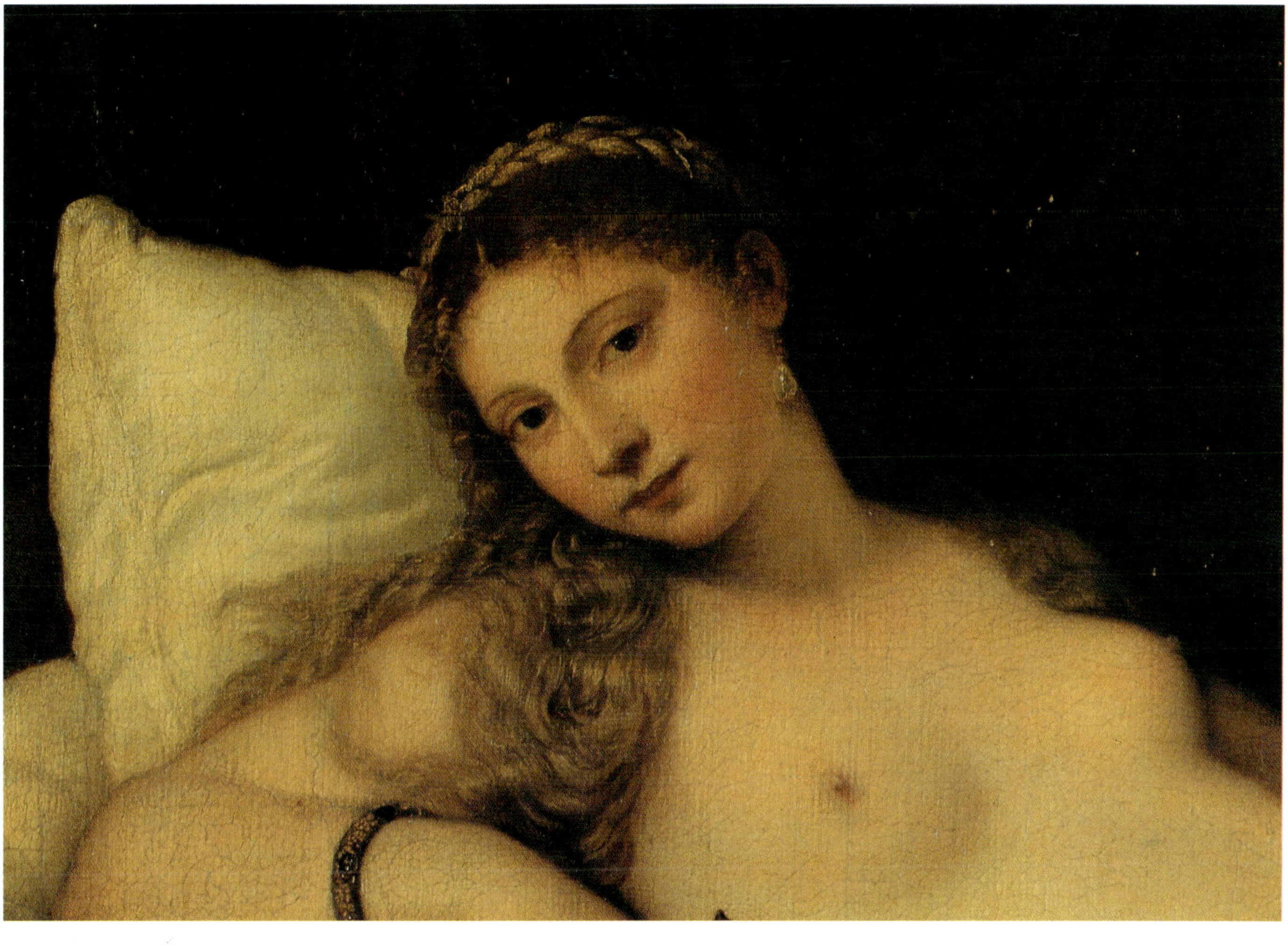

Titian and Mannerism

In 1539 Titian completed the *Presentation of the Virgin at the Temple* for the 'Scuola Grande' of Santa Maria della Carità, now the Accademia Gallery of Venice. The painting is remarkable for its glowing colours and for the careful depiction of naturalistic detail. The architectural vistas, inspired by stage-sets for the theatre, play a fundamental rôle in the work. It is evident from this use of perspective and from other stylistic clues that Titian was receptive to the influence of Tuscan-Roman painting filtered through the work of Porta and Salviati who arrived in Venice in 1539 and, later, through Vasari himself who came to Venice for the first time in 1541 to stage Aretino's play *Talanta*.

Titian's relationship with these artists in particular and Mannerist painting in general has been explored in various ways. For instance, in comparison with Pordenone (the painter considered to be the promotor of the Mannerist style in the Venetian area) Titian was more independent in adopting the imported Michelangelesque foreshortenings and it is worth remembering that he had used such devices before in his Frari *Assumption*. However, Titian's Mannerist leanings seem to be more a con-

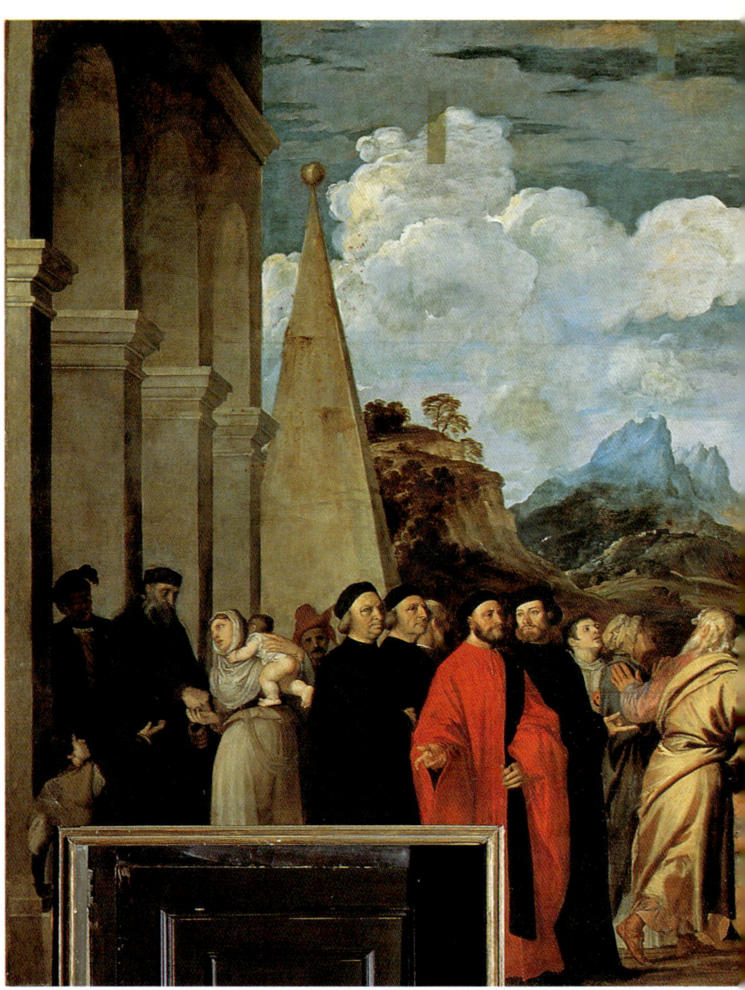

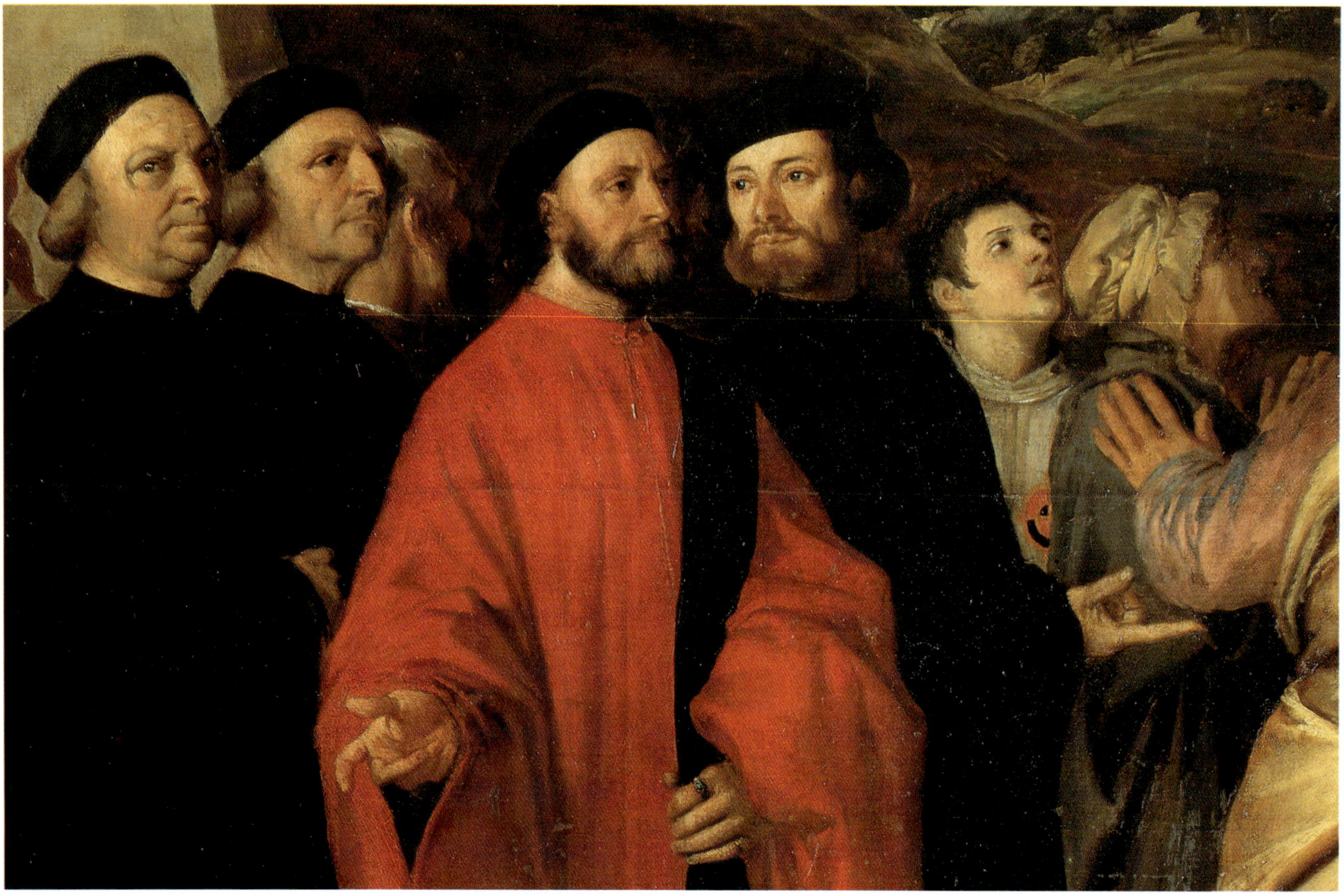

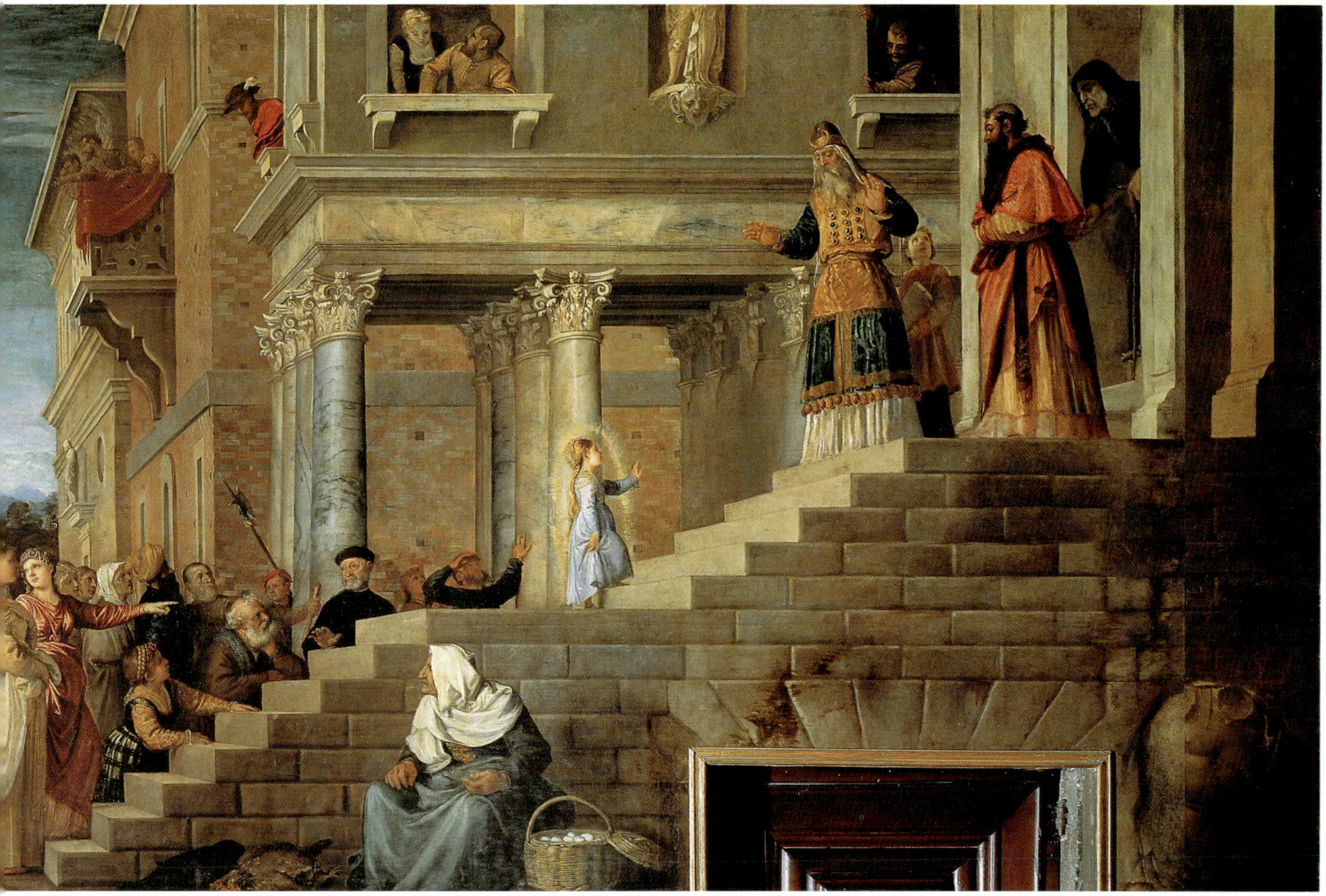

51-53. Presentation
of the Virgin at
the Temple (1539)
345x775 cm
Venice, Academy
Gallery

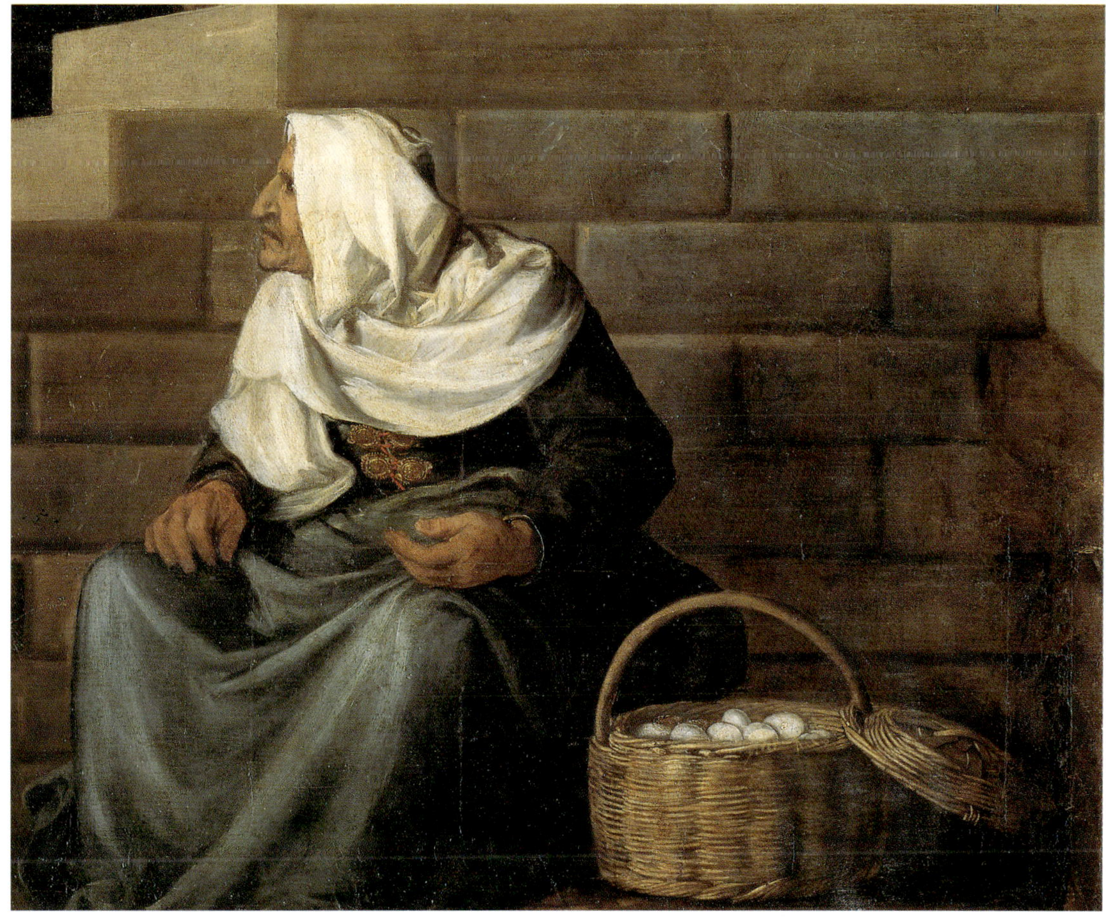

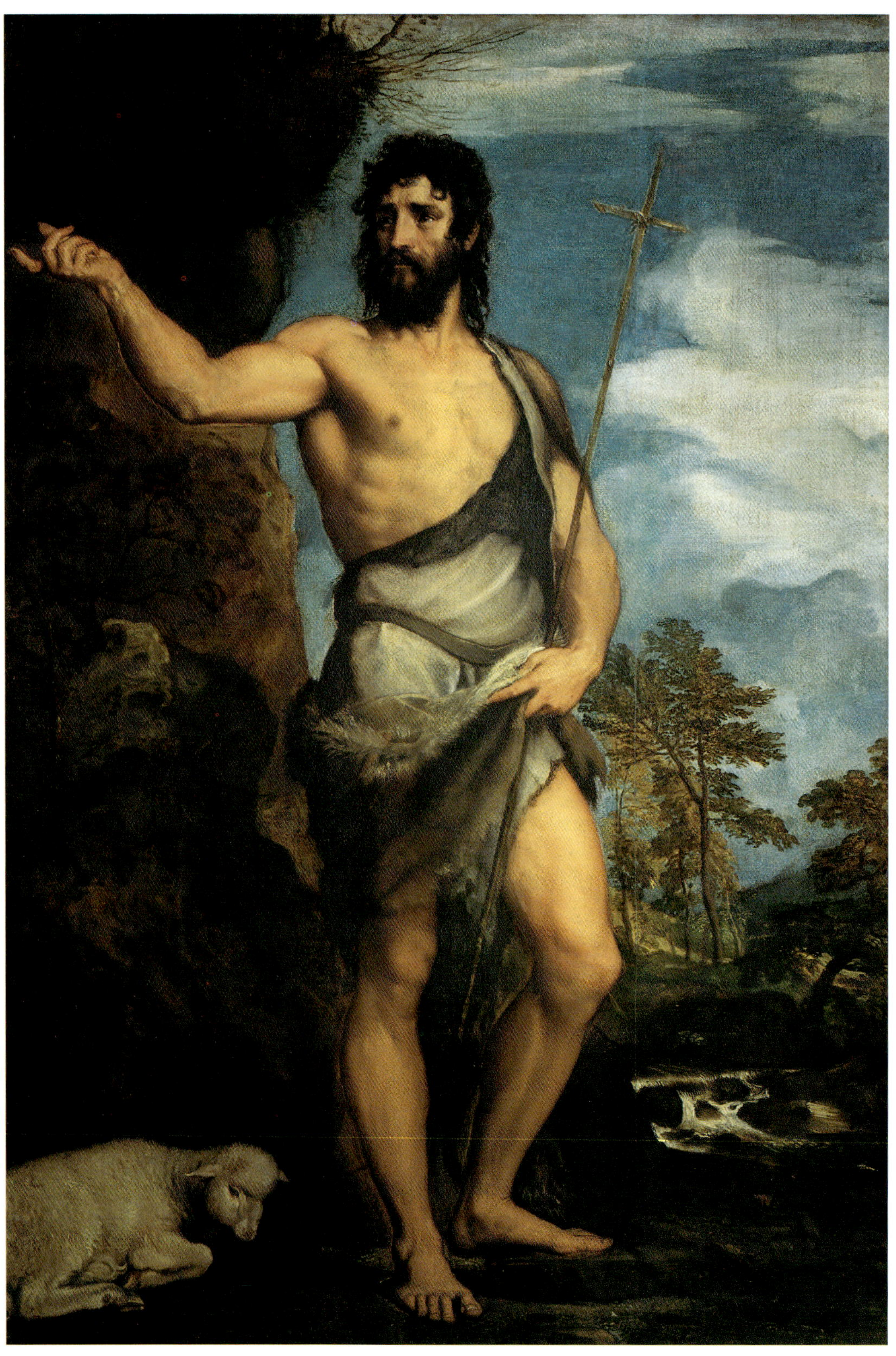

cession to fashion than the result of a conversion to the style. After all, Salviati, Porta and Vasari had been called to Venice by members of the aristocratic intellectual elite who had close political ties with the papal court. It is Giulio Romano who probably exerted the greatest influence on Titian who had direct experience of his Mantuan works. In fact, Titian's repertoire of muscular nudes derives from Giulio Romano rather than from Tuscan artists present in Venice. The same is true of the spiralling movement of figures, the counterpoised poses and the strong intersecting diagonals in works such as the Louvre *Crowning with Thorns* (1540), the Accademia *St John the Baptist* of the same year and the ceiling paintings of 1542-1544 for Santo Spirito in Isola, now in the sacristy of the church of Santa Maria della Salute. In these canvases, as well as in works with secular or mythological subjects such

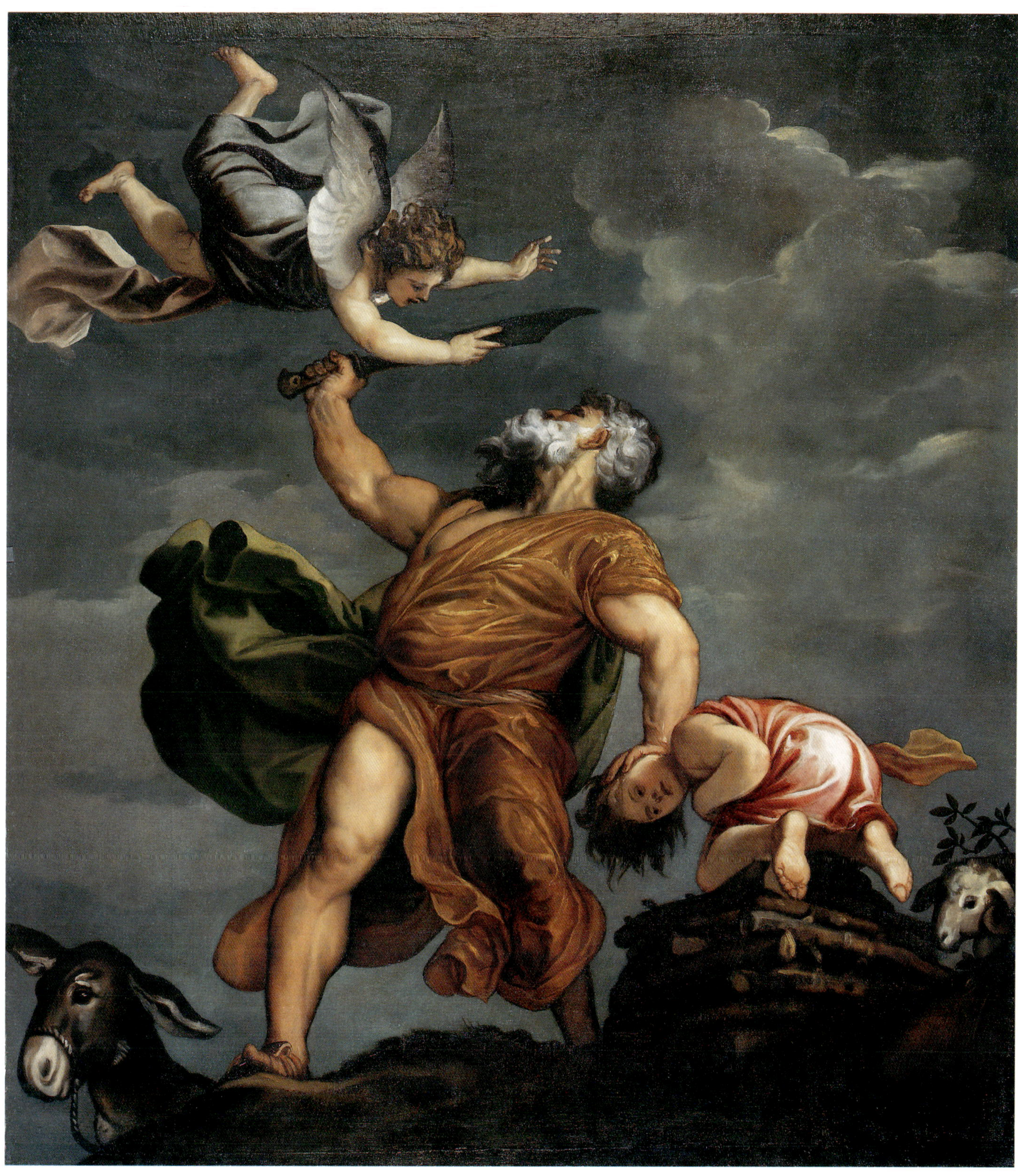

54. *St John the Baptist (1540)*
201x134 cm
Venice, Academy Gallery

55. *Sacrifice of Isaac (1542/1544)*
328x284.5 cm
Venice, Church of Santa Maria della Salute

as *Alfonso D'Avalos Addressing his Troops* (1540-1541) and the so-called *Pardo Venus*, we see Titian's Mannerism at its height. Often verging on the brutal and bombastic, it is a style which saturates his work with intense drama. Yet it is worth noting how the three-dimensional clarity of Titian's figures, the bold effects of foreshortening and the strong contrasts of light and shade manage to achieve a perfect synthesis with the

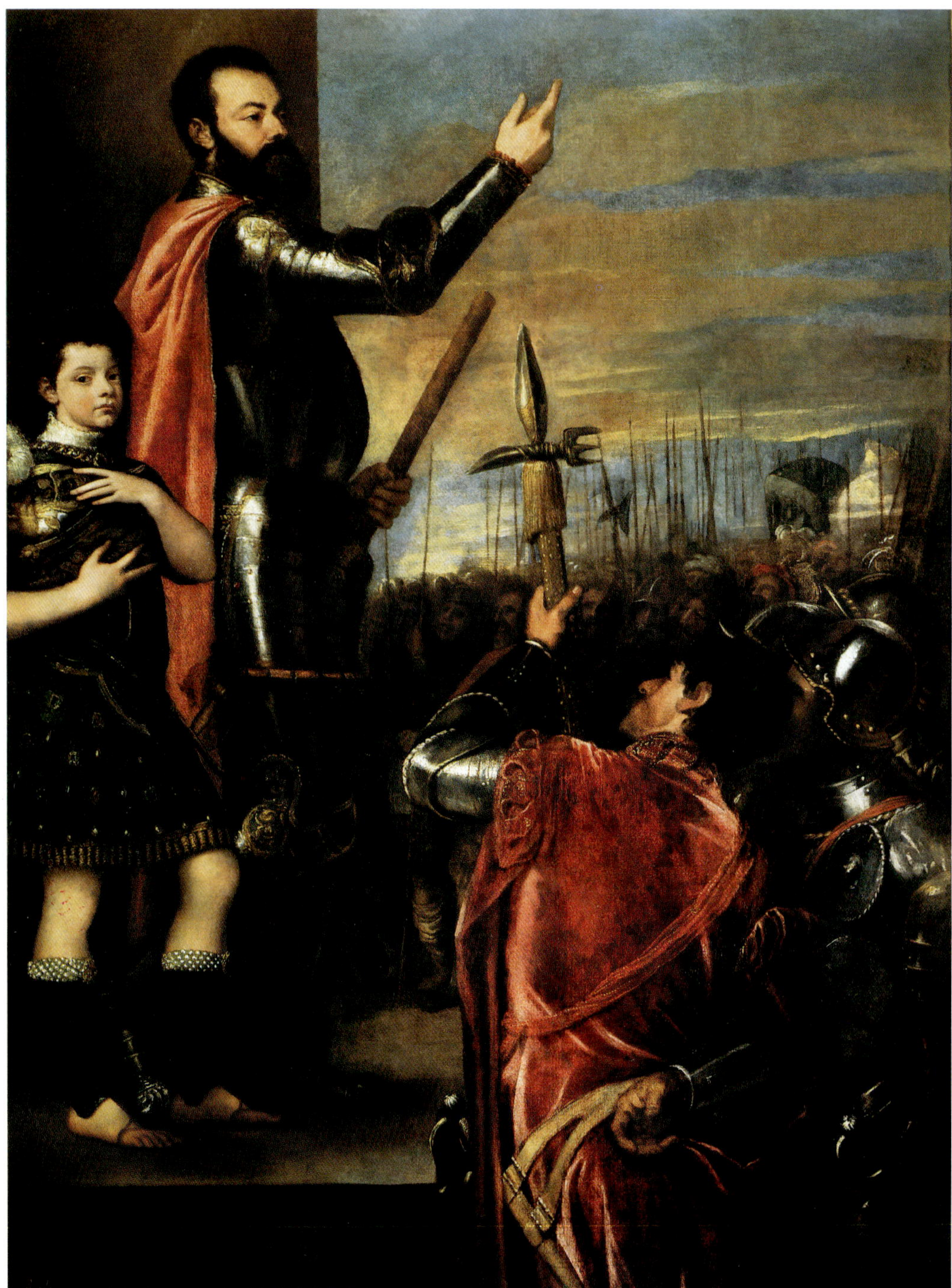

continual dominance of colour in his work.

A series of magnificent portraits belong to the period of Titian's so-called "Mannerist crisis". These include the Washington portrait of *Cardinal Pietro Bembo* datable to 1539-1540 and that of *Ranuccio Farnese*, probably executed in Venice in 1542, when the twelve-year old grandson of the Pope was nominated Prior of San Giovanni dei Furlani, the property of the Knights of Malta. This series of portraits include the Naples *Portrait of Paul III Farnese* and the Pitti *Portrait of a Nobleman*, the latter known as the *Young Englishman* because of the sitter's intensely blue eyes. The Washington *Portrait of Doge Gritti*, painted some years after his death in 1538, and the portrait of Titian's friend *Pietro Aretino* (Pitti) also belong to these years. In these works Titian lays bare, with a forcefulness which borders on the cynical, not only the physical features of his sitters, but also their psychological state. And so we are presented with the heroic moral tension of the warrior Doge, the overbearing arrogance of the Tuscan poet, the deeply-felt piety of the pope and the rigorous austerity of the "Young Englishman", all expressed in a stunning symphony of colour.

From 1539 onwards Titian established strong ties with the all-powerful Farnese family, which included Pope Paul III. As we have seen, Titian had ex-

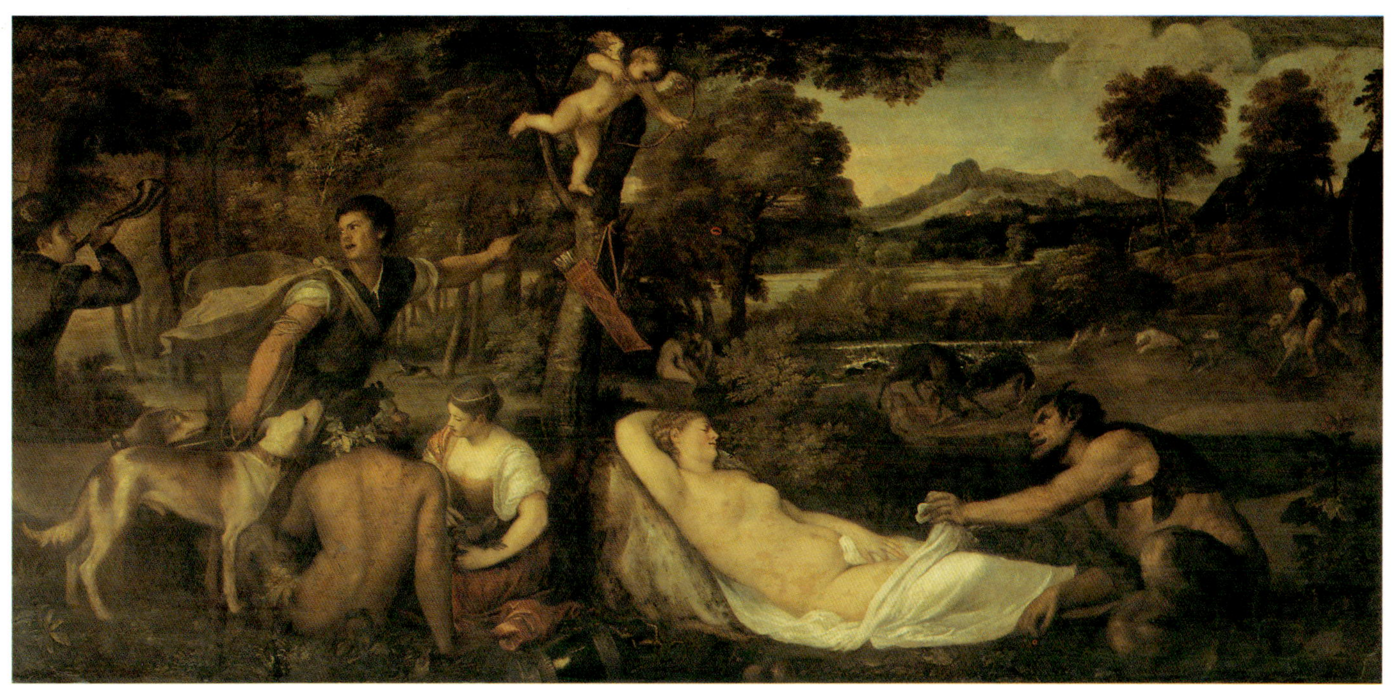

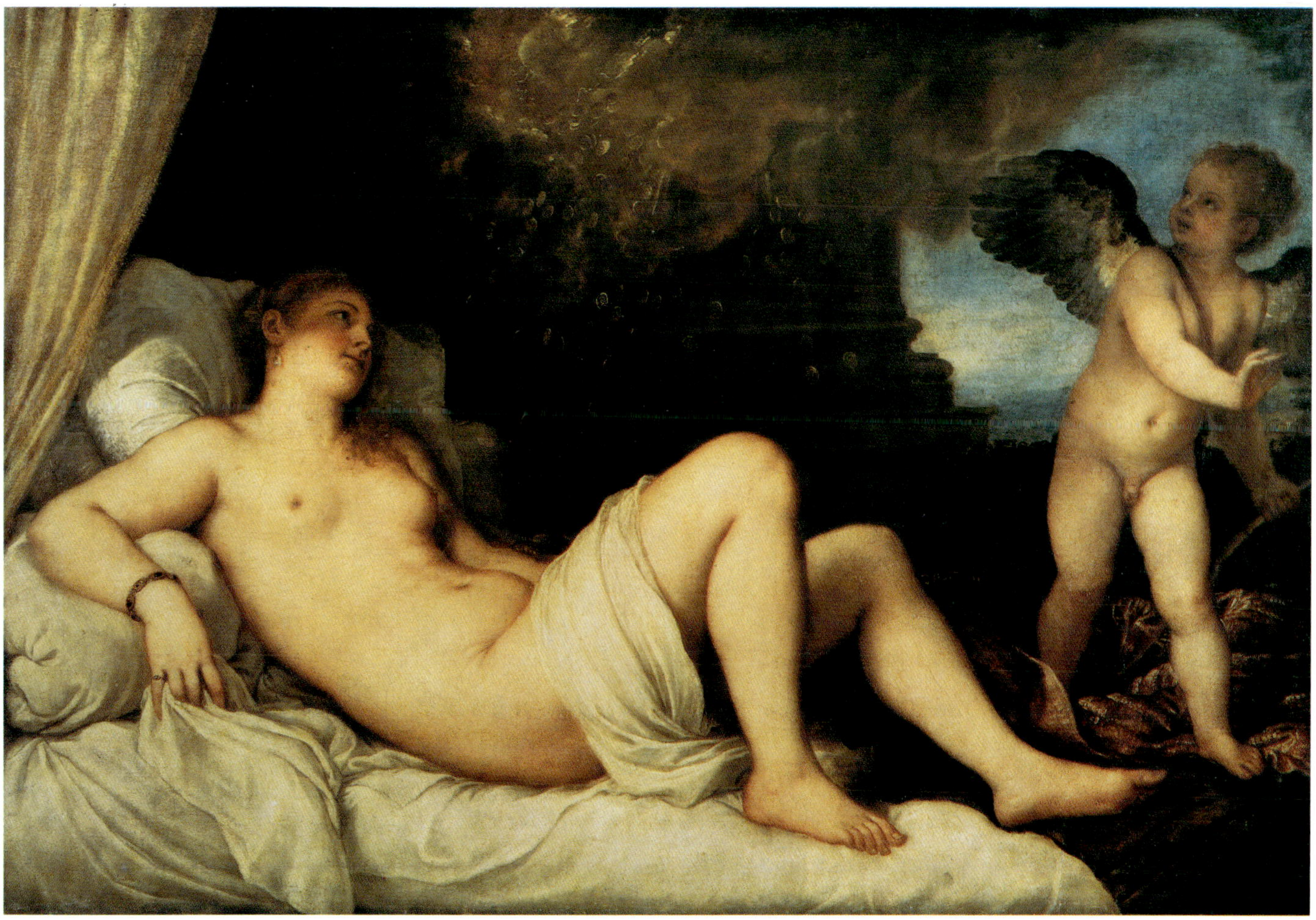

57. Pardo Venus (1540)
196x385 cm
Paris, Louvre

58. Danaë (1544)
117x69 cm
Naples, Capodimonte National Gallery

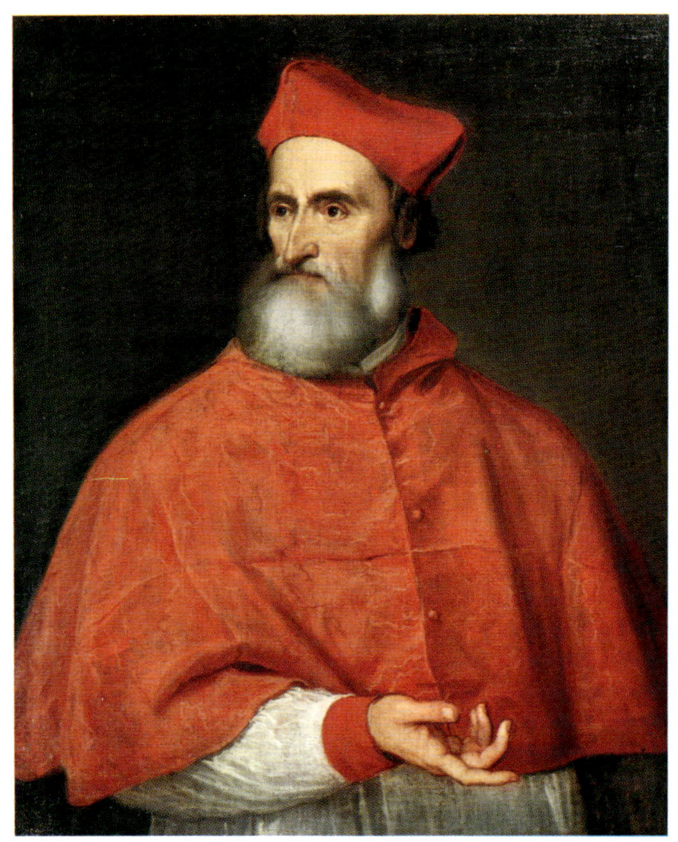

ecuted portraits of the young Ranuccio Farnese and of the Pope himself. In 1545 Titian at last agreed to go Rome, accepting the invitation of the Pope's nephew, Cardinal Alessandro Farnese, who had promised the painter benefices for his son Pomponio, who was a priest. He departed from Venice in September of that year and after a brief stay in the Marches, as guest of the Duke of Urbino, he reached Rome on 9 October. It seems likely that at this point in his career Titian would have felt himself almost obliged to experience at first hand the origins of the Mannerist style, which was rooted in the works of Raphael and Michelangelo. Nevertheless one has the impression that Titian had overcome his "Mannerist crisis" of the early 1540's even before setting out for Rome. Indeed, he carried with him the remarkable Naples *Danaë*, painted for Ottavio Farnese, which he had completed shortly before his departure. This work constitutes the clearest evidence of a decisive stylistic change of direction in Titian's painting at this time. The powerful physicality of the *St John the Baptist* or the athletic protagonists which throng the biblical narratives for

59. Portrait of Pietro Bembo (1539/1540)
94.5x76.5 cm
Washington, National Gallery of Art

60. Portrait of a Gentleman known as "The Young Englishman" (1544/1545)
111x96.8 cm
Florence, Galleria Palatina, Pitti Palace

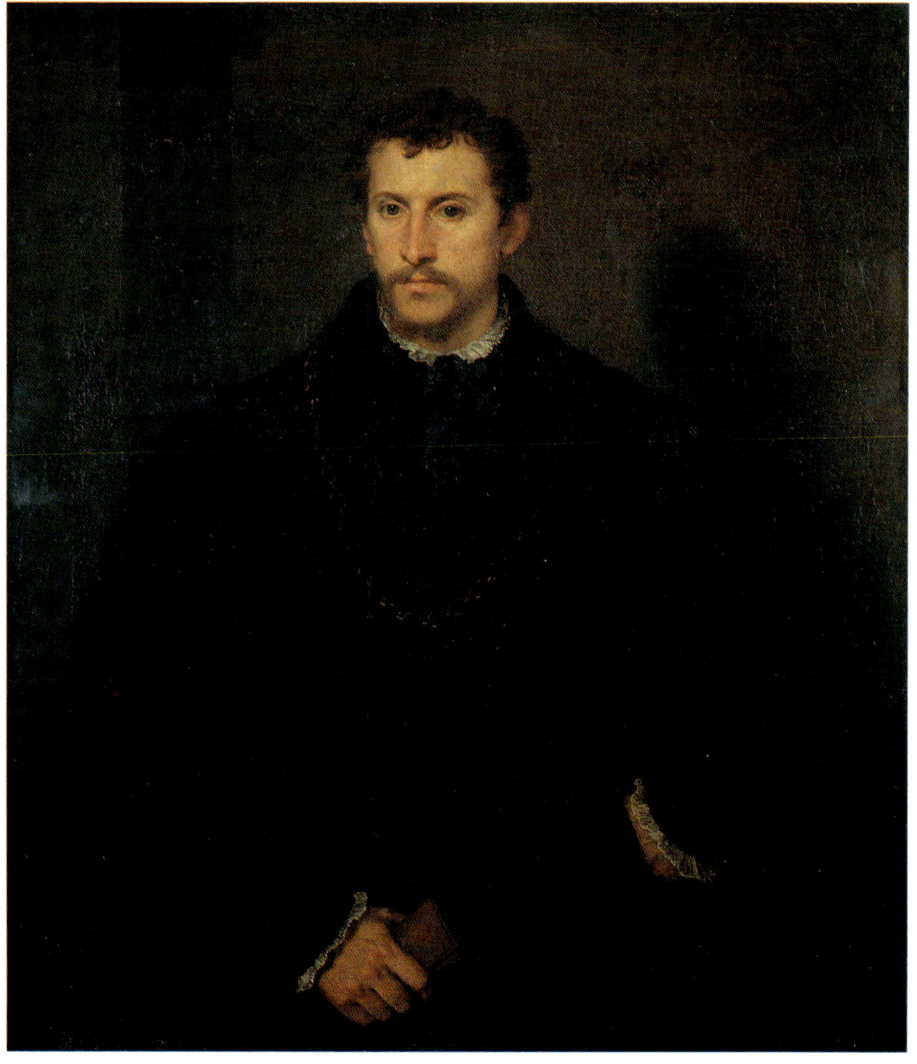

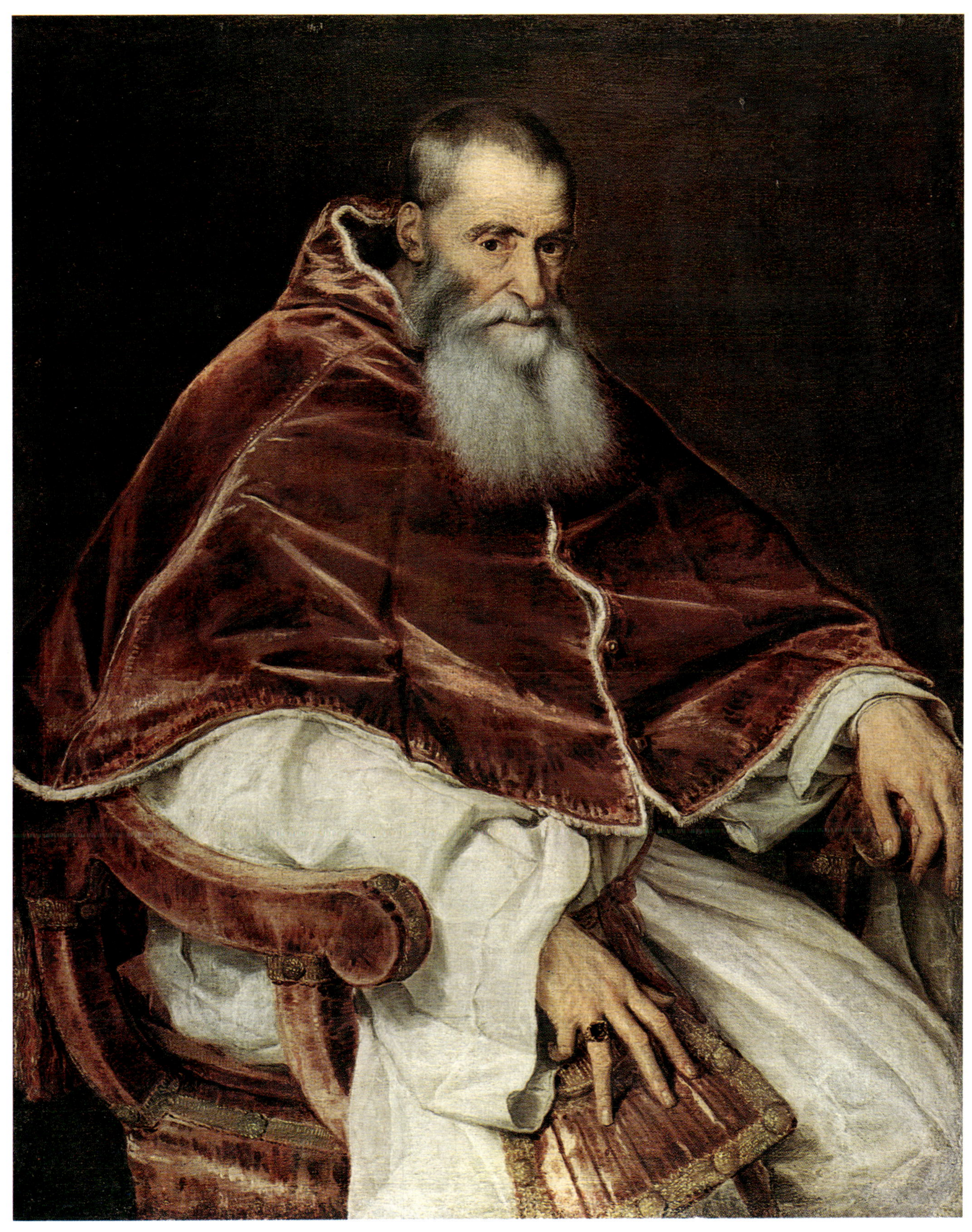

61. Portrait of Pope Paul III (1545/1546)
106x85 cm
Naples, Capodimonte National Gallery

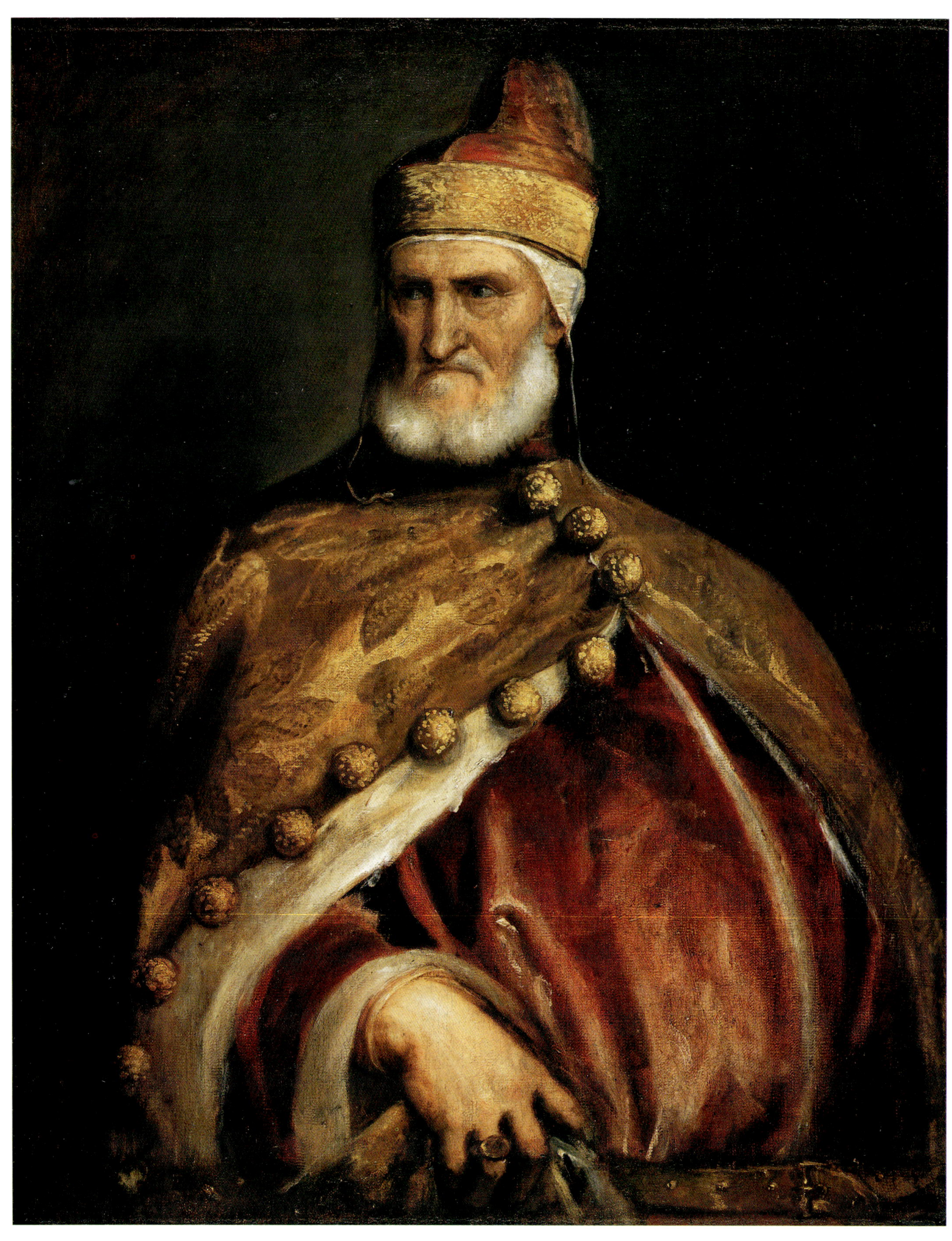

62. *Portrait of Doge Andrea Gritti (1544/1545)*
133.6x103.2 cm
Washington, National Gallery of Art

63. *Portrait of Pietro Aretino (1545)*
96.7x77.6 cm
Florence, Galleria Palatina, Pitti Palace

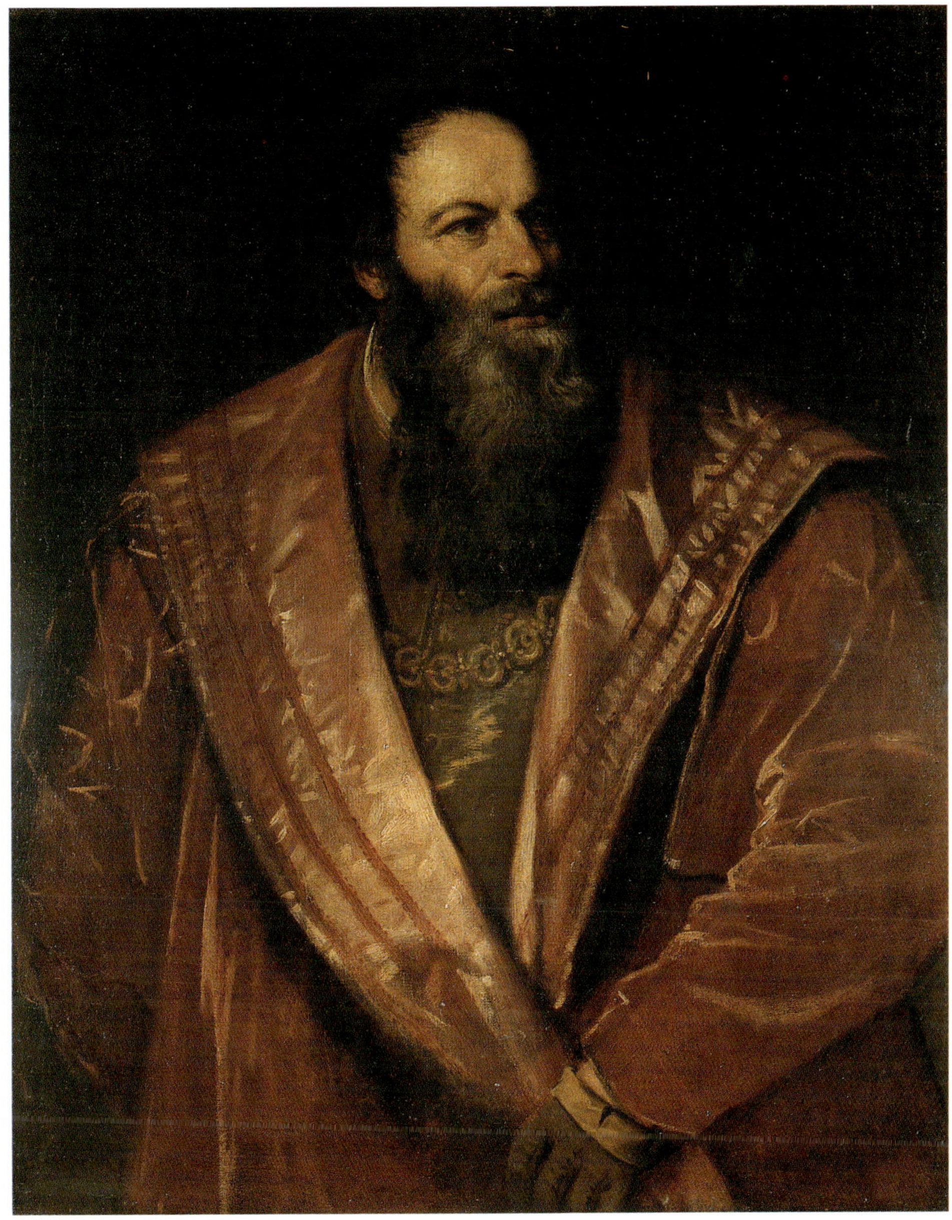

Santo Spirito in Isola give way to a sensuous naturalism which reveals a renewed interest in the unconstrained use of rich colour, especially in the landscape.

It is clear that a work such as the *Danaë* could never have been fully appreciated in the artistic climate of contemporary Rome. Indeed, Vasari recounts how the great Michelangelo went to pay his respects to Titian in his rooms and, having seen the *Danaë*, praised its "colouring and style". On leaving the painter's house, however, Michelangelo could not resist adding that "it was a shame that in Venice they did not learn to draw well from the beginning and that those painters did not pursue their studies with more method".

It was highly unlikely that Titian's sojourn in Rome would herald any significant change in his work, given the great divide which separated his painting — on the conceptual as well as stylistic lev-el — from the style dominant in the papal city. He did, however, stay on in Rome for several months, partly because he was still hoping (in vain as it turned out) for the benefices promised to his son Pomponio. Titian painted three portraits for the Farnese family, the most important of which is the one of *Pope Paul III with his Nephews Alessandro and Ottavio*, now at Capodimonte. This is a masterpiece of psychological insight in which the resonance of the colours plays its part by creating a feeling of distress.

The Roman interlude is only thinly documented in Titian's surviving correspondence. We have only one letter — to Emperor Charles V — in which the painter mentions his interest in the monuments of antiquity: "I am learning — he wrote — from these marvellous ancient stones". His stay in Rome came to an end in the early months of 1546; on 19 March he received honorary citizenship at a ceremony at

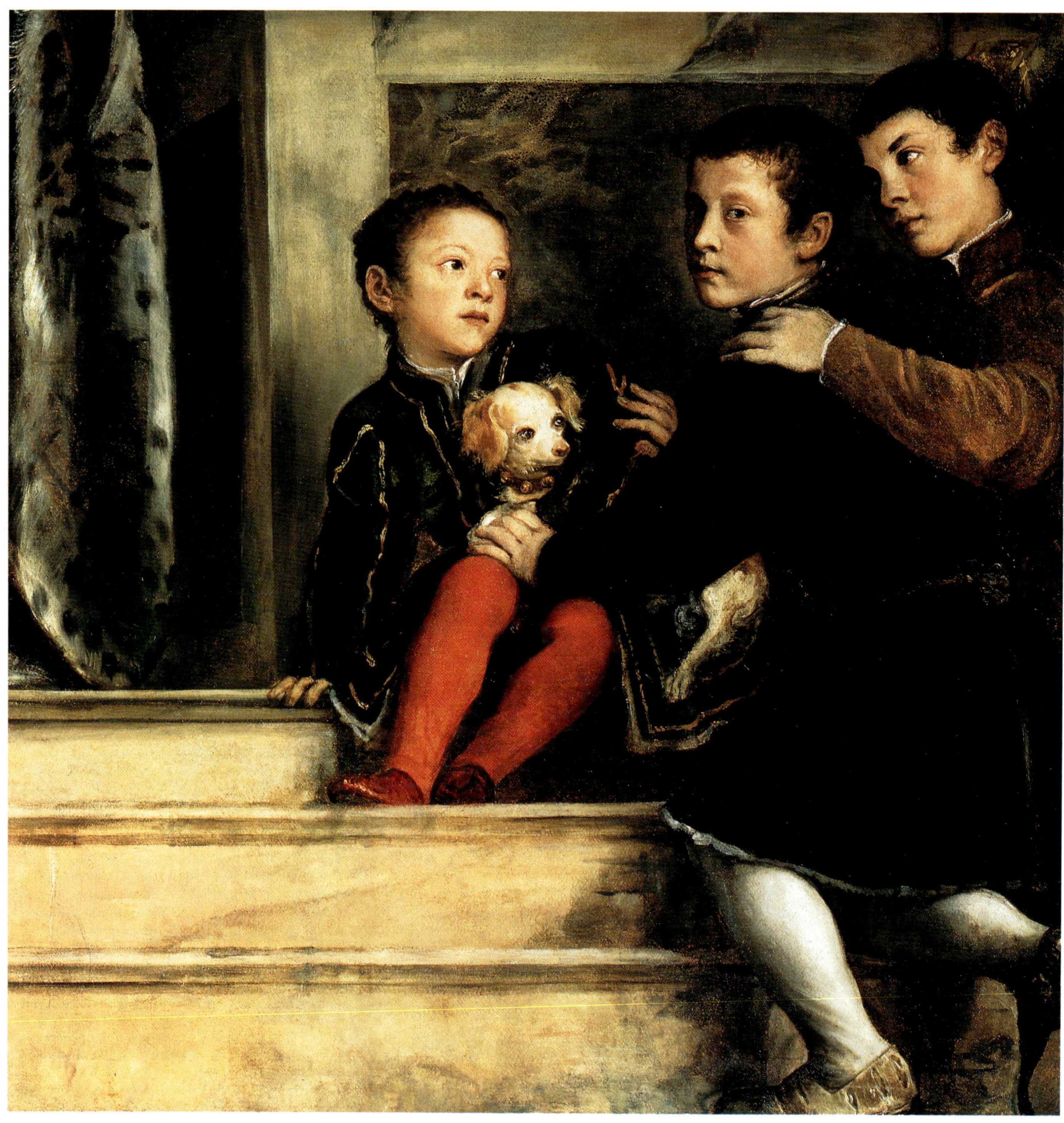

the Capitol and left for Florence shortly afterwards — the first stage of his rapid return journey to Venice.

On his return Titian was faced with a number of works left incomplete at his sudden departure for Rome. Among these was the resplendent *Votive Portrait of the Vendramin Family*, now in London; begun in 1543, it was only now brought to completion. In this work Titian takes up once more that scheme of composition experimented with twenty years earlier in the Pesaro altarpiece for the Frari church. Here, depicted with great realism and calm monumentality, the elderly Gabriele Vendramin, surrounded by his sons and grandsons, kneels before the altar which bears the sacred reliquary of the True Cross — property of the confraternity of Saint John the Evangelist. As in the earlier work, it is Titian's use of bright colour — vibrant notes of intense hues — which dominates the painting.

At the same time Titian was working on the central canvas for the ceiling of the meeting-hall in the 'Scuola Grande' of Saint John the Evangelist, leaving his assistants to finish the decoration. He also completed, with workshop assistance, the altarpiece for the church of Serravalle, begun in 1542.

64, 66. Votive
Portrait of the
Vendramin Family
(1547)
206x301 cm
National Gallery,
London

65. Pope Paul III
with his Nephews
Alessandro and
Ottavio (1546)
214x174 cm
Naples, Capodimonte
National Gallery

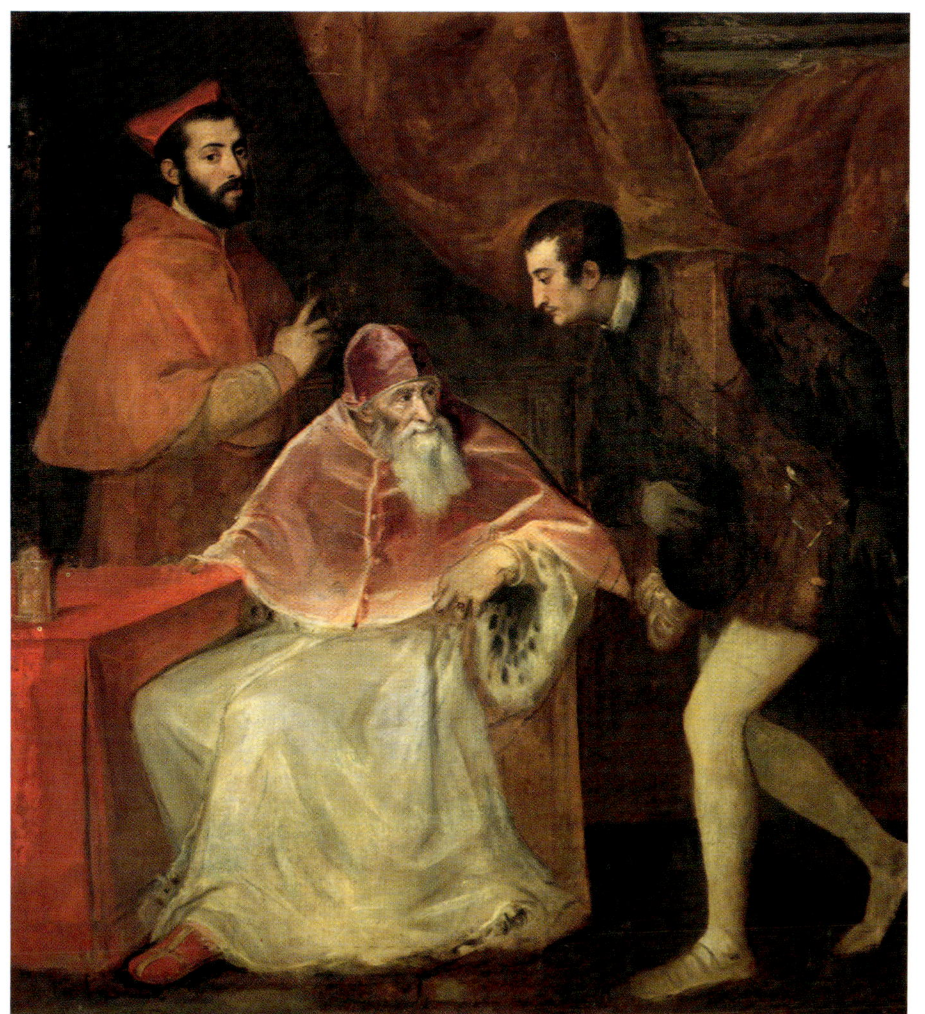

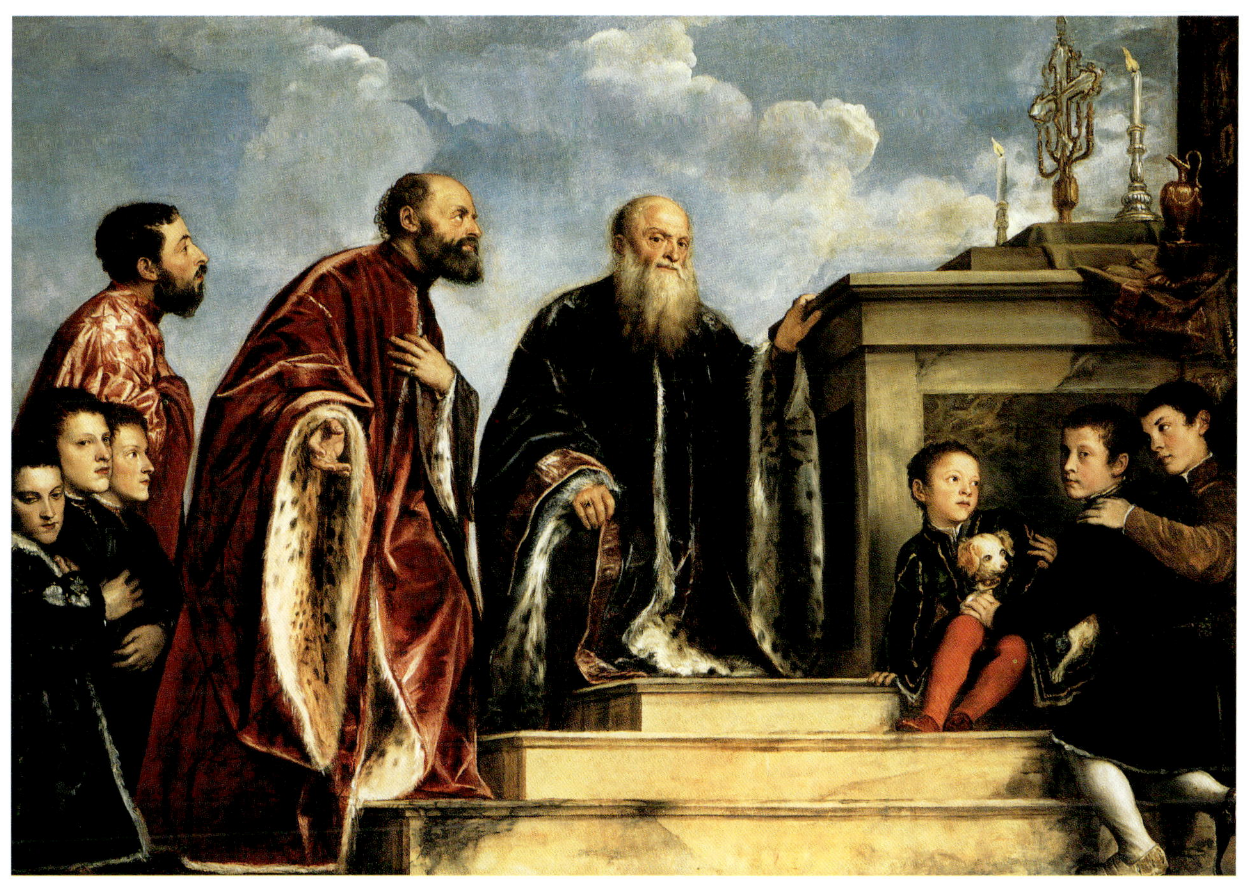

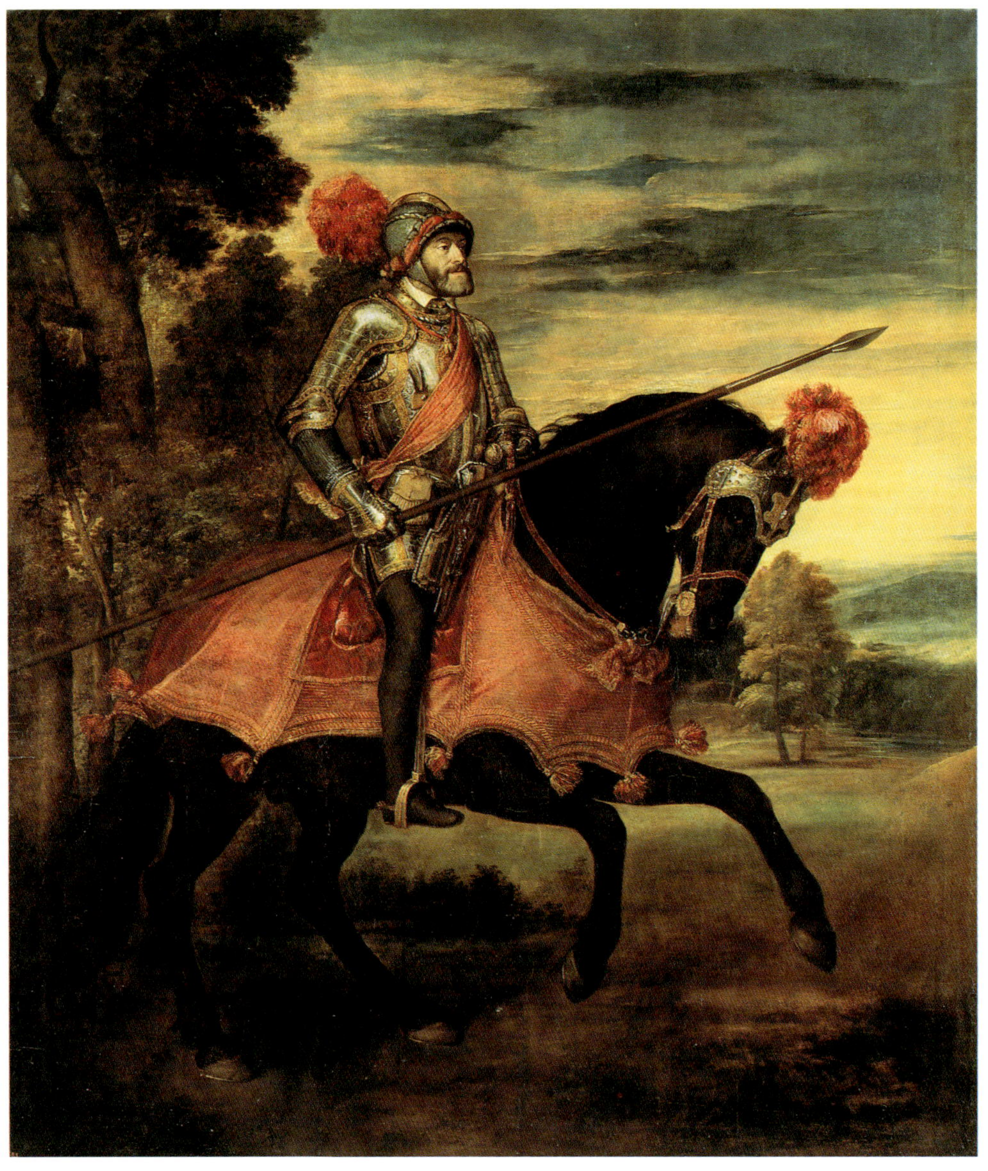

Charles V and Philip II

At the beginning of 1548 Titian left Venice once more, this time for Augsburg where he met Charles V, fresh from his great victory over the Protestant League at Mühlberg. Titian was accompanied by his son Orazio and Lambert Sustris, a young Dutch painter who had only recently joined his workshop. At Augsburg (where he remained until October 1548) he was kept frantically busy painting, chiefly, portraits of the Emperor and important members of his court. Of the Emperor's portraits the Prado *Charles V on Horseback* stands out. Here Titian displays the warrior virtues of this proud old monarch in clear contrast to the melancholy and slightly pained image of the same Emperor in the Munich *Charles V Seated*, where he seems weighed down by the cares of state and religion.

Apart from the portraits, Titian also worked on the first version of the Prado *Venus with Organist and Small Dog*, one of his most successful compositions and destined to be repeated often by Titian and his workshop. At Augsburg he also received a commission from Queen Mary of Hungary to paint four ceiling canvases for her summer residence at the castle of Binche in Flanders. These

67. Portrait of Charles V on Horseback (1548)
332x279 cm
Madrid, Prado

morality-paintings were to depict the famous legendary torments of the 'Damned': those of Tityus, Sisyphus, Tantalus and Ixion. On his return to Venice Titian painted the *Tityus and Sisyphus* which were complete by June 1549. It is possible that he never executed the remaining two canvases. The most obvious characteristics of the two paintings despatched to Flanders and now in Madrid is the evidence of a return to the expressive vocabulary of Mannerism, which derives ultimately from Michelangelo. Moreover, here Titian painted 'lightning flash' effects of light and used a thicker 'impasto' of colour which makes these canvases quite different from the somewhat monochromatic flatness of the earlier ceiling paintings for Santo Spirito in Isola.

The altarpiece for the church of San Giovanni Elemosinario in Venice belongs to this stylistic phase, although the date of the work has long been a matter of debate. However, the fiery colours, offset by the white gleam of the saint's robe, leads one to place this complex painting (in which there are still echoes of Pordenone's approach to composition) close to the Prado 'Damned'.

At the beginning of November 1550 Titian, who was then more than sixty years old, undertook a second journey to Augsburg to meet the Emperor. Charles V had called a meeting of the Diet at Augsburg and had used the occasion to announce his intention to abdicate in the near future, leaving the Imperial crown to his brother Ferdinand and that of Spain to his son, Prince Philip, who from that moment became the most important of Titian's patrons. Immediately Titian painted a full length portrait of Philip, now in the Prado. This is a remarkable exercise in court portraiture. with the deathly pale figure of the prince, confined within his splendid armour, who emerges imperiously from the shadows in a glow of light; in the same way a shaft of light picks out the great plumed helmet placed on the red velvet covering of the table behind the prince. The portrait can be considered as a sort of heraldic image, a symbol of the military and political power of the prince, but at the same time Titian gives us a psychological insight into this introverted personality, who would turn out to be indecisive in affairs of state and torn between a fanatic religious faith and a tortured, repressed sexuality.

Titian returned to Venice in August of 1551. From this time on he considerably reduced his work for local patrons, making way for painters of the younger generation, Tintoretto, Paolo Veronese and Jacopo Bassano, while he himself concentrat-

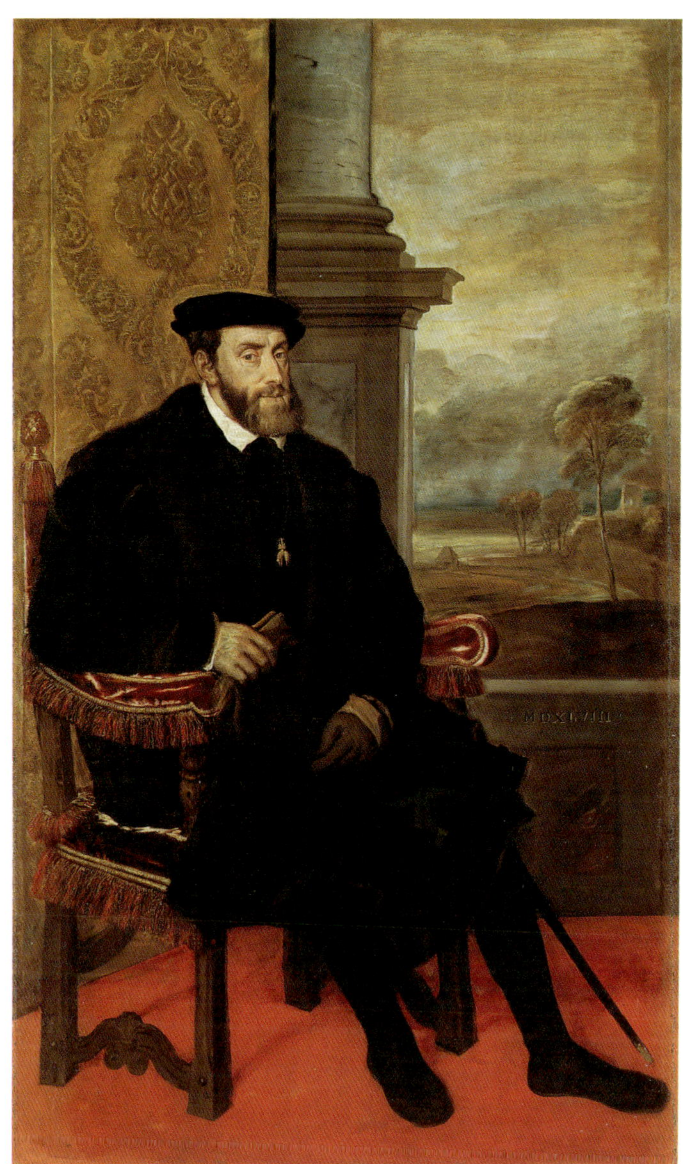

68. Portrait of Charles V Seated (1548)
205x122 cm
Munich, Bayerische Staatsgemäldesammlungen

ed on the numerous commissions from the Hapsburgs and their *entourage*. Titian's connection with Philip II (who ascended the throne in 1556) and the Spanish court was not financially rewarding, as is made clear in the many letters Titian wrote to the king in his frequently unsuccessful efforts to obtain money promised him. On the other hand the relationship was extremely positive from the artistic point of view, in that he was left at liberty to experiment with the inventiveness, interpretation and execution of the works asked of him.

He continued to paint portraits of dignitaries connected with the Imperial court. These include the bishop prince of Trent, *Cristoforo Madruzzo*, now in São Paulo and the *Captain with Cupid and a Dog*, now in Kassel. The importance of these per-

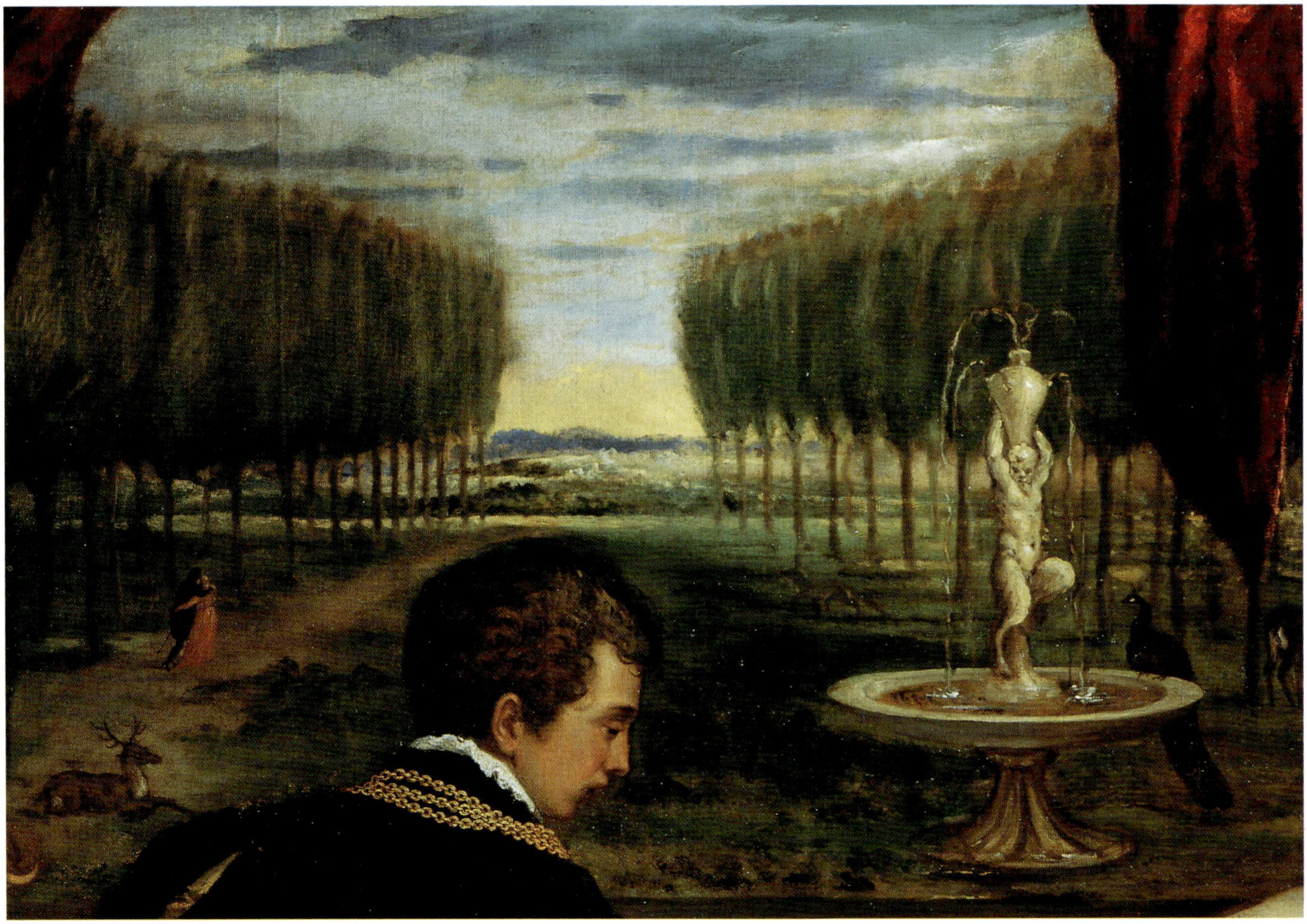

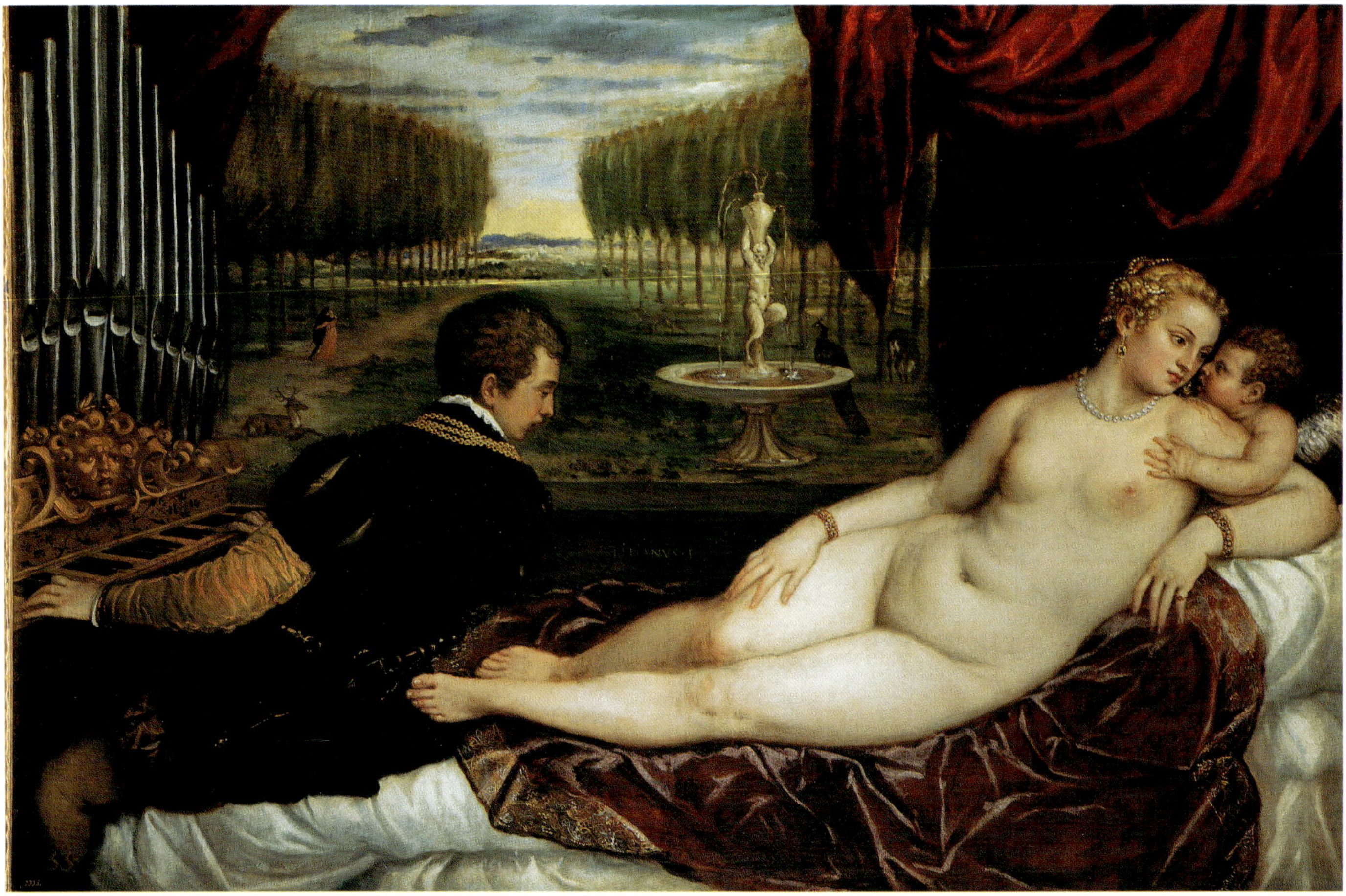

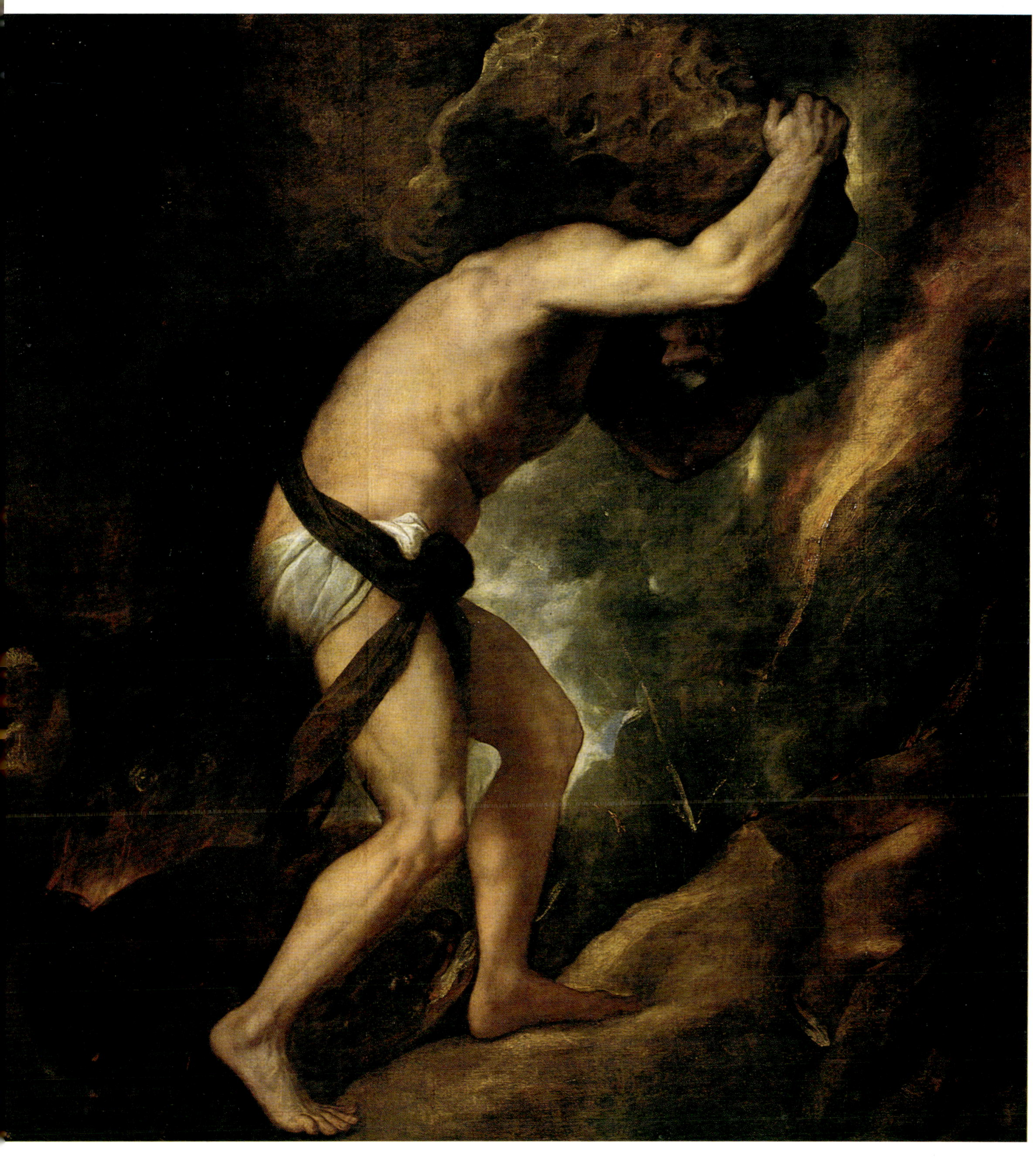

69, 70. *Venus with Organist and Cupid (1548)*
148x217 cm
Madrid, Prado

71. *Sisyphus (1549)*
237x216 cm
Madrid, Prado

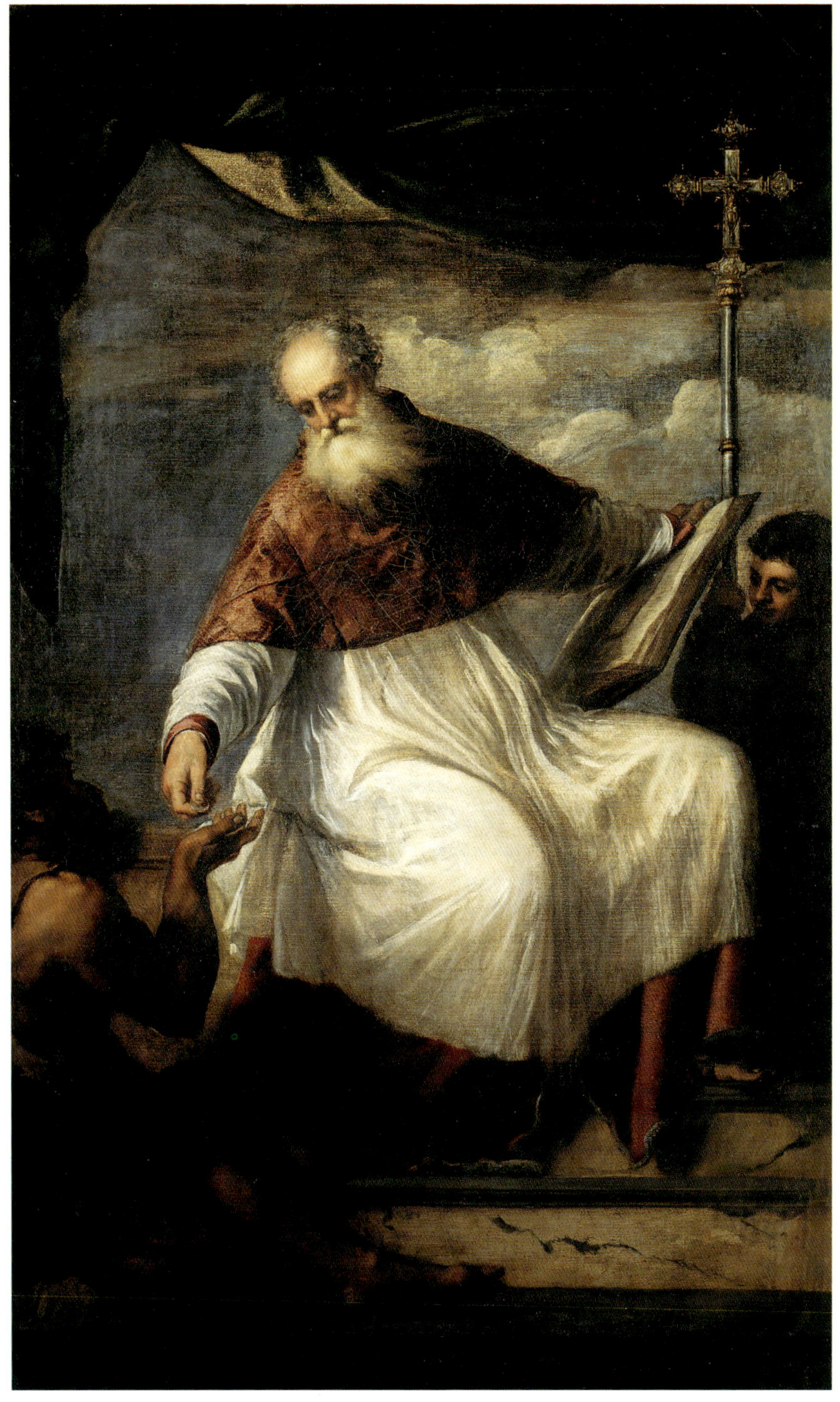

sonalities is made explicit by the fact that they are depicted full-length, which previously had been the case only with Titian's portraits of Charles V and Philip II. At the same time Titian was working on the *Trinity in Glory*, now in the Prado. This huge canvas was commissioned by Charles V during his stay at Augsburg and Titian had taken almost four years to complete it. The complex iconography (centred on the glorification of the Spanish court which is identified here with the heavenly court) has lent itself to various interpretations, from a *Paradise* to a *Last Judgement*. In the right margin of the painting appears Titian's foreshortened self-portrait. He places it below the figures of Charles V, his wife Isabella, Prince Philip and other notables, as if the painter wished to testify that he was accepted as part of their world.

Again for the Hapsburgs, Titian executed between 1553 and 1554 two "mythological fables" of clearly erotic intent — the *Venus and Adonis* and the *Danaë*, both now in the Prado. The latter is really a variation on the canvas painted ten years earlier for the Farnese family. With greater fidelity to Ovid's text, the Cupid has now been replaced by the elderly nurse who attempts to use her apron to gather the shower of gold into which Jupiter had

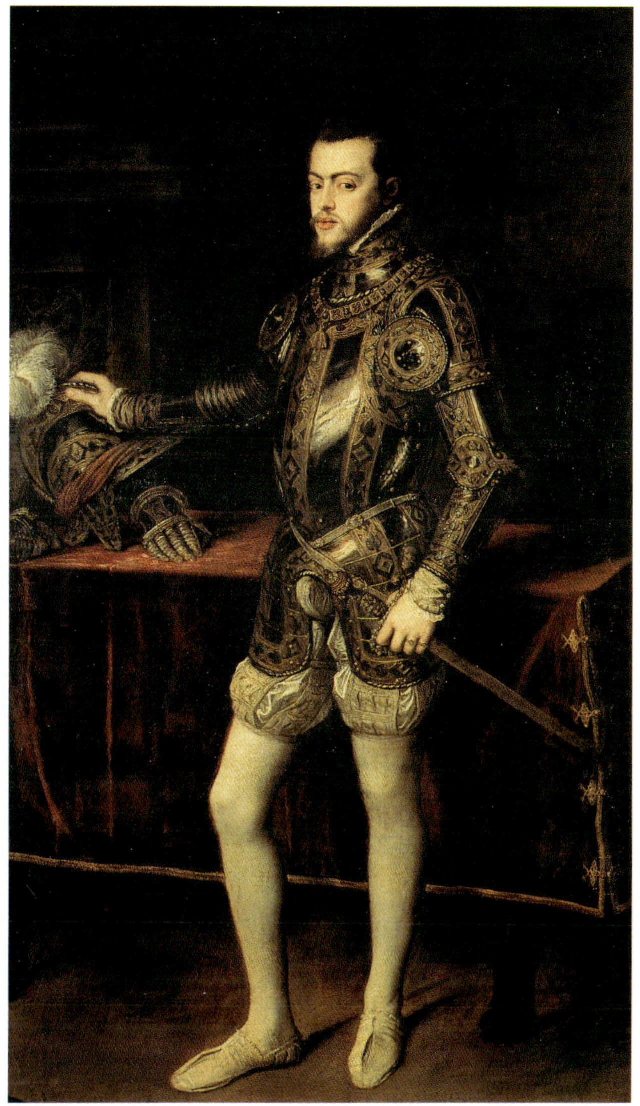 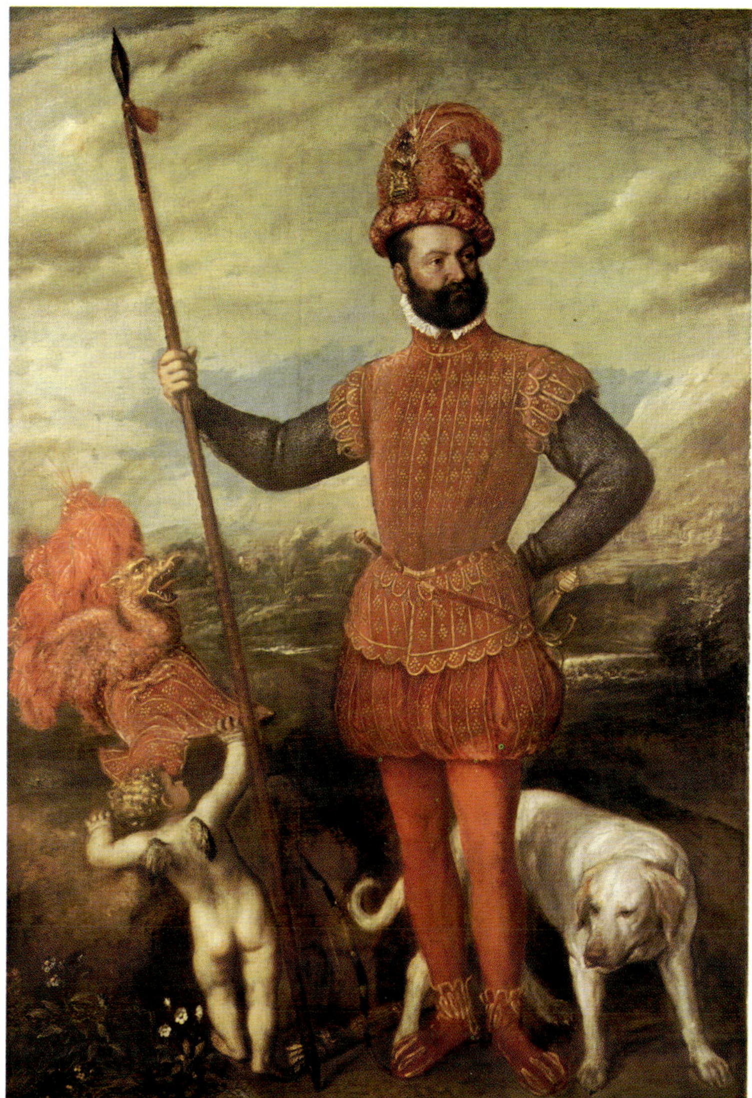

72. St John the Alms-Giver (1548/1549)
264x148 cm
Venice, Church of San Giovanni Elemosinario

73. Portrait of Philip II in Armour (1551)
193x111 cm
Madrid, Prado

74. Captain with Cupid and a Dog (1551)
223x151 cm
Kassel, Gemäldegalerie

transformed himself in order to possess the young woman. The *Venus and Adonis*, on the other hand, became the prototype for a whole series of replicas of this subject. In both paintings the scene of the union of the lovers is bathed in the warm light of sunset, where the diffuse softness of the colours holds sway. The female nudes reveal the continuing inspiration of Michelangelo's sculpture, such as the *Dawn* and *Night* from the Medici tombs in Florence. But what is entirely personal to Titian is the

quality of the colour, which fragments into patches of dazzling luminosity — a perfect complement to the ecstatic sensuous abandon of the figures.

Of the same high poetic quality is the Washington *Venus at her Toilet*, which can probably be dated to 1554-1555; the figure of the goddess derives from the celebrated Roman statue of Venus owned by the Medici family.

In the late 1550's Titian executed three altarpieces of great importance. In 1557 he completed the *Annunciation* for the church of San Domenico Maggiore in Naples, in 1558 the *Crucified Christ with the Virgin Mary, Saint Dominic and Saint John* for the church of San Domenico at Ancona and, in 1559, the *Martyrdom of St Lawrence* for the Venetian Crociferi church (subsequently the Jesuit church) which had been commissioned by Lorenzo Massolo back in 1548. The three paintings are stylistically similar although the Venetian altarpiece stands out for its very fine quality. In each of them Titian handles nocturnal scenes with a completely new technique of painting. In fact, he achieves

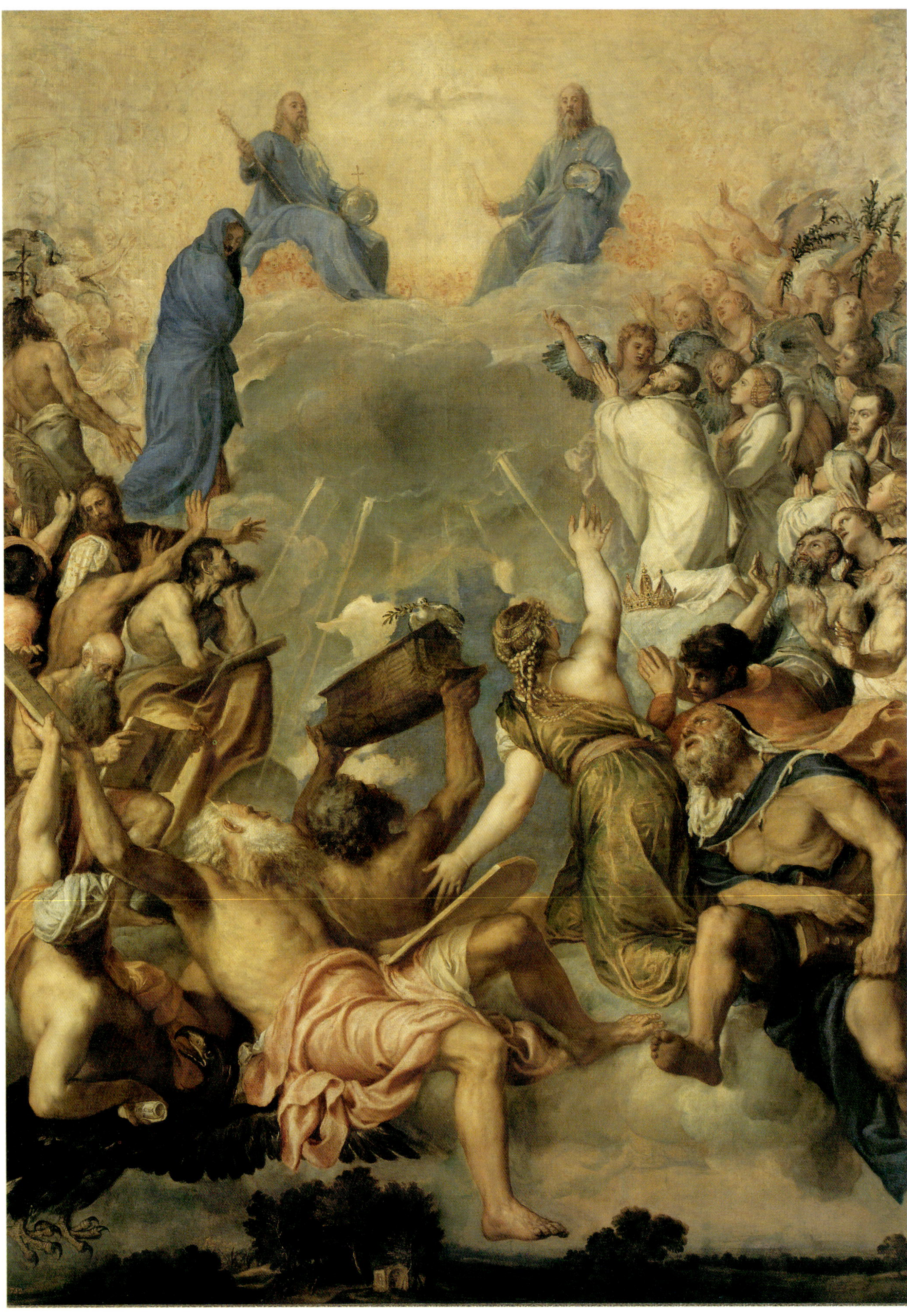

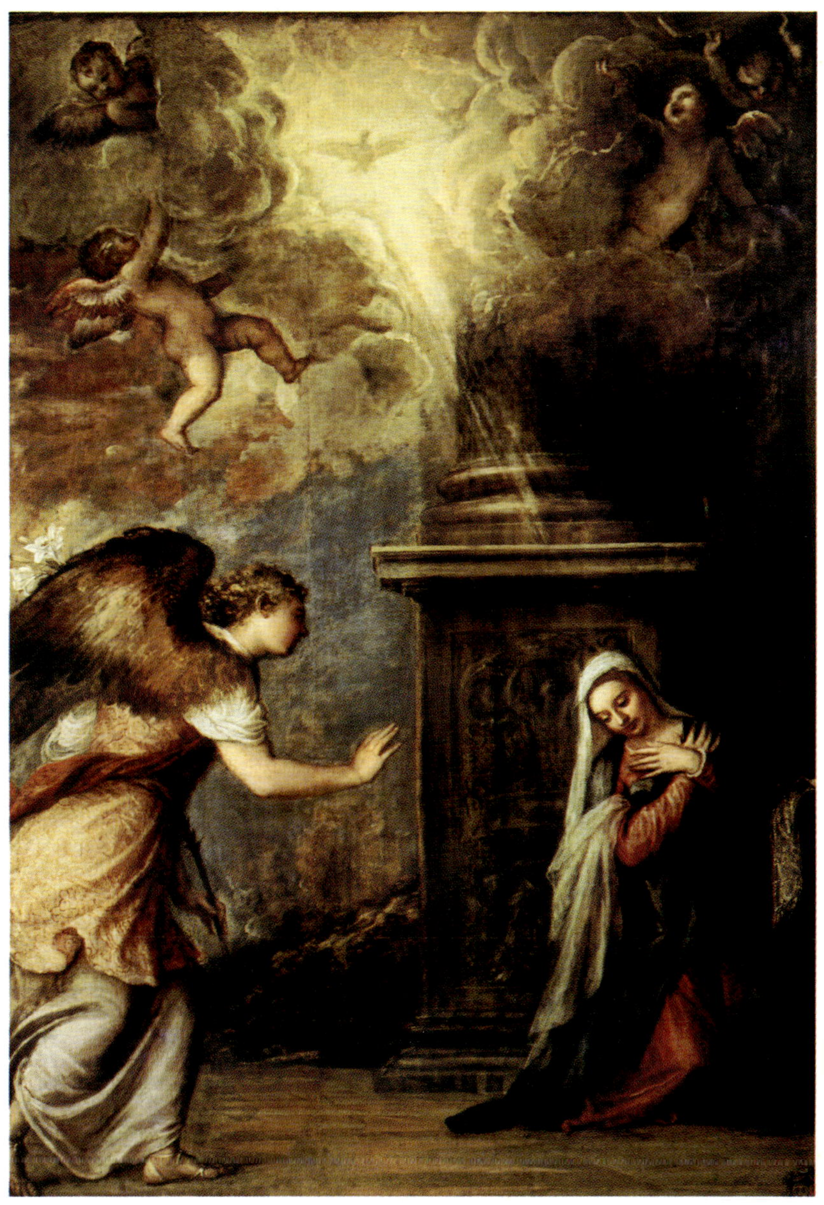

75. *The Trinity in Glory (1554)*
346x240 cm
Madrid, Prado

76. *Annunciation (1557)*
232x190 cm
Naples, Capodimonte National Gallery

those effects of strong light coming from within the dark backgrounds of the paintings by applying blobs of luminous pigment (white leads, lacquer reds, bright yellows, blood-red crimsons) onto a thickly layered, smokey background. This technique, which Titian was to use for the rest of his life, is beautifully described in a seventeenth century text by Marco Boschini, who based his account on the testimony of Palma the Younger, a pupil of Titian in his youth: "He began his paintings with such an unbroken layer of colours that this served (so to speak) as a bed or base for the images which he would then create on them. I have seen massive strokes of colour with streaks of pure red-ochre for the half-tones; at other times he used a splash of white-lead with a brush already stained with reds, black and yellow, to outline light areas, and with a few touches a figure of rare promise would appear. After laying these foundations he would turn the paintings to the wall, sometimes leaving them for months without looking at them. When he decided to work on them again he subjected them to a rigorous examination as if they were his mortal enemies, seeing if anything particularly struck him, or if he could discover anything that did not conform with his careful conception of the works. Like a benevolent surgeon tending a patient, ascertaining whether it was necessary to bleed a swelling or reduce an excess of flesh, he brought them

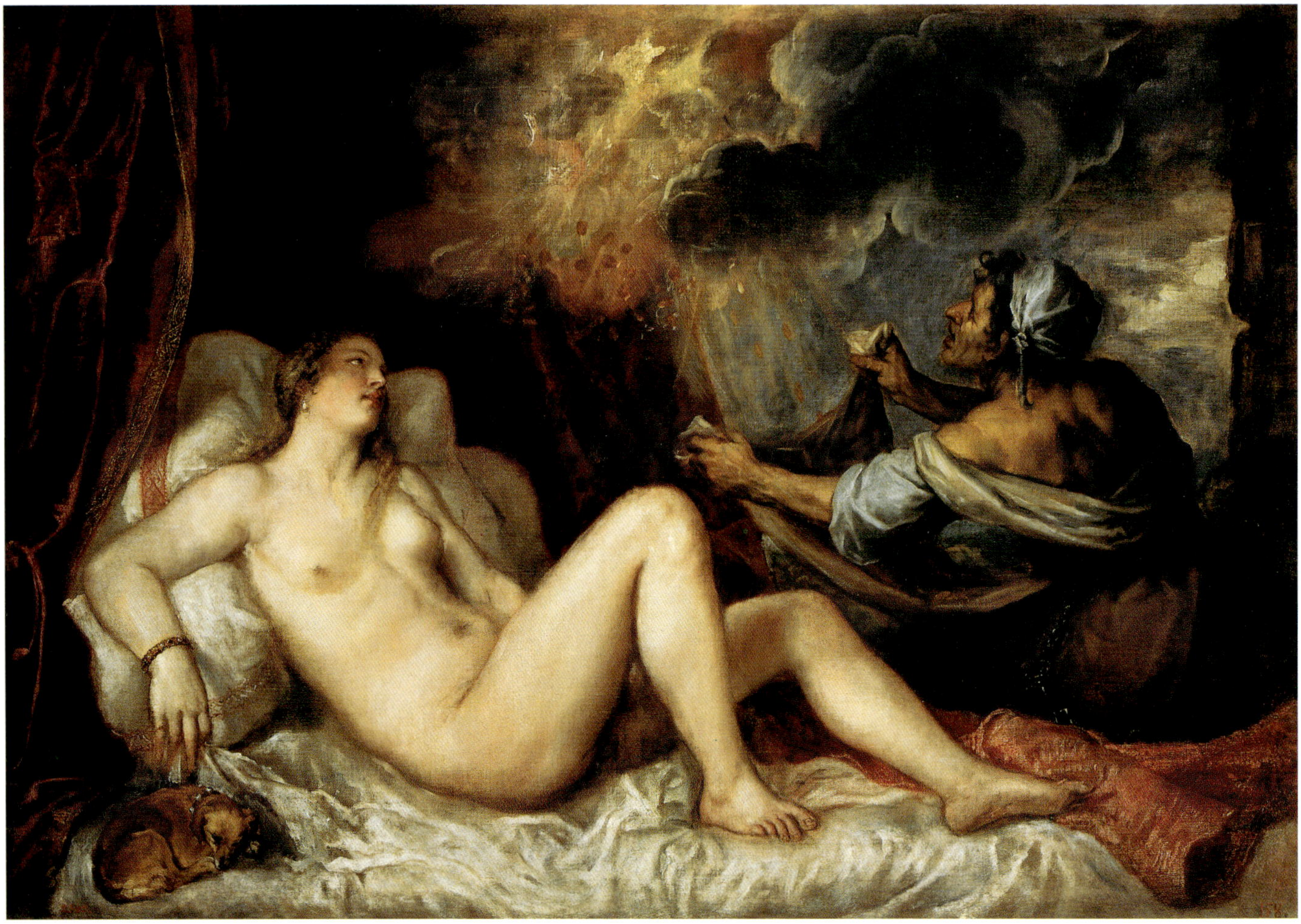

77. *Danaë (1553/1554)*
129x180 cm
Madrid, Prado

78. *Venus at her Toilet (1554/1555)*
124.5x105.5 cm
Washington, National Gallery of Art

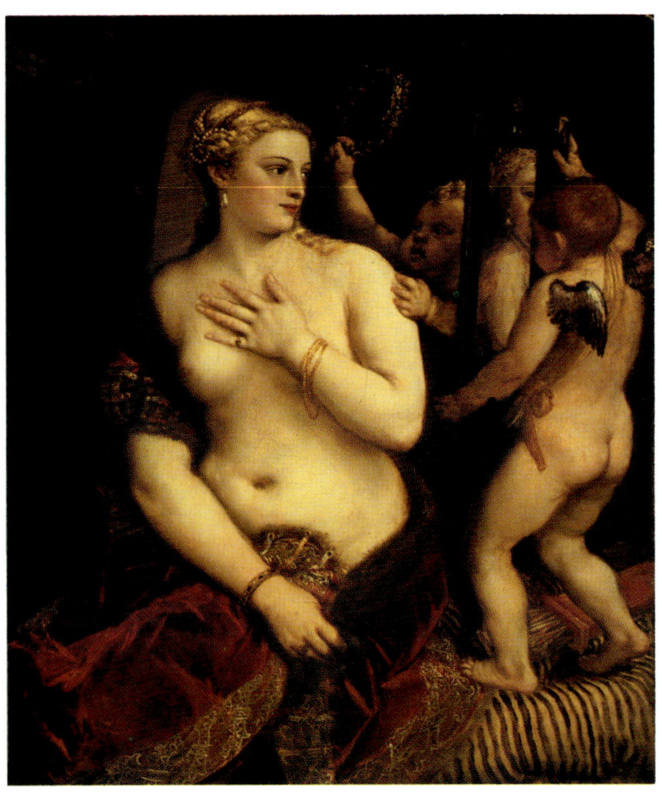

to the perfection of nature and of art and having done this he would leave the canvas to dry and turn to another painting to do the same thing. And every so often he would flesh out the figures, going over them many times, until they lacked only the breath of life, and never completing a figure in a single stage… but for the final touches he would blend the transitions from highlights to half-tones with his fingers, merging one tint with another, or with a smear of his finger he would apply a dark accent in some corner to strengthen it, or with a dab of red, like drops of blood, he would enliven the surface, and so he continued to transform and perfect his life-filled figures, And Palma swore to me that in the final stages of the work Titian painted more with his fingers than with his brush."

And so Titian disintegrates that process of building up figures through drawing and a sculptural sense of the three-dimensional. The definition of detail and the homogeneous use of colour which had characterized his painting for so long, now gives way to a method based solely on colour, applied with broad brushstrokes and completed by working the pigments with the fingertips just like a sculptor modelling in clay.

This stylistic phase, which has been defined as "magical impressionism", was not fully appreciated by Titian's contemporaries. Some of them attributed this rapid and abbreviated way of painting to the physical decline of the old painter and in particular to his failing sight. Never was such an ungenerous judgement levelled at an artist. Consider, for example. a work such as his Prado *Entombment*, sent to Philip II in 1559: a profoundly moving masterpiece of great psychological intensity which became something of a prototype for the religious paintings pervaded by a bitter pathos that Titian was to produce in the last years of his life.

Of similar style are two celebrated mythological paintings painted for Philip II and now in Edinburgh: *Diana and Callisto* and *Diana and Actaeon*. Here, too, the tragic stories (the huntsman Actaeon accidently discovers the grotto where Diana and her nymphs are bathing and because of this he is transformed into a stag and torn to pieces by his hounds; Callisto was one of Diana's nymphs and as such had to be as chaste as the goddess; made pregnant by Jupiter and found out by Diana, she is driven away) push Titian towards a dramatic emphasis in which vibrant colours play their part with their rich hues and strong contrasts. The following years were particularly busy ones for Titian; he painted other mythological pictures for Philip II, in-

79. Venus and Adonis (1553/1554)
186x207 cm
Madrid, Prado

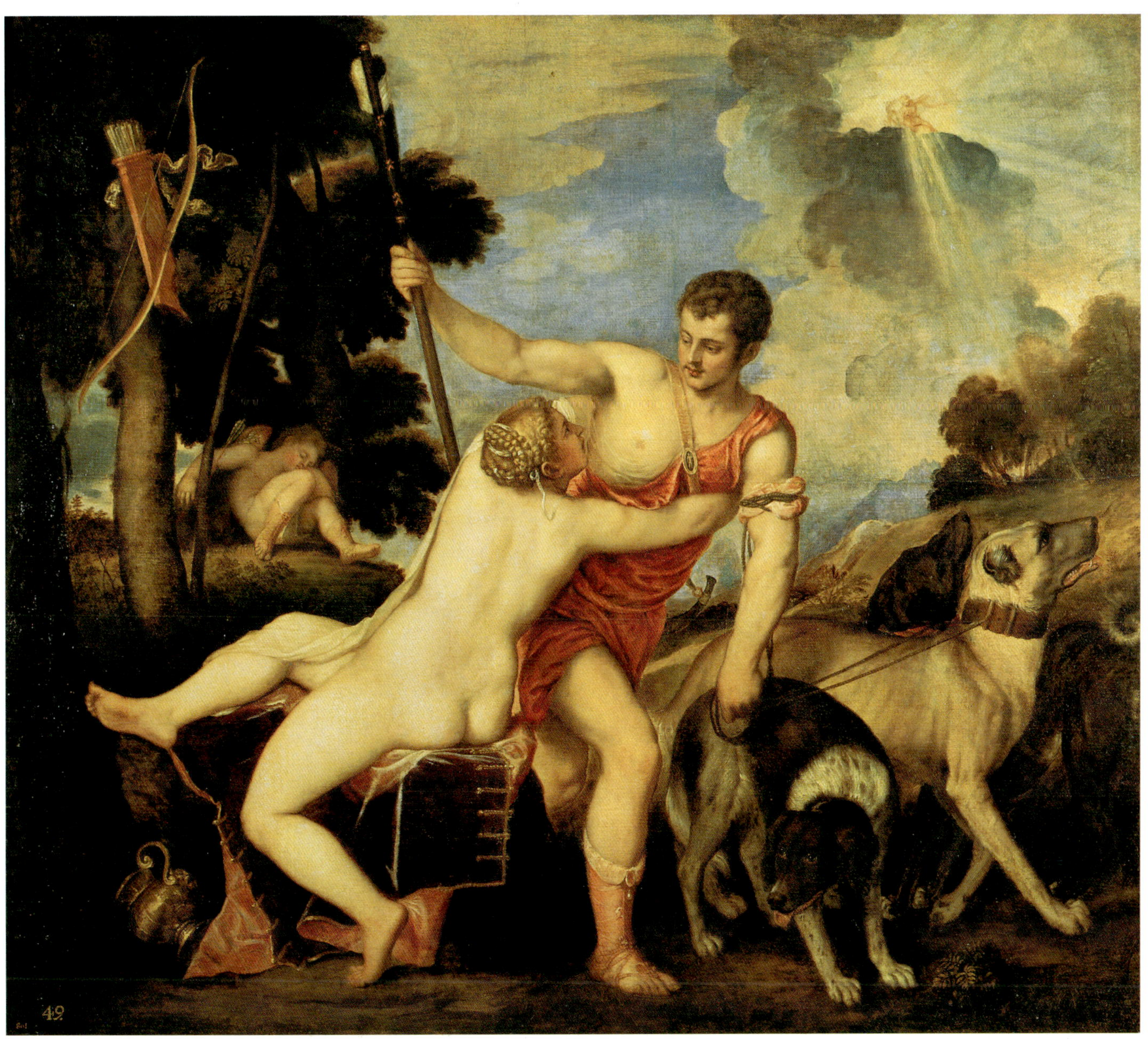

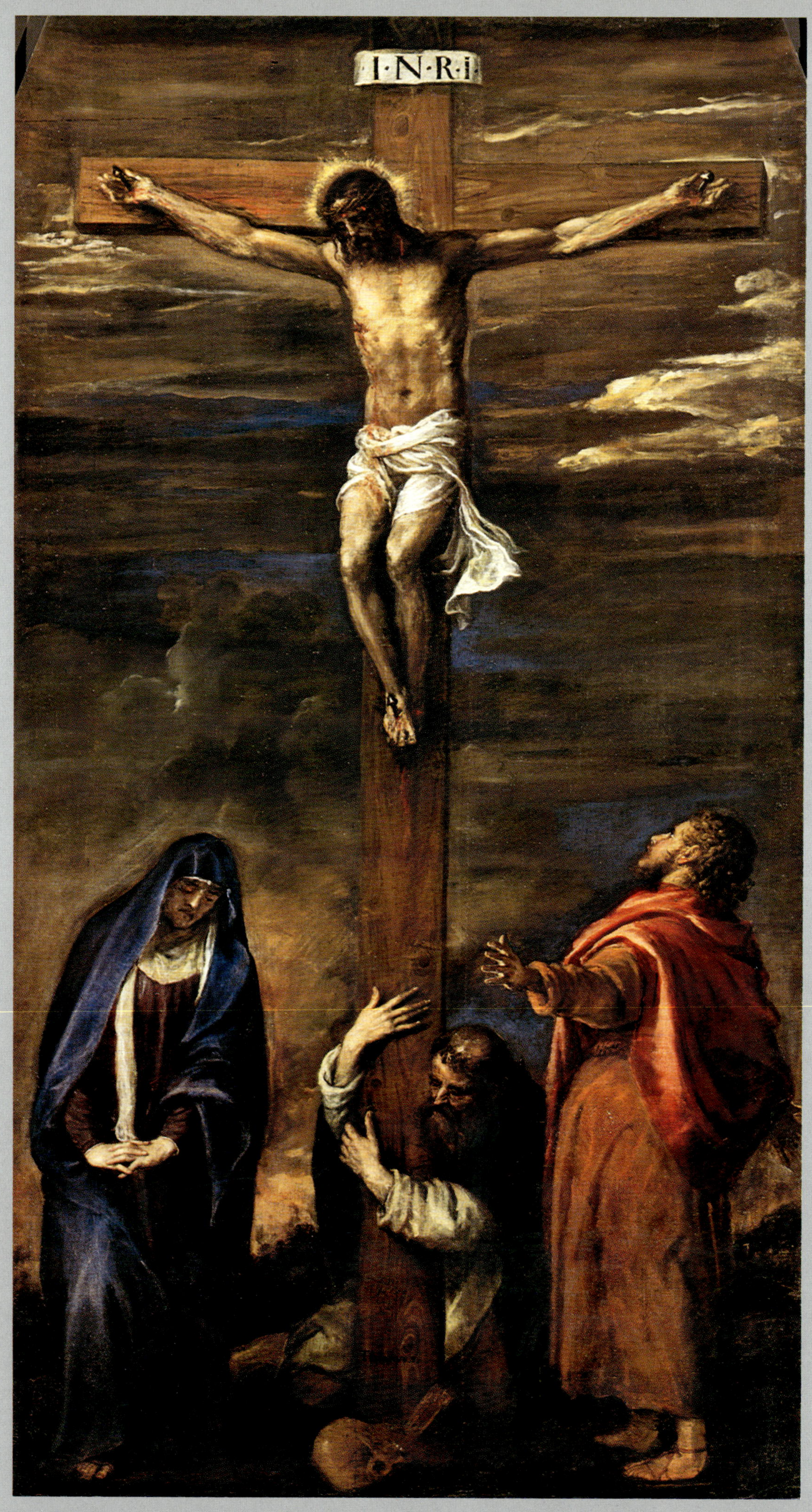

I · N · R · i

cluding the splendid *Rape of Europa* in Boston.
Painted between 1559 and 1562, it also reveals
a profound sense of tortured despair, as does the
London *Death of Actaeon*. Here the dramatic
scene of the young hunter attacked and ripped
apart by the pack of dogs takes place in a landscape of livid colours heavy with premonition. To
these years belongs the Wallace Collection *Perseus
and Andromeda* (1562-1563) with its sublime
depiction of the monster rising at night from the
billowing moonlit waves.

The year 1562 almost certainly saw the production of two exceptionally fine works: the Berlin *Self-
Portrait* and the *Annunciation* for the Venetian
church of San Salvador. The former presents us
with the image of the painter (then over seventy)
emerging majestically from the shadowy background like some ghostly apparition. Titian is
dressed in a voluminous white shirt topped by a
fur-edged robe; nothing in the painting alludes spe-
cifically to his craft but the great gold chain he wears
is a proud reminder of the honour bestowed on him
in 1533 when Charles V made him a Knight of the
Golden Spur. This was long assumed to be an unfinished work because of the fragmented brushstrokes and the lack of firm outlines so typical of
the late works of Titian. But there is nothing casual
in the seeming incompleteness of this and other
contemporary works. It was a conscious artistic de-

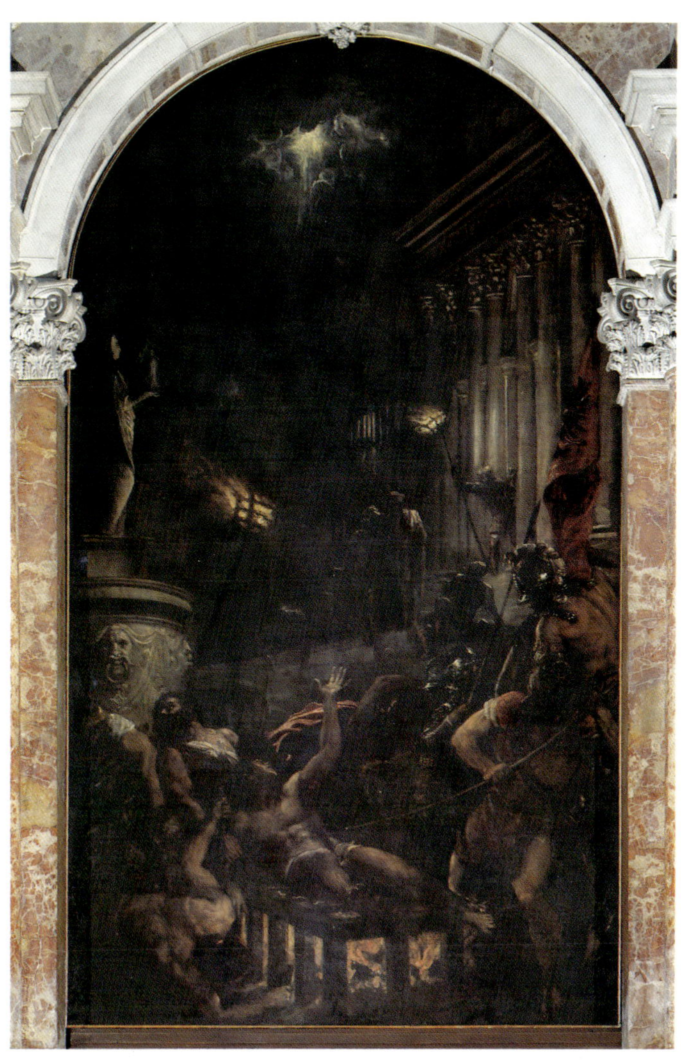

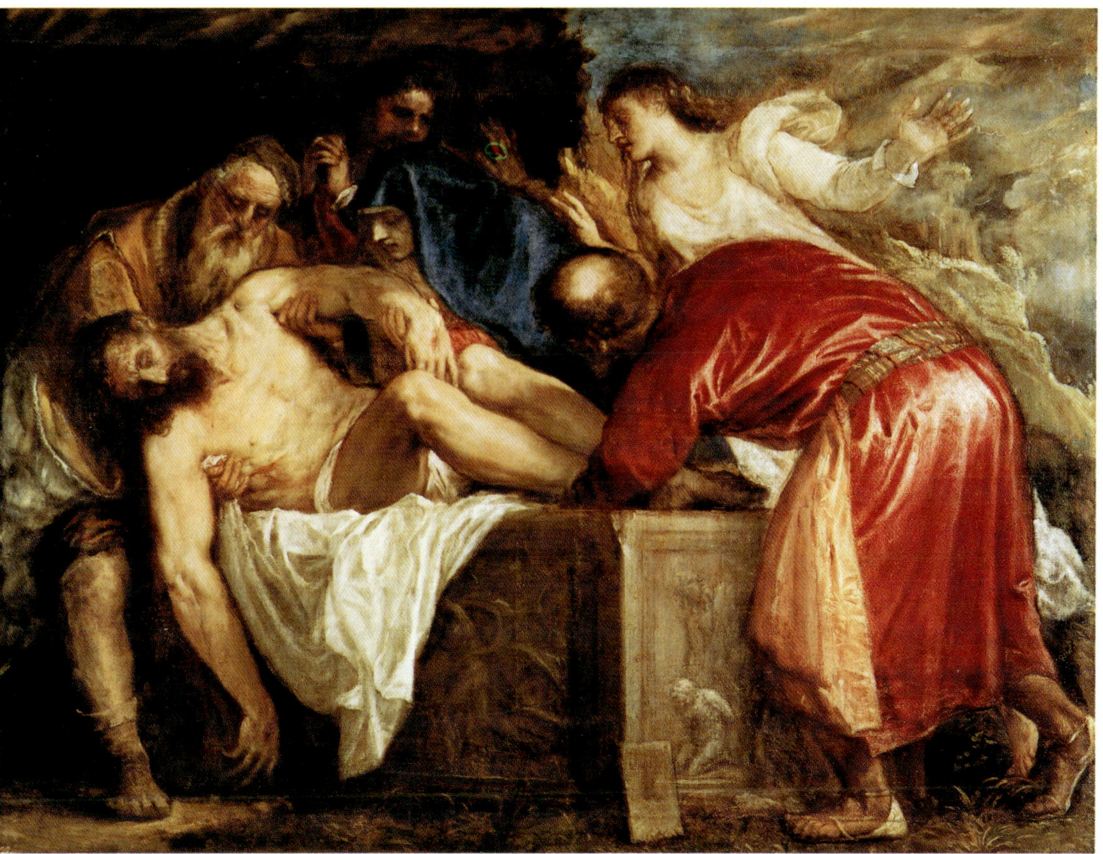

80. *Crucified
Christ with the
Virgin Mary and
Saints Dominic
and John (1558)*
375x197 cm
Ancona, Church
of San Domenico

81. *Martyrdom of
St Lawrence
(1559)*
493x277 cm
Venice, Jesuit
Church

82. *Entombment
(1559)*
137x175 cm
Madrid, Prado

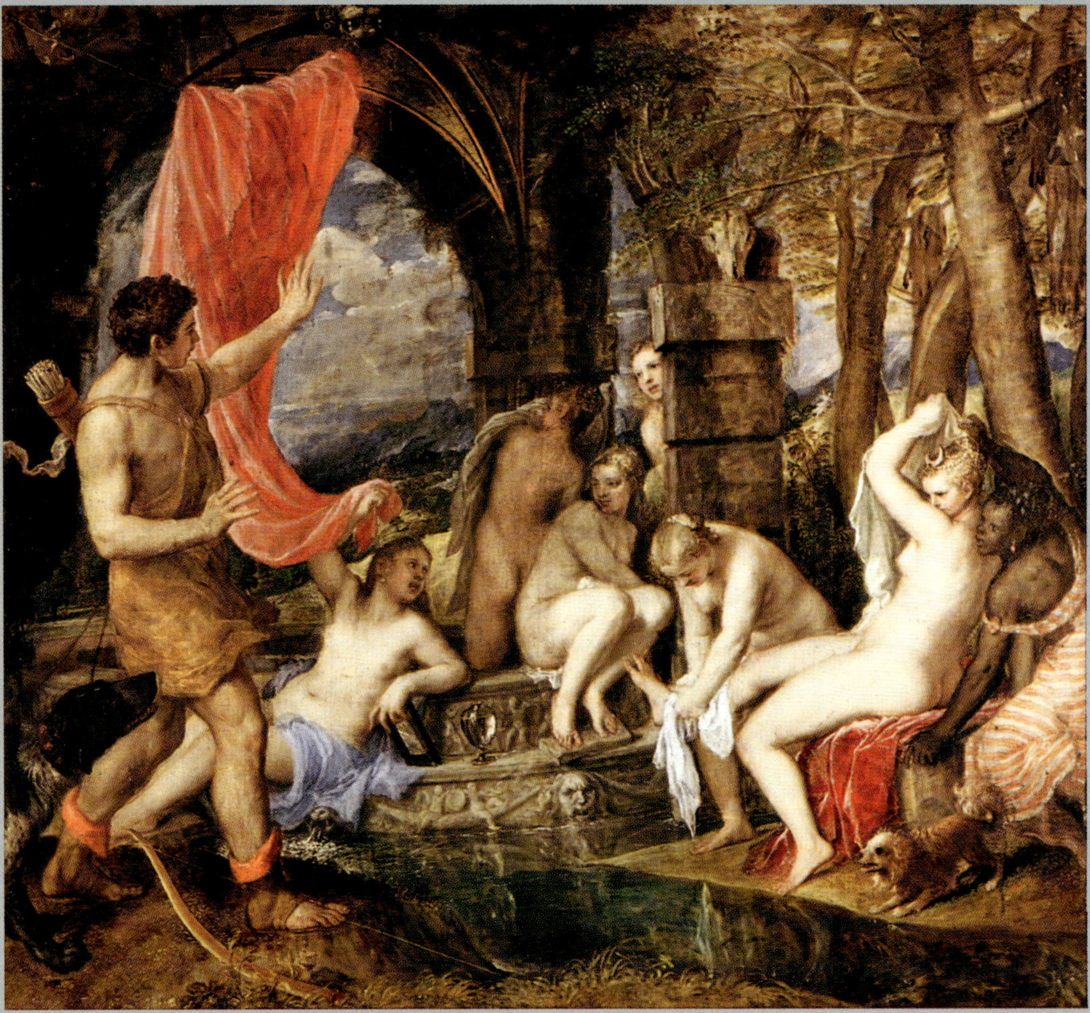

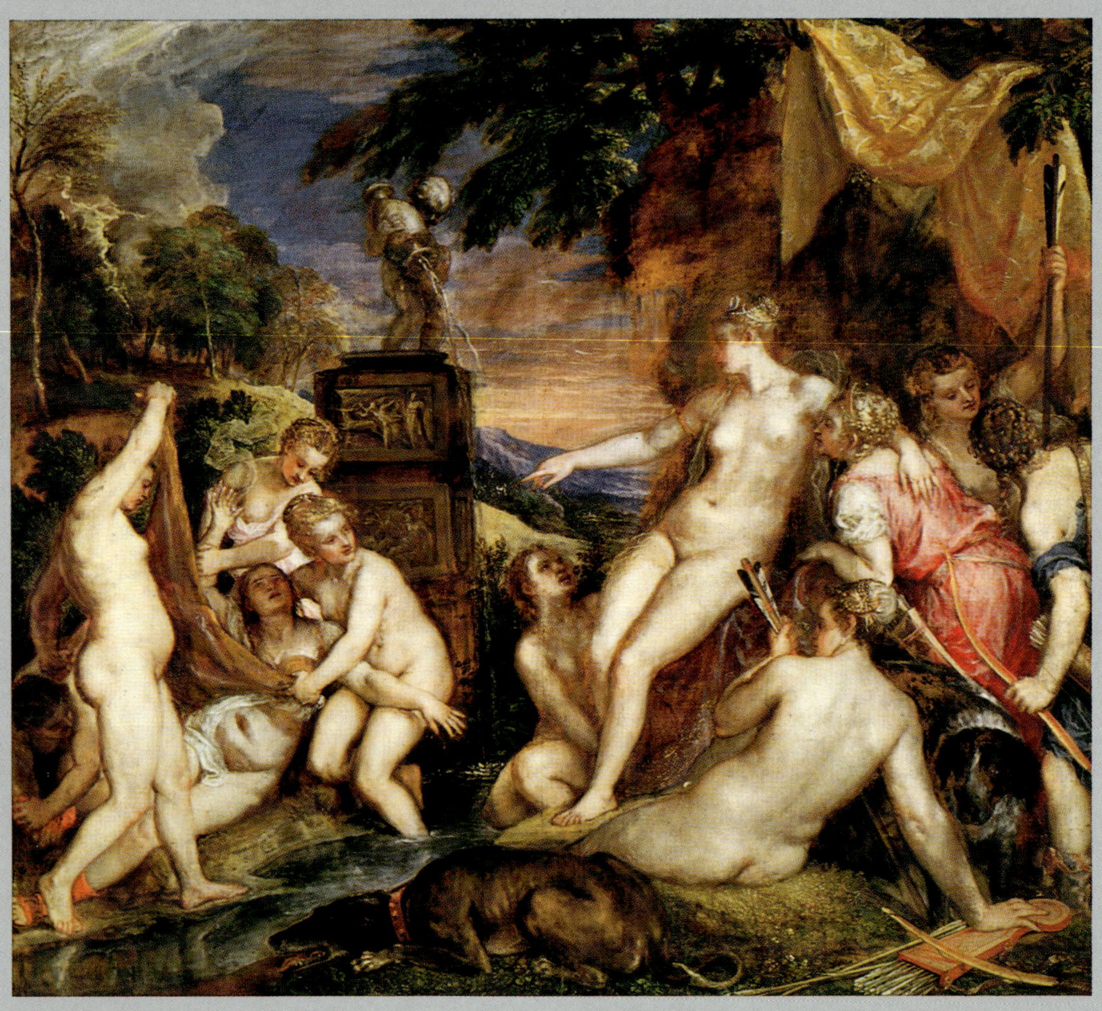

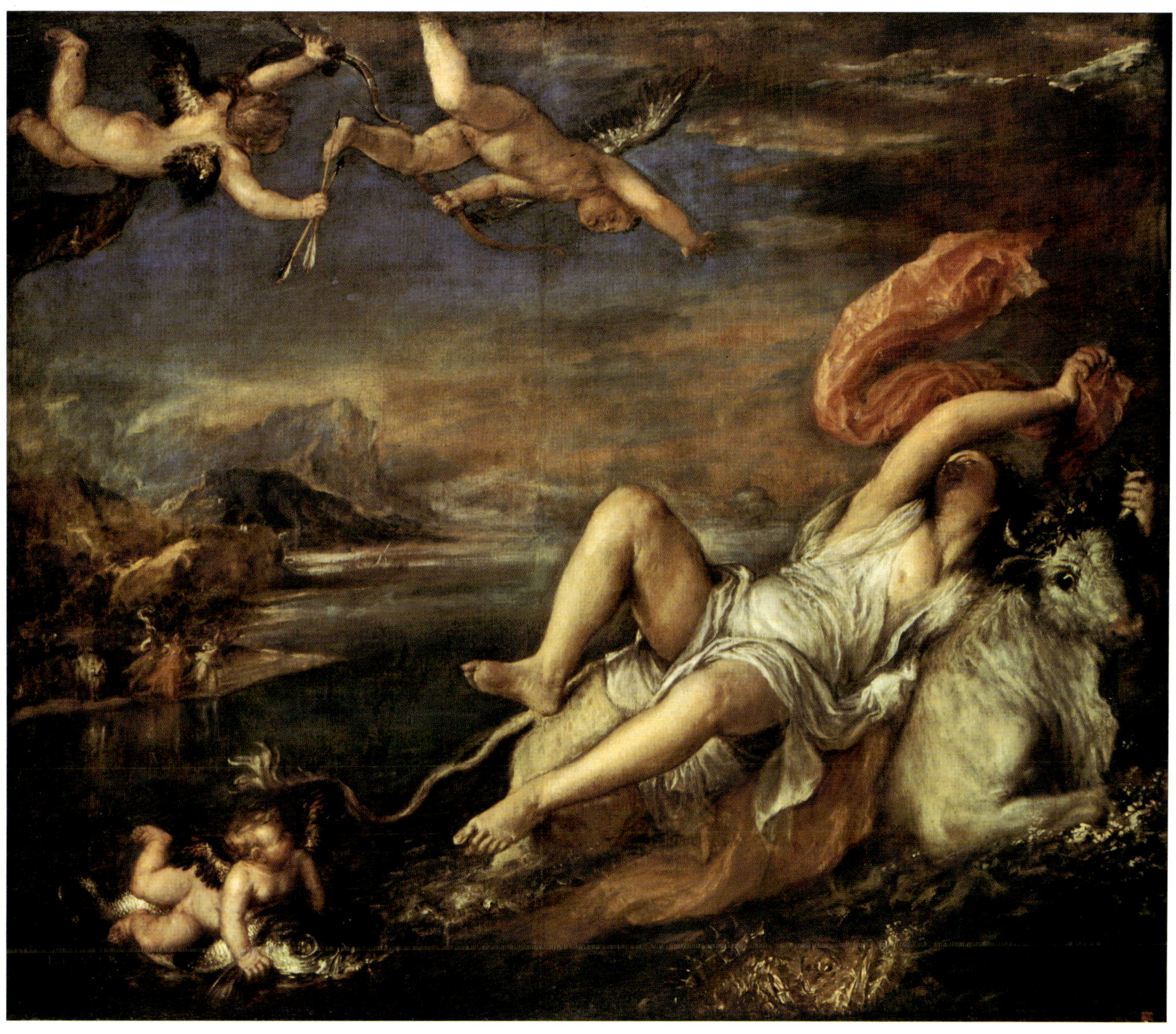

83. *Diana and Actaeon (1559)*
190.3x207 cm
Edinburgh, National Gallery of Scotland (on loan
from the Duke of Sutherland Collection)

84. *Diana and Callisto (1559)*
187x205 cm
Edinburgh, National Gallery of Scotland (on loan
from the Duke of Sutherland Collection)

85. *Rape of Europa (1559/1562)*
185x205 cm
Boston, Isabella Stewart Gardner Museum

cision on the part of Titian, who finds direct emotional communication through these luminous effects, and through that very "unfinished" quality of the painting, which becomes a vehicle for the expression of what may be seen as the unquiet, questing soul of the elderly painter. Once more Titian's superb technical expertise becomes a tool for the expression of profound feeling; and it is precisely this quality which has been appreciated by modern critics, resulting in a reassessment of the final phase of Titian's artistic career. Vasari was certainly wrong in equating incompleteness with imperfection when he wrote about the incandescent *Annunciation* for the church of San Salvador, commissioned in 1559 by the wealthy merchant Antonio Cornovì della Vecchia and probably completed in 1562. This painting must be considered as one of the greatest of Titian's final works, replete with

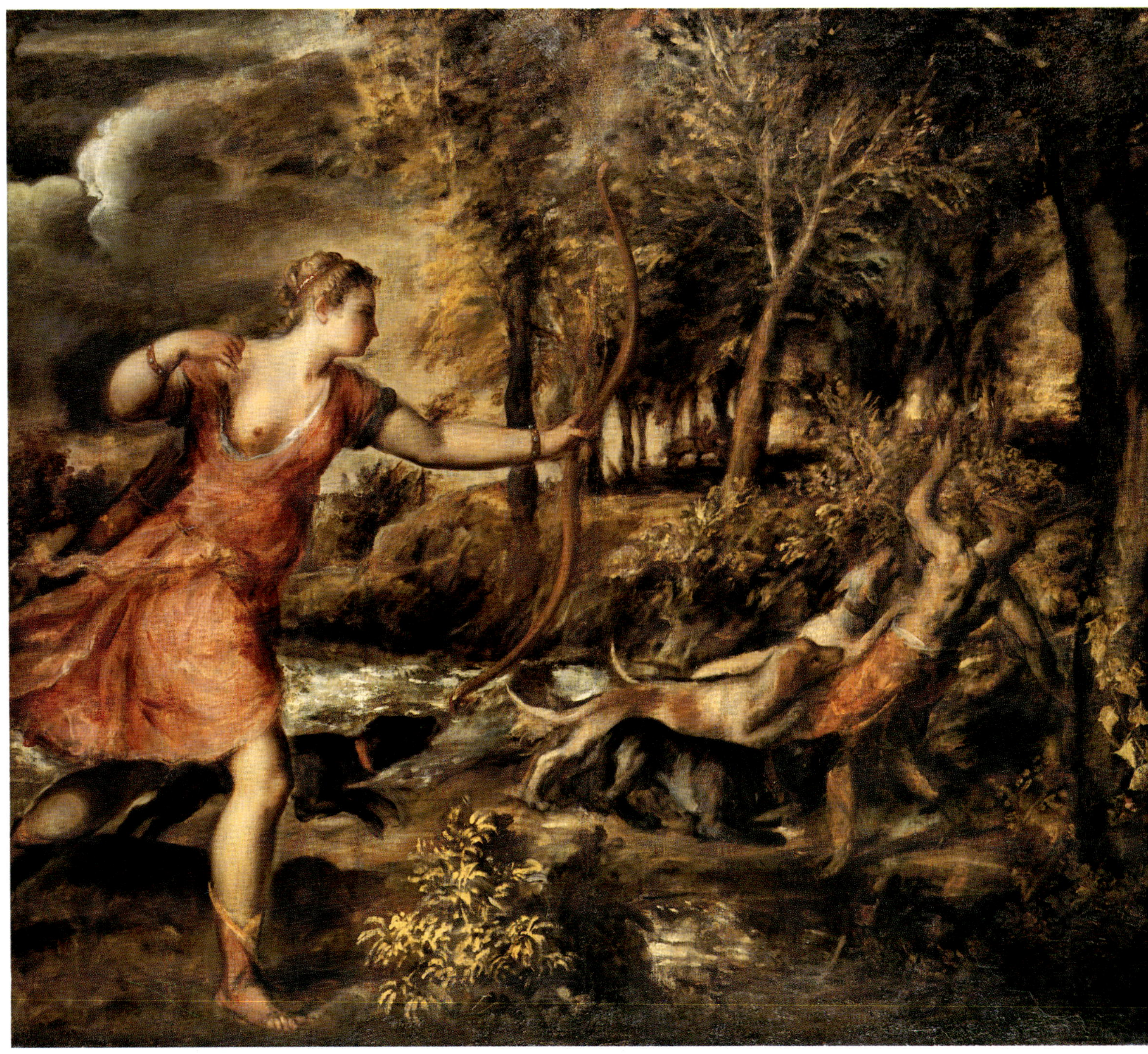

the ingredients typical of his late style: the restrained
sensuality of the glowing angel whose hair and great
open wings seem made of molten gold in the flash-
ing light; the broken brushstrokes which do not seek
to define form; the dark chasm of the background
which opens up into a vision of fiery heaven with
its pyrotechnic display of cherubs encircling the
dove of the Holy Spirit.

86. Death of Actaeon (1562)
179x189 cm
London, National Gallery

87. Annunciation (1559/1562)
403x235 cm
Venice, Church of San Salvador

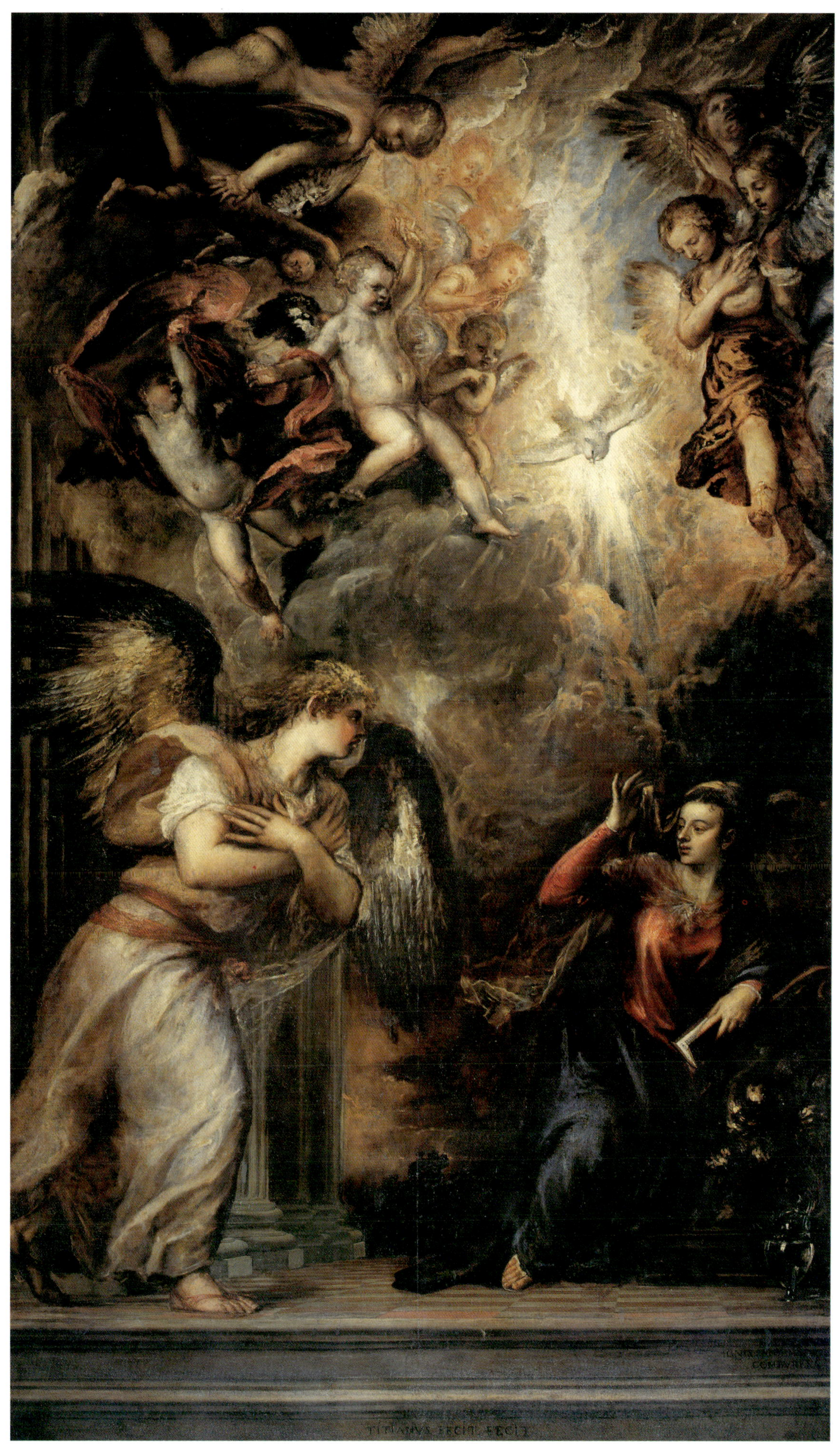

The Final Years

The elderly Titian's final years are marked by the anguish of personal tragedy. The year 1556 saw the death of his close friend of thirty years, Pietro Aretino. In 1558 Charles V died in the solitude of the monastery of St Yuste; sentiments of gratitude and respect had long bound Titian to his old patron. A year later his brother Francesco died — a trusted and unobstrusive collaborator on countless painting projects. The effect these losses had on Titian is clear in some of his letters to Philip II but his paintings remain the most eloquent testimony of his distress in these years. Take, for example, the Prado *Entombment* of 1565 (similar in its composition to the version sent to Philip II in 1559) where the disjointed gestures of the onlookers communicate their strident grief at the death of the Saviour. Even potentially joyous mythological sub-

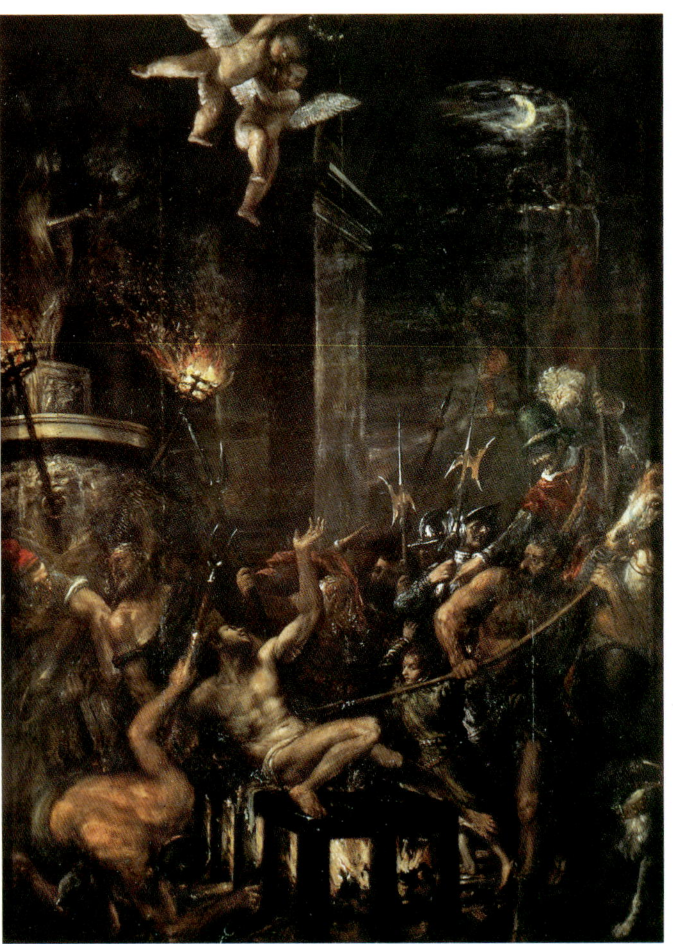

88. *Martyrdom of St Lawrence (1567)*
175x172 cm
Escorial, Monastery of St Lawrence

jects such as *Venus Blindfolding Cupid*, painted around 1565 and now in Rome, is pervaded with a degree of tension which is clearly evident in the sad and pensive expressions and in the intense colours of the fiery sky.

In the same period Titian handled his various versions of the *Penitent Mary Magdalene* with a similar dramatic intensity. This is particularly evident in a comparison of the St Petersburg canvas — considered the prototype for the series — with the early Pitti *Mary Magdalene* painted for the Duke of Urbino in 1533. In December of 1567 Titian sent to Spain his second *Martyrdom of Saint Lawrence*, destined for the high altar of the monastic church of St Lawrence at the Escorial. Here too, he repeats the composition used earlier for the altarpiece of the same subject for the church of the Crociferi, completed in 1559, but handles it in a more tortured way, giving free rein to the expressiveness of his late style. In this period, which saw Titian focussing his attention on religious themes, he still found the energy to paint portraits. Between 1567 and 1568 he produced two of his greatest masterpieces in this field: the Prado *Self-Portrait* and the *Portrait of Jacopo Strada* in Vienna.

In the new *Self-Portrait* Titian departs completely from the scheme of the earlier one in Berlin. He depicts himself in profile, dressed in black and holding a paintbrush in clear allusion to his craft. Around his neck is the gold chain which reminds us that he held the rank of Knight of the Golden Spur. But, above all, the impression of inner strength and self-assurance exuded by the Berlin self-portrait has disappeared. In just a few years there has been a marked physical decline and, more significantly, the portrait suggests an erosion of the aging painter's self-confidence.

The portrait of the well-known antiquarian *Jacopo Strada* is of the very highest quality. It is painted in energetic dabs of brown and ochre yellow, offset by the black velvet jerkin with a silver fox fur flung around the shoulders. The careful depiction of the details which allude to the profession of the sitter (the statuette, the coins, the cartouche and the books) do not distract from the characterization of Strada, who is looking enquiringly at someone outside the painting.

Connected to these paintings is the London *Allegory of Time Governed by Prudence*, where portraits of Titian, his son Orazio and his grandson

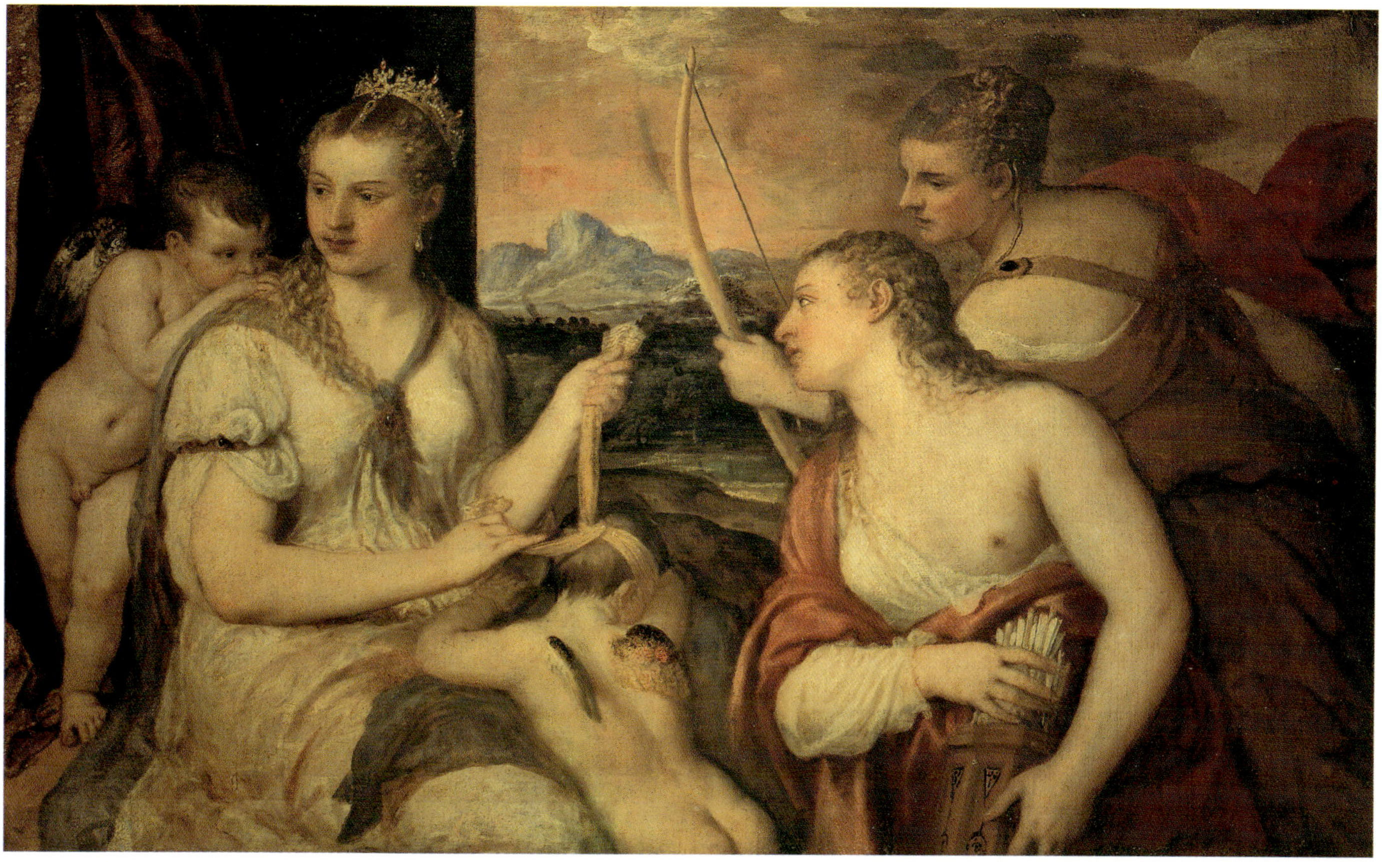

89. *Venus Blindfolding Cupid*
(c. 1565)
118x185 cm
Rome, Borghese Gallery

90. *Penitent Mary Magdalene*
(c. 1565)
118x97 cm
St. Petersburg, Hermitage

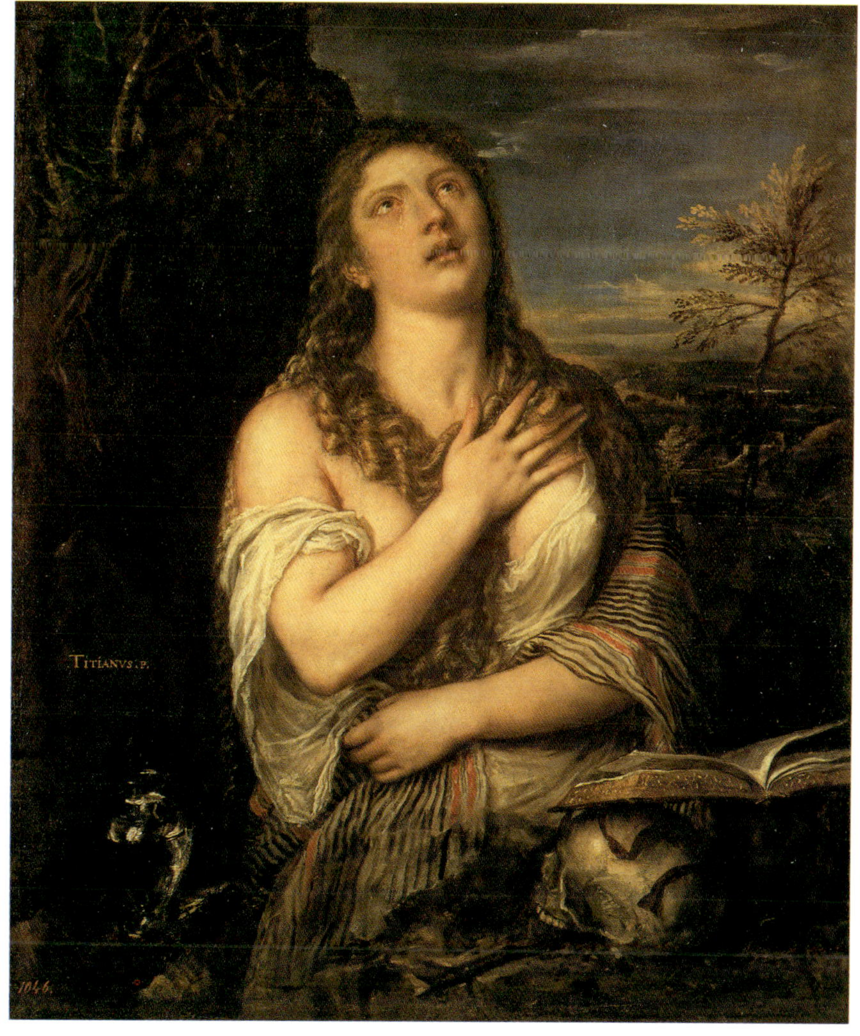

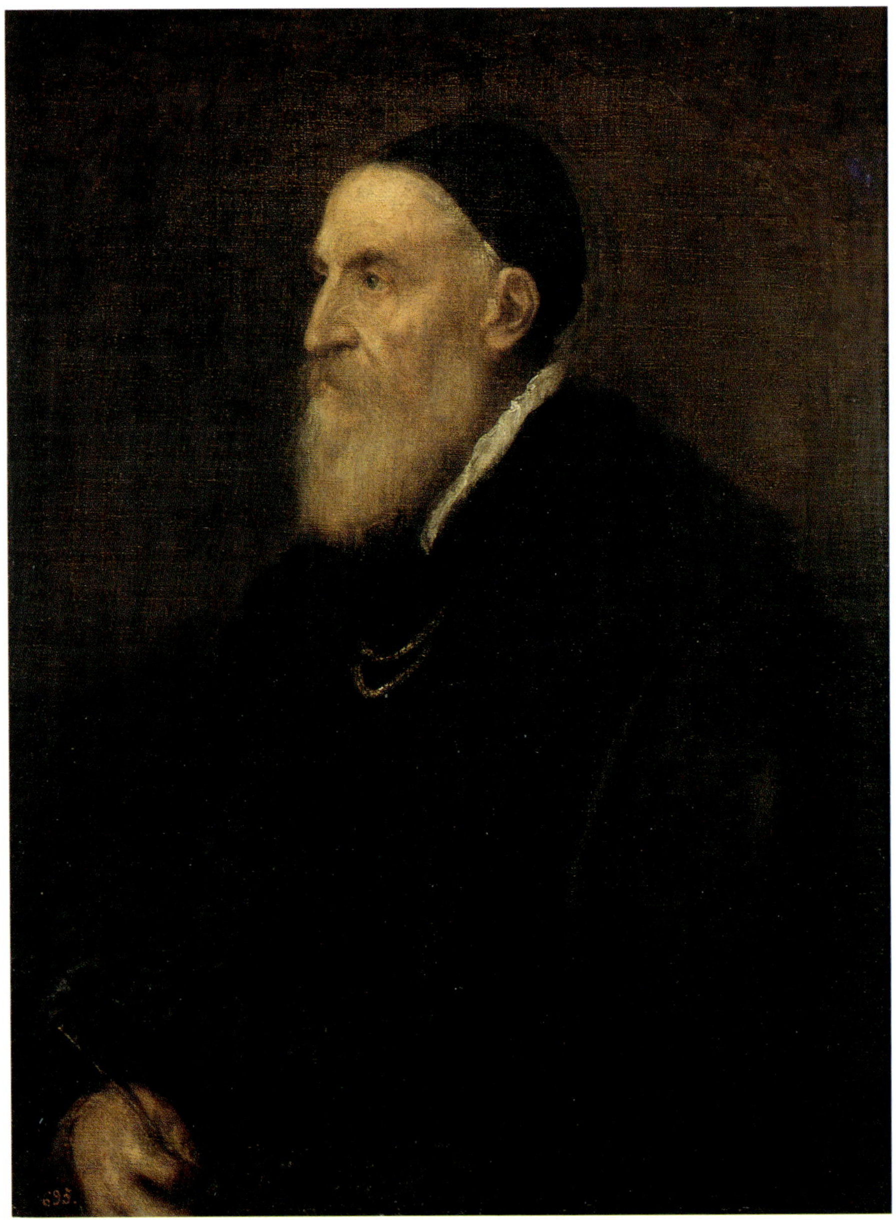

91. *Self-Portrait (1567/1568)*
86x69 cm
Madrid, Prado

Marco are each coupled with an animal head: respectively a wolf, a lion and a dog, symbolizing the past, present and future. In the upper part of the painting there is an inscription which is the key to the complex allegorical meaning of the work: "EX PRAETERITO PRAESENS PRUDENTER AGIT, NI FUTURUM ACTIONE DETURPET" ("From the (experience of the) past, the present acts prudently, lest it spoil future action").

Approaching the eighth decade of the century the chronology of Titian's works becomes less clear chiefly because of their stylistic similarity. There are numerous devotional paintings, including the deeply felt *Madonna and Child* in London and the small *Altarpiece*, probably executed by 1566 for the Vecellio family chapel in the archidiaconal church of Pieve di Cadore. The series of paintings dedicated to the passion of Christ are outstanding. These include: the Munich *Crowning with Thorns*, the Saint Louis *Mocking of Christ*, the St Petersburg *Ecce Homo* and the two versions of *Christ Carrying the Cross* in St Petersburg and in Madrid. In these works, pervaded with immense dramatic power, the brushstrokes gradually dissolve into rapidly applied dabs of pigment. The aim is no longer to reproduce nature but to directly convey the raw emotion of the painter, who is participating fully in the tragic subject of his picture. This explains, in the Munich painting, the depiction of the tortured body of Christ, drenched in blood and sweat, and the sinister sulphurous flashes

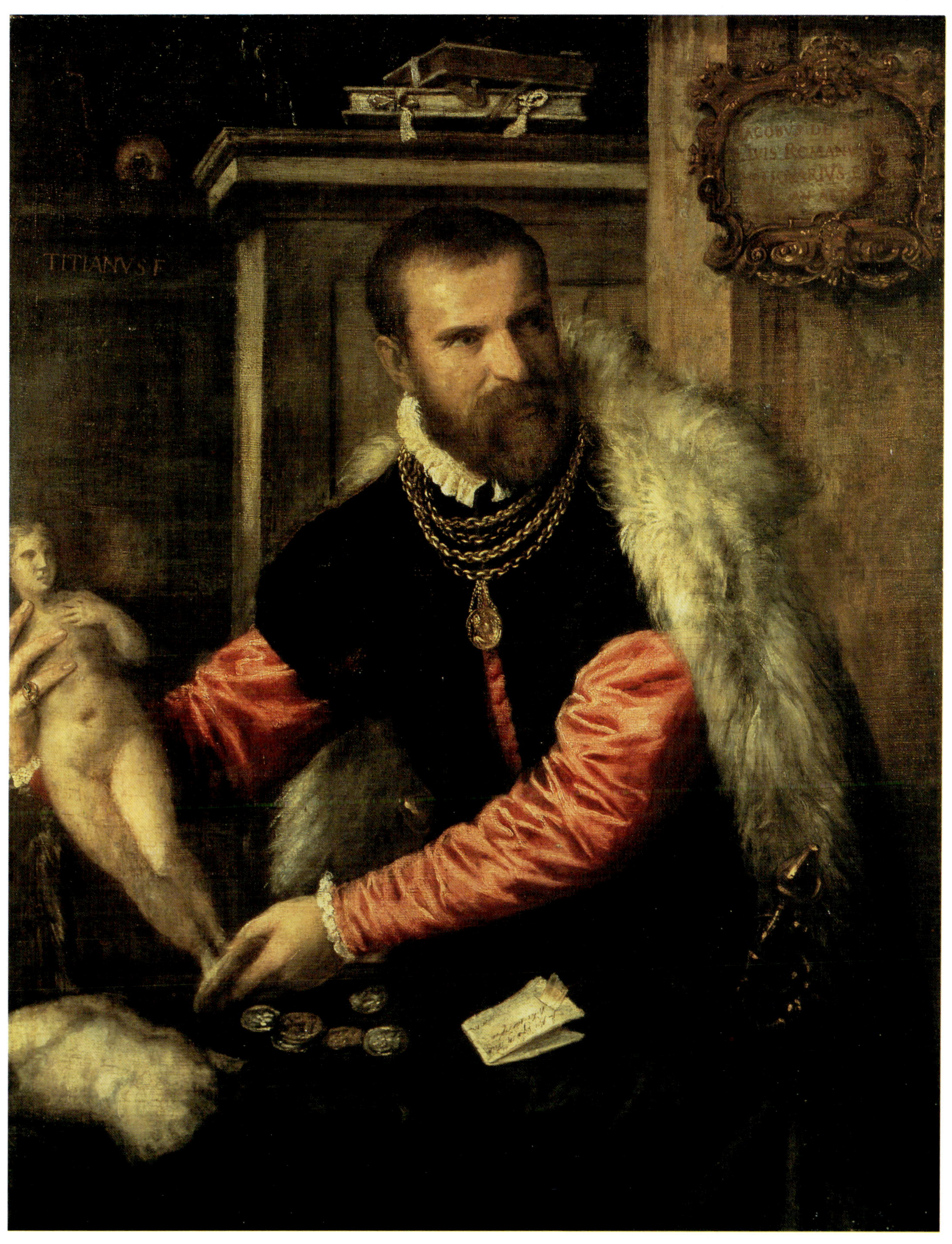

92. Portrait of Jacopo Strada (1567/1568)
125x95 cm
Vienna, Kunsthistorisches Museum

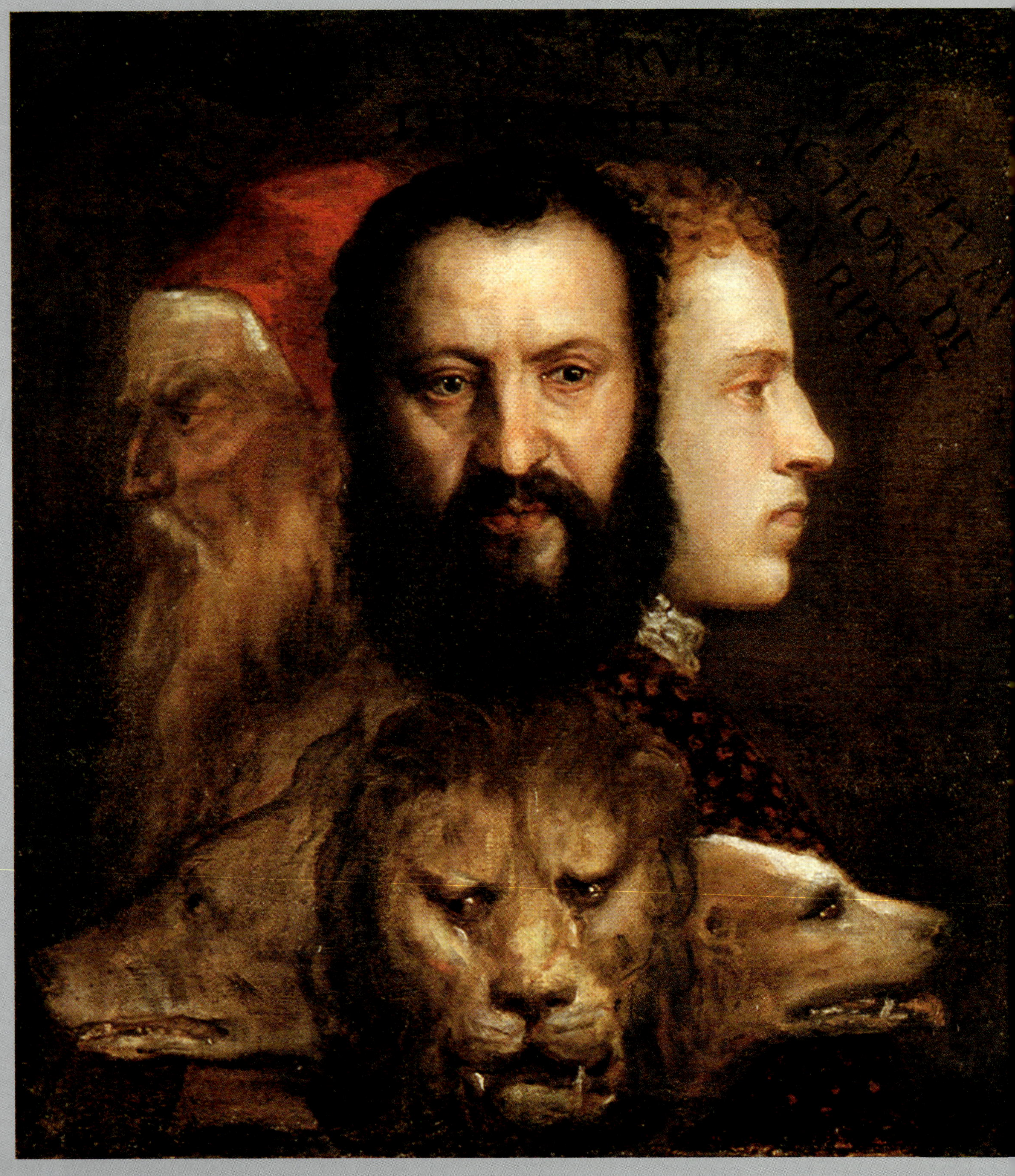

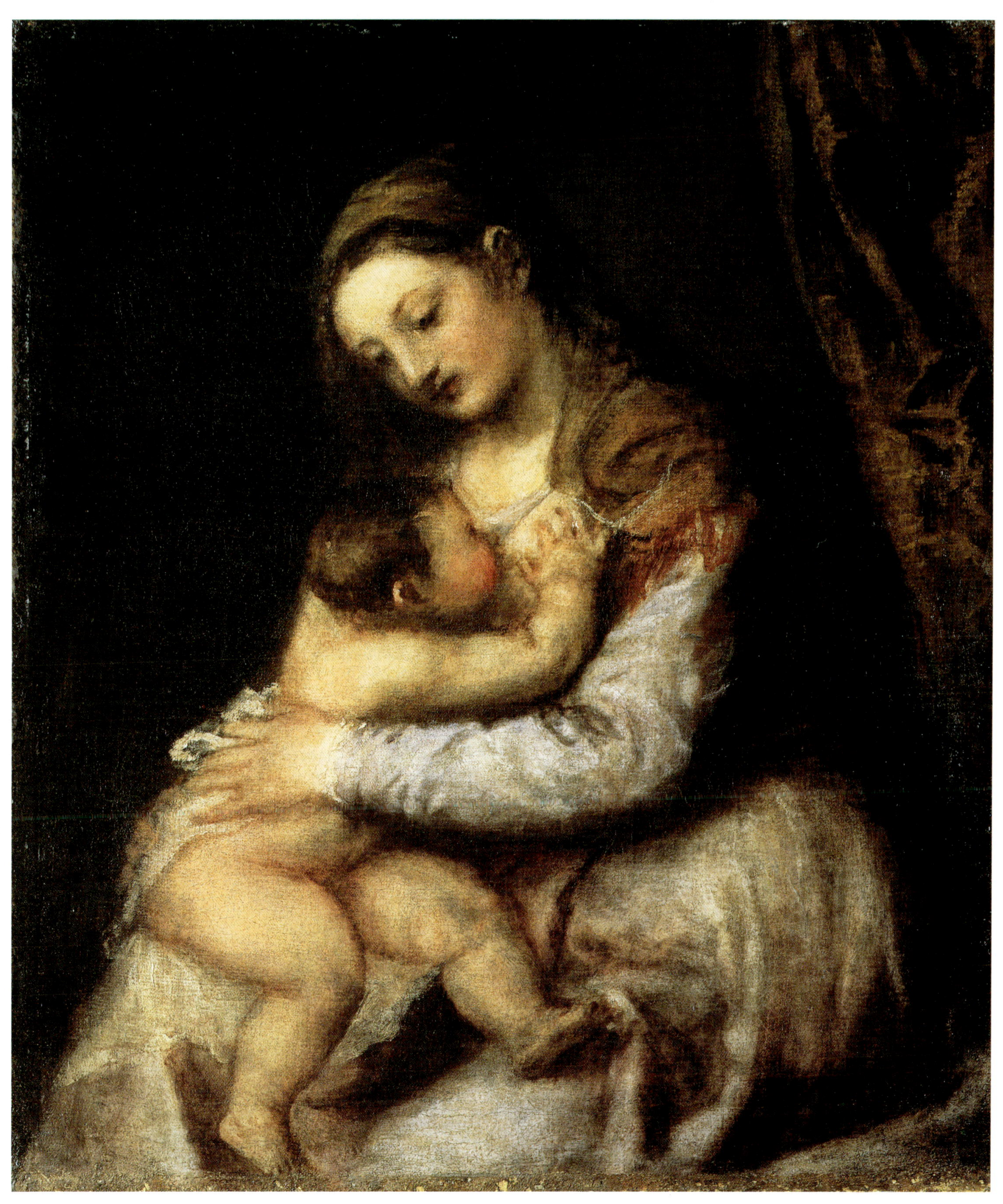

93. *Allegory of Time Governed by Prudence*
(1565/1570)
75,6x68,7 cm
London, National Gallery

94. *Madonna and Child (1565/1570)*
75x63 cm
London, National Gallery

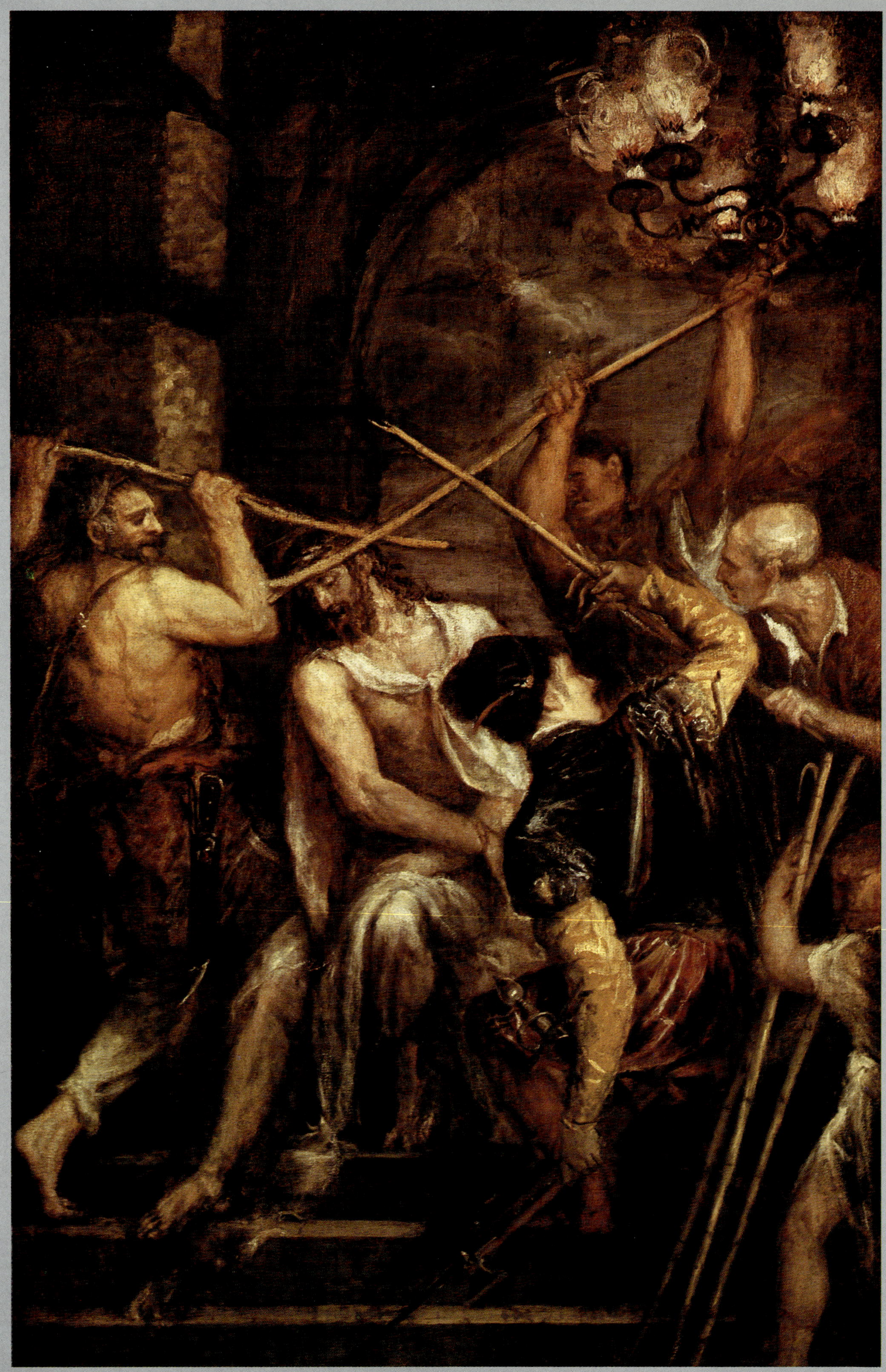

95. *Crowning with Thorns*
(1570/1575)
280x182 cm
Munich, Alte Pinakothek

96. *Mocking of Christ*
(1570/1575)
109x92 cm
Saint Louis, The Saint Louis
Art Museum

97. *Christ Carrying the Cross*
(1570/1575)
98x116 cm
Madrid, Prado

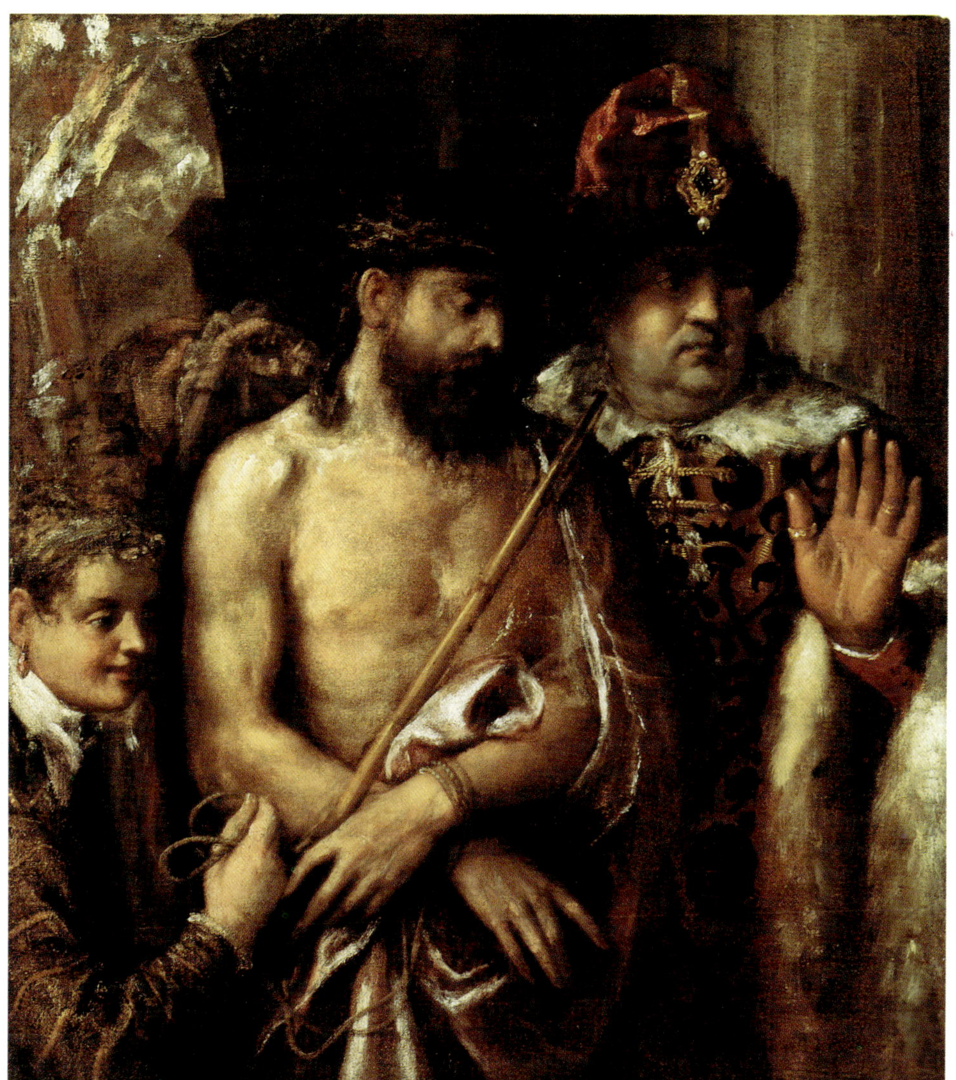

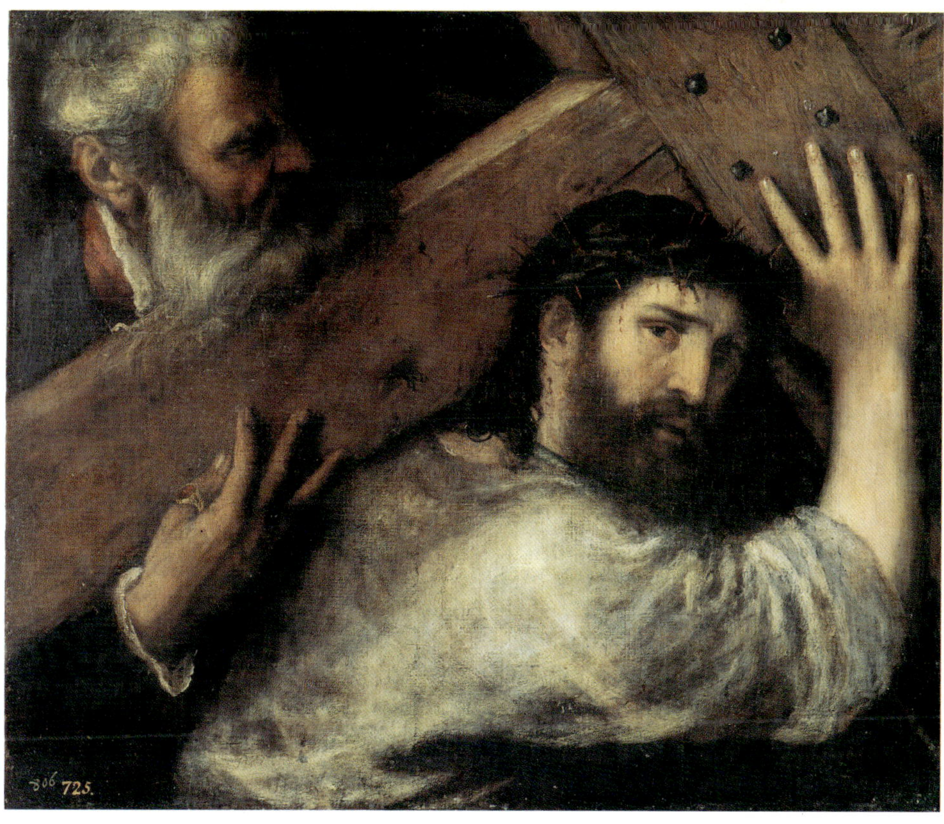

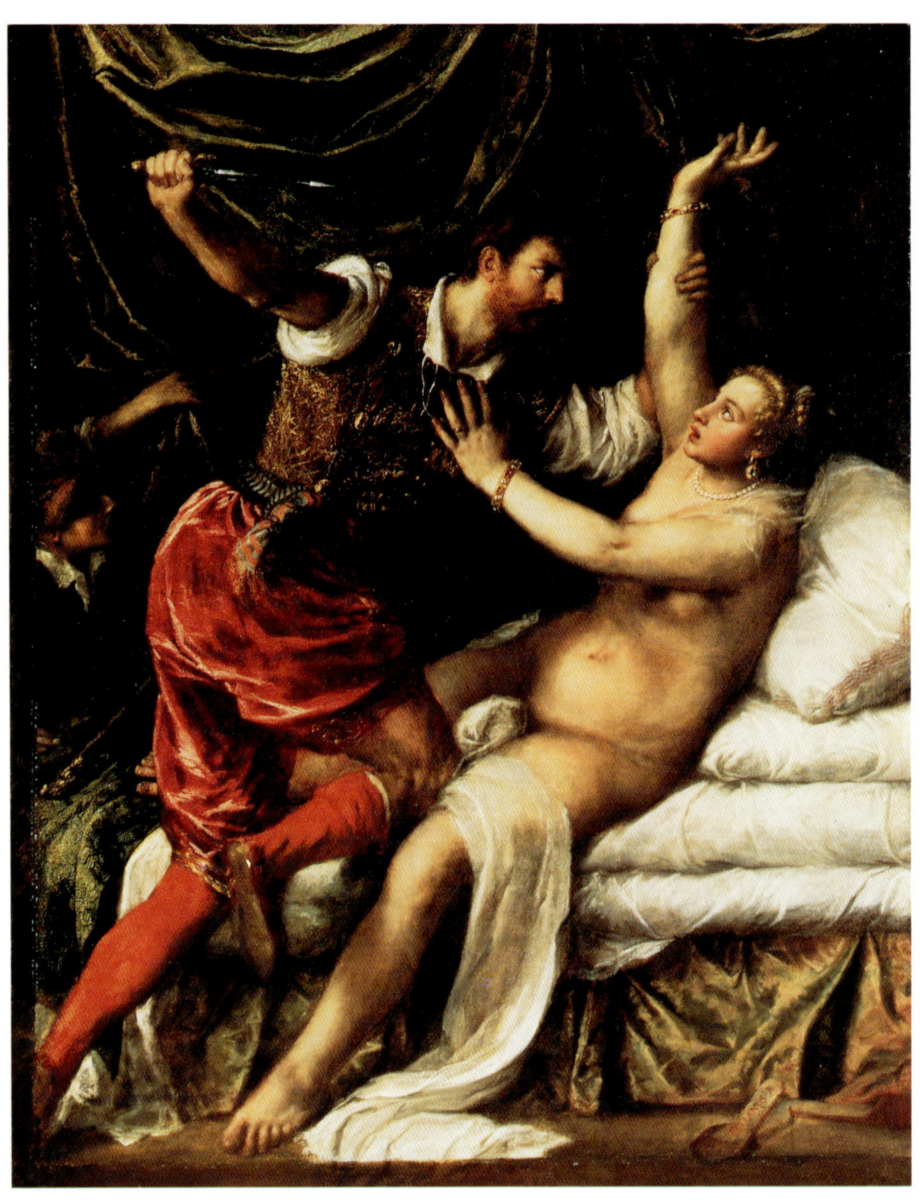

98. *Tarquin and Lucretia* (1571)
189.9x145.4 cm
Cambridge, Fitzwilliam Museum

99, 100. *Doge Antonio Grimani*
Kneeling before the Faith
(1575/1576)
373x496 cm
Venice, Doges' Palace

101. *Spain Succouring Religion*
(c. 1575)
168x168 cm
Madrid, Prado

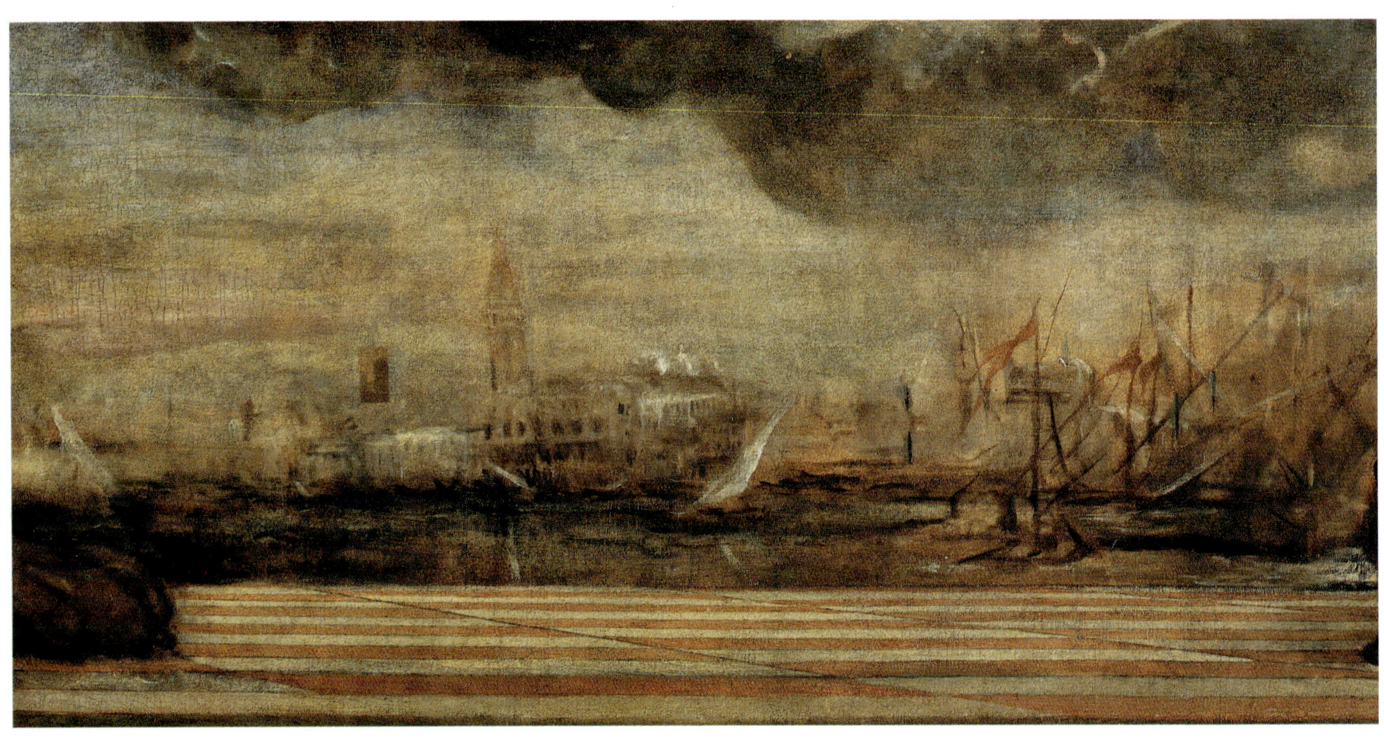

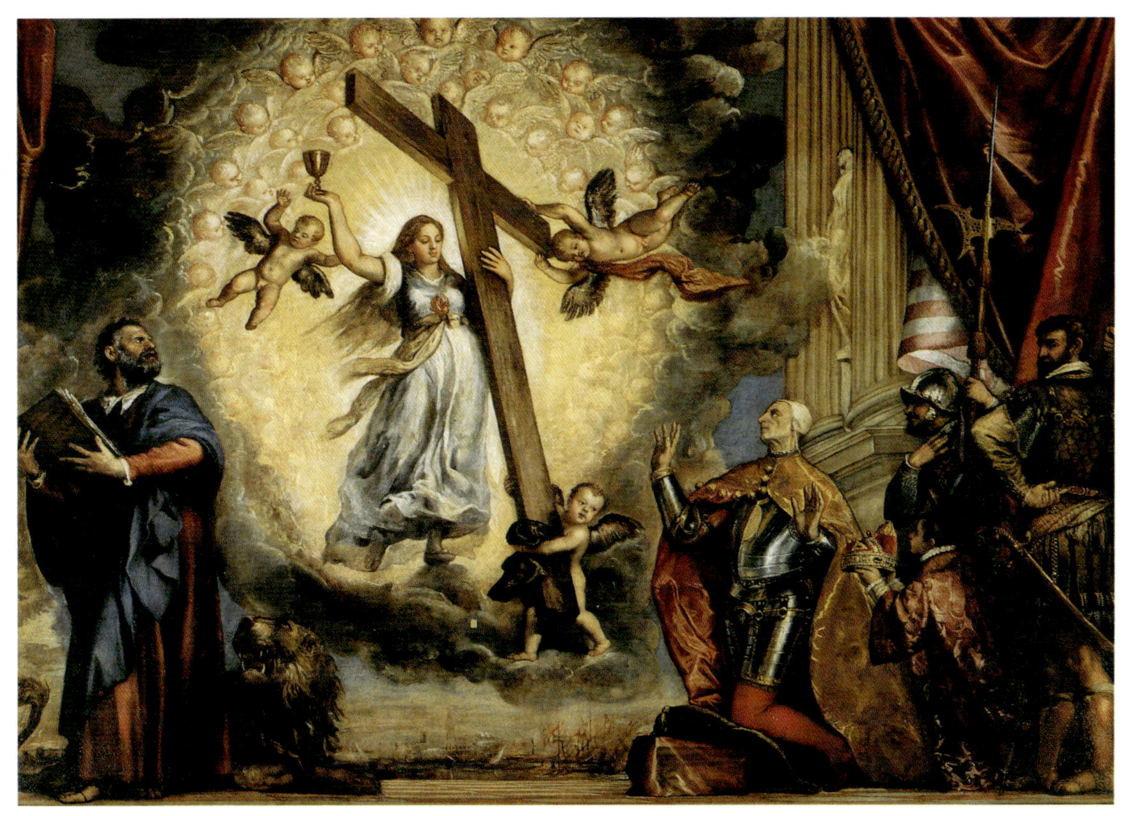

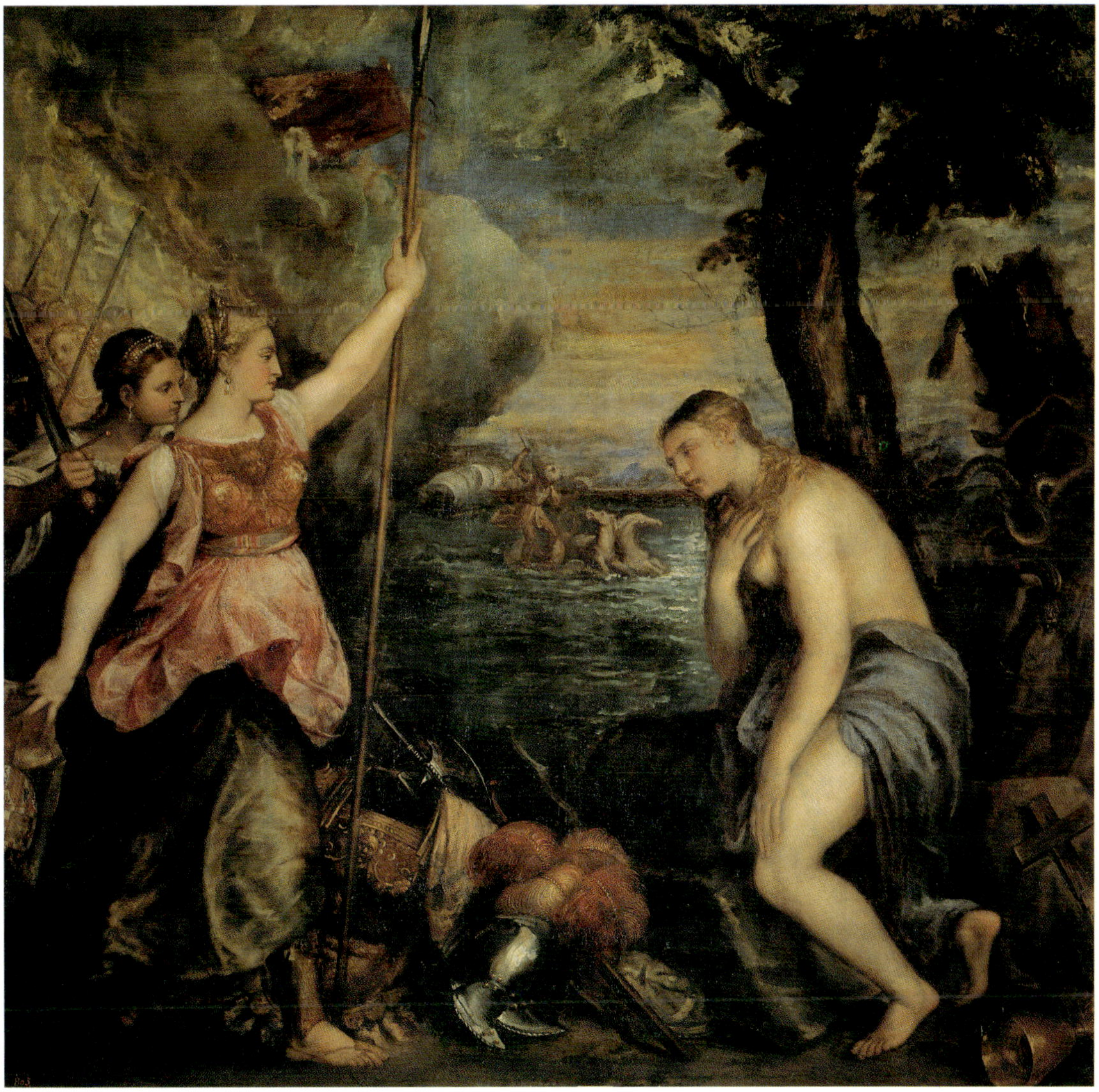

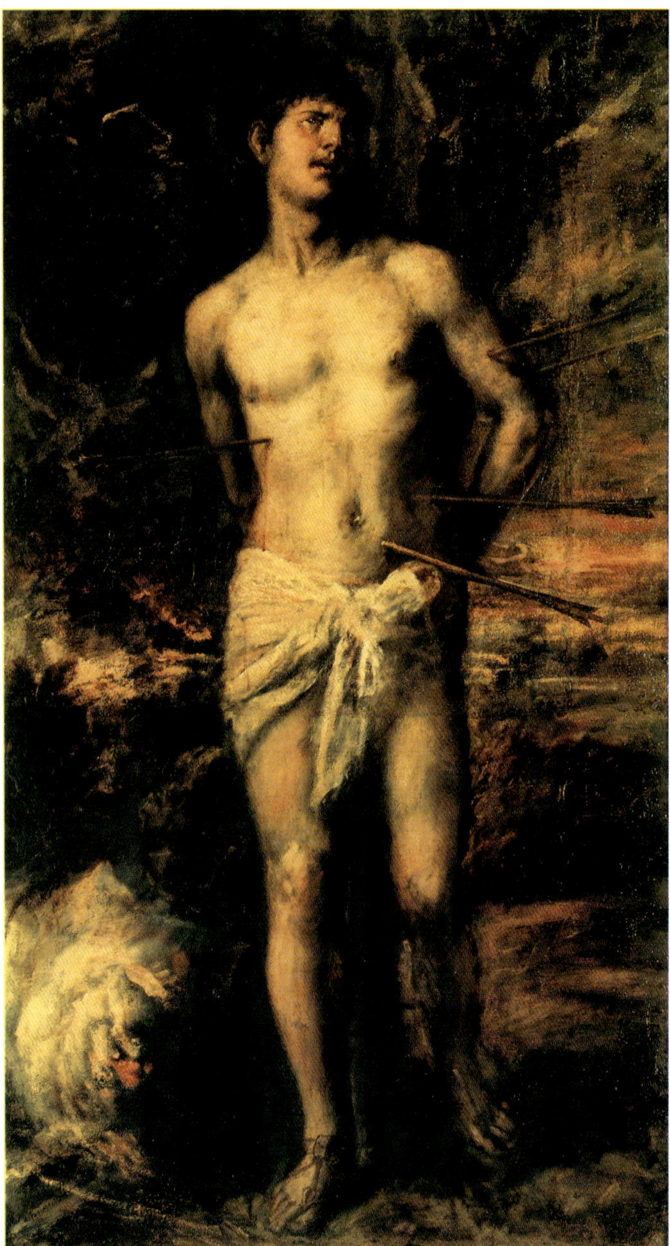

102. *Saint Sebastian (c. 1575)*
212x116 cm
St Petersburg, Hermitage

ject in Vienna represents Titian's first thoughts for this painting and it is here, more than in any other picture, that it is easy to imagine Titian giving the final touches to his work by rubbing in the pigments with his fingertips in the way recounted by Palma the Younger.

Titian's very last works were produced between 1575 and 1577. Two were official commissions: one, for the Doge's palace, depicting *Doge Antonio Grimani Kneeling before the Faith in the Presence of Saint Mark*, clearly carried out with the help of assistants and the second, which is entirely autograph, sent to Philip II. depicting *Spain Succouring Religion* and commemorating the participation of the Spanish fleet at the Battle of Lepanto. The remaining works of Titian's *oeuvre* belong to the final months and days of his life. For the most part they were in his studio at his death and were then sold off to various Venetian collectors by his son Pomponio. Amongst these were the hellish *Saint Sebastian* in St Petersburg, a masterpiece of painterly skill which reaches heights of virtuosity in the exceptional landscape background; the disturbing *Youth with Dogs* in Rotterdam, whose mysterious subject matter critics have failed to decipher; and the evocative *Shepherd and Nymph* in Vienna, streaked with glowing light.

An awareness of impending death weighs heavily on two paintings Titian was working on in the summer of 1576, when Venice was devastated by a terrible plague which was to kill his favourite son Orazio. The iconography of the *Flaying of Marsyas* in Kroměříž derives from a Giulio Romano fresco of the same subject in the Sala delle Metamorfosi of the Palazzo Te in Mantua, but Titian accentuates the terrifying savagery of the mythological scene through the churning background of ruddy-browns, and the gloomy colours fitfully lit by sudden flashes of light. The "hidden" meaning of the painting has been variously interpreted; however the presence of Titian himself, in the guise of King Midas, has favoured a reading of the painting as the painter's meditation on his own life and on his illusion that he could "transform material into precious painted images, an illusion extinguished by his final realization that artistic accomplishments are as nothing in the face of the misfortunes of history".

This was exactly the case with his *Pietà*, in the Venice Accademia, which Titian painted for the Chapel of Christ in the Frari church on the understanding that he would be buried there. But when the old painter died on the 27 August 1576 the painting was still incomplete; it passed into the hands of Palma the Younger who merely added

of light which appear in the small Saint Louis canvas.

Titian's connection with Philip II continued right up to the painter's final days. Amongst the last pictures sent to Spain was the important *Tarquin and Lucretia*, now in Cambridge. It displays remarkable invention in the breath-taking speed with which the action takes place, emphasised by the rivulets of streaming light in the foreground of the painting. It is probable that the canvas of the same sub-

103. *Youth with Dogs*
(c. 1575/1576)
99.5x117 cm
Rotterdam, Museum Boymans
van Beuningen

104. *Shepherd and Nymph*
(1575/1576)
150x187 cm
Vienna, Kunsthistorisches
Museum

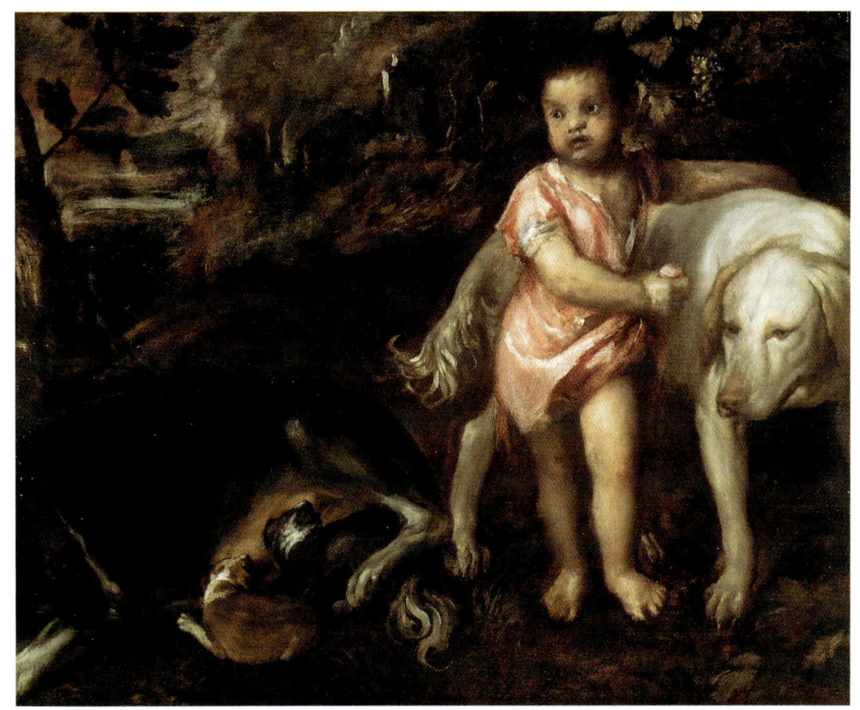

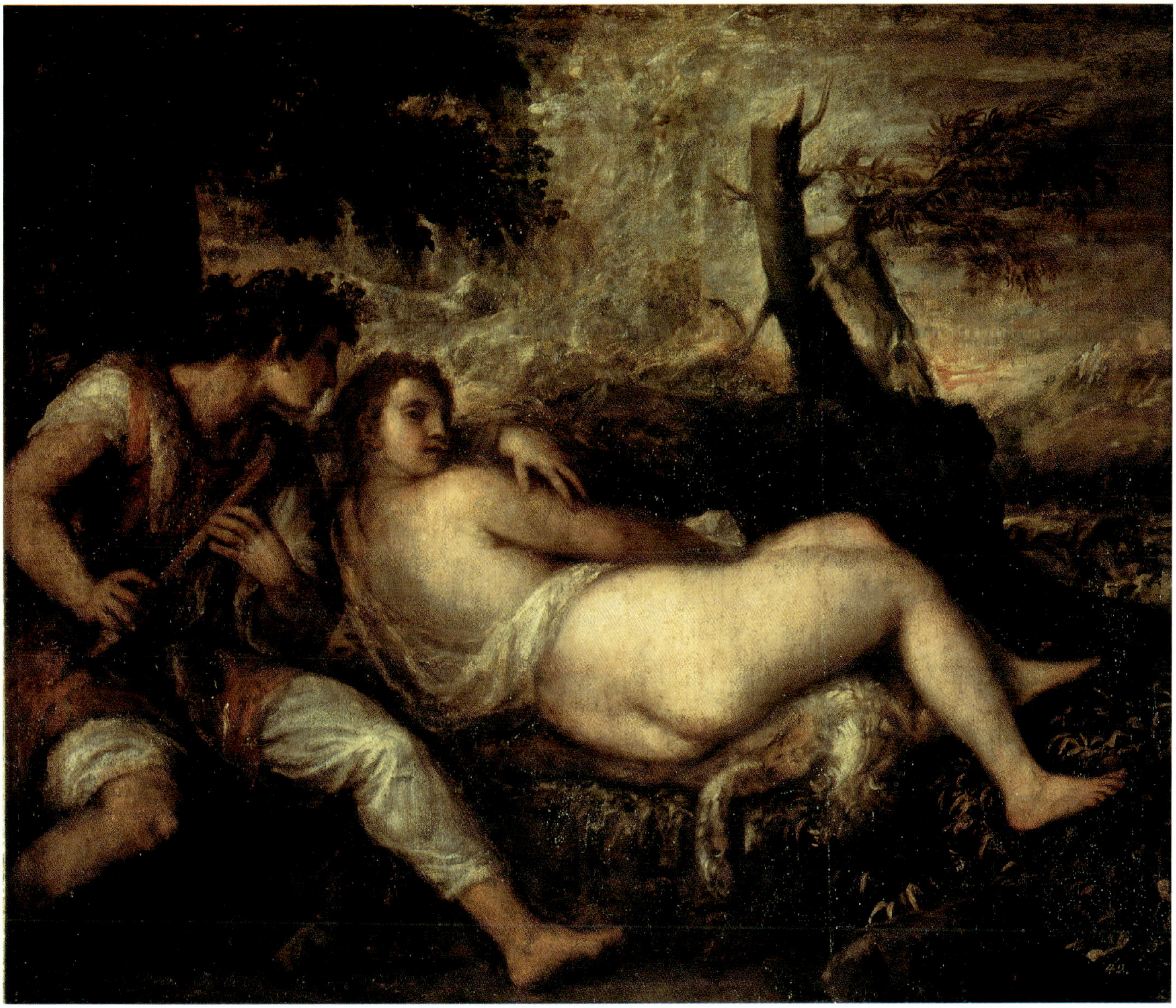

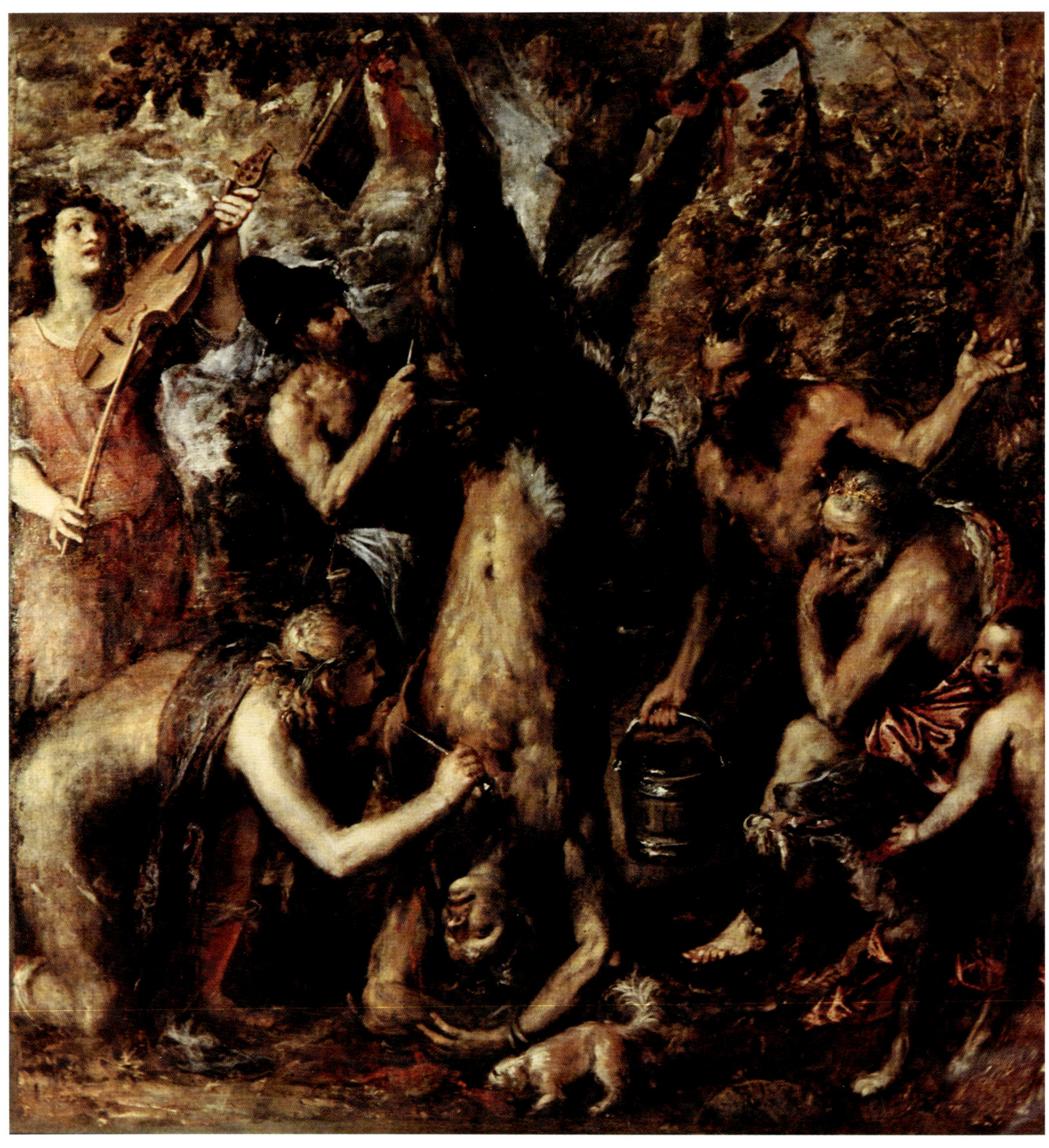

some glazing and the minimum of retouching. In
this grandiose canvas, which is centred on the
themes of death, the eucharistic sacrifice and resurrection, we can read the artistic testament of Titian. As in the other paintings from this period, the
Pietà is imbued with a feeling of intense drama, a
repressed anguish which is given vent in the tragic
figure of Mary Magdalene screaming her despair
and in details such as the horrendous lions' heads
(which serve as bases for the statues), symbolic of
the terrifying mysteries of the hereafter. And over
the whole canvas the brush and fingers of the old

105. The Flaying of Marsyas (1575/1576)
212x207 cm
Kroměříž, State Museum

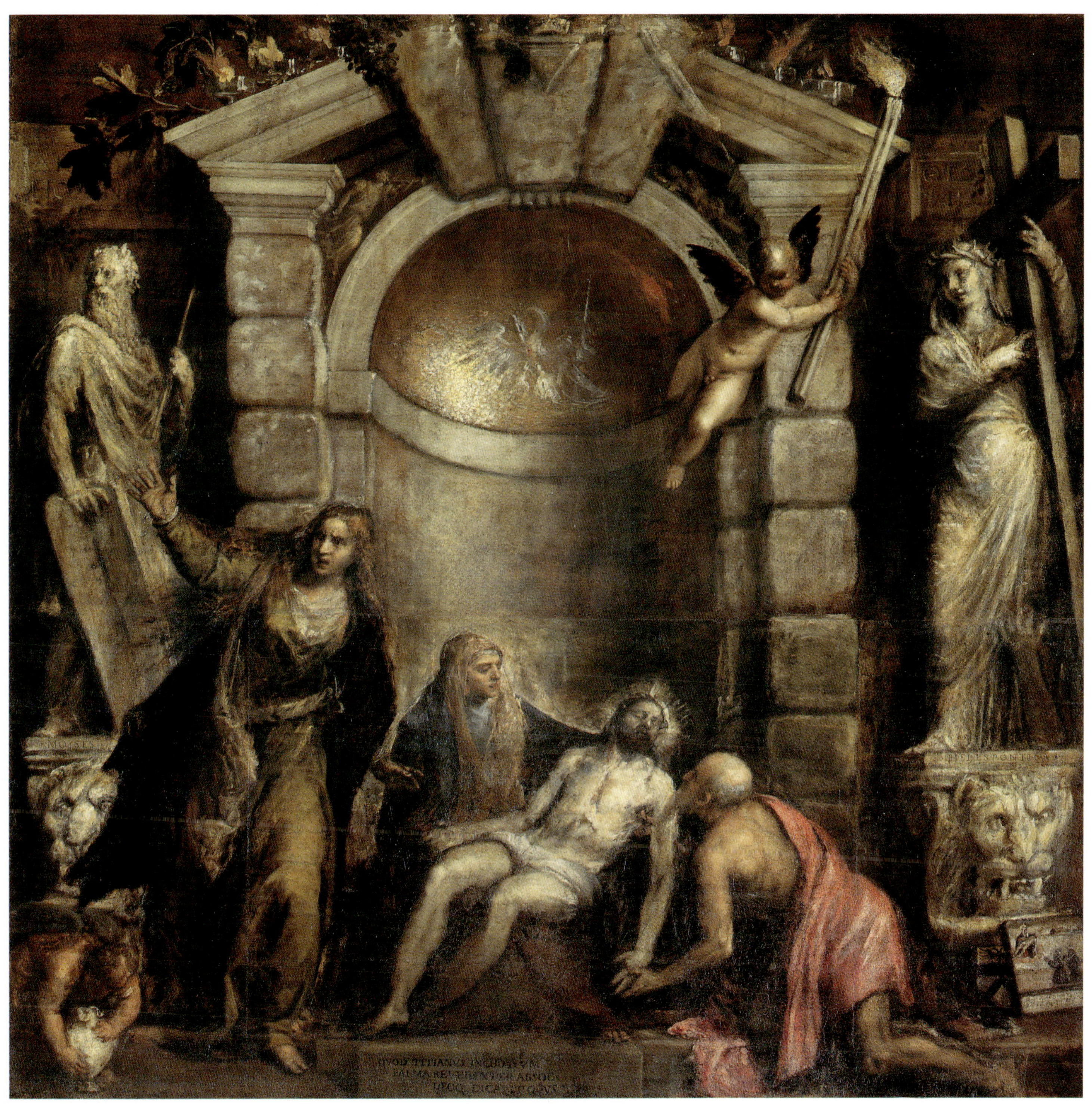

106. *Pietà (1576)*
353x348 cm
Venice, Academy Gallery

artist have skimmed tremulously, bestowing touches of light to the figures silhouetted against the silvery architectural backdrop.

Historical Events

1502 Victory of the Venetian and papal fleets over the Turks at Levkas.

1503 Julius II, newly elected to the papal throne, condemns the Venetian conquests in Romagna.

1504 Treaty of Blois between Louis XII of France and Emperor Maximilian against Venice.

1508 League of Cambrai against Venice.

1509 Venetians defeated at Agnadello by the armies of the League of Cambrai. Andrea Gritti retakes Padua and defends it from Imperial attack.

1510 Devastating plague in Venice.

1513 Pope Julius II dies; succeeded by Leo X.

1516 The Venetians retake Brescia after allying themselves with France against the papacy and Spain.

1519 Emperor Maximilian dies and his successor, Charles V, unifies the Empire with the kingdom of Spain.

1521 Doge Leonardo Loredan dies and is succeeded by Antonio Grimani.

1523 Doge Antonio Grimani dies and is succeeded by Andrea Gritti.
Venice allies herself with Charles V against France.
Clement VII is elected Pope.

1527 Sack of Rome carried out by the Imperial troops.

1528 Venice allies herself with France against Charles V.

1529 Treaty of Cambrai between France and Charles V; Venetian neutrality.
The Peace of Bologna ratifies the dominion of Spain over Italy.

1530 At Bologna Pope Clement VII crowns Charles V King of Italy and Holy Roman Emperor.

1534 Paul III ascends the papal throne.

1536 Another outbreak of the plague in Venice.

1538 Death of Andrea Gritti.
Defeated at the Battle of Prevesa, the Venetians lose the Peleponnese to the Turks.

1539 Pietro Lando elected Doge.
The wife of Charles V, Isabella of Portugal, dies in Toledo.

Titian's Life and Works

1488-90 Born at Pieve di Cadore.
1508-09 He works on the frescoes for the Fondaco dei Tedeschi.
1510-11 He works on the frescoes for the 'Scuola del Santo' in Padua.
Fête Champêtre (Louvre) and the *Interrupted Concert* (Pitti).
1513 After rejecting Pietro Bembo's invitation to go to Rome, Titian offers his services to the Venetian Republic, asking for the 'Senseria' of the Fondaco dei Tedeschi (the sinecure of the office of broker which carried with it status as offical painter).
He opens a workshop at San Samuele.
1516 Titian makes contact with the D'Este court and visits Ferrara. He is given the commission for the *Assumption*.
1517 On the death of Giovanni Bellini Titian obtains the 'Senseria'.
1518 Unveiling of the *Assumption*.
1519 He is given the commission for the *Pesaro Altarpiece*.
He travels to Ferrara to deliver the *Worship of Venus*.
1520 *Gozzi Altarpiece* (Ancona).
Another trip to Ferrara.
He works on the *Averoldi Polyptych*.
1522 He signs and dates the *Averoldi Polyptych*.
1523 He delivers the *Bacchus and Ariadne* to Alfonso d'Este in Ferrara.
He works in the Doge's Palace.
1524-25 Another sojourn in Ferrara.
1525 Marriage to Cecilia by whom he already has two sons.
1526 Unveiling of the *Pesaro Altarpiece*.
1528 He receives the commission for the *Martyrdom of Saint Peter Martyr* for the church of Santi Giovanni e Paolo.
1529 He meets Charles V at Parma.
1530 He delivers the *Saint Peter Martyr Altarpiece*.
Death of his wife Cecilia following the birth of a daughter, Lavinia.
1531 He works for Federico Gonzaga.
He moves to a house at Biri Grande, in the parish of San Canciano, where he will live for the rest of his life.
1533 At Bologna he meets Charles V who makes him a Count and a Knight of the Golden Spur. Titian declines the offer to move to Spain.
1536 He works for Francesco Maria della Rovere.
1537 The nuns of the convent of Santa Maria degli Angeli reject the *Annunciation* which Titian then gives to the Empress Isabella.
1538 He delivers the *Battle of Cadore*.
The sinecure of the 'Senseria' of the Fondaco dei Tedeschi is revoked.
Venus of Urbino.

Cultural Events

1500 Leonardo da Vinci is in Venice for a brief period.
Jacopo de' Barbari publishes the *Pianta di Venezia* (Map of Venice).
Carpaccio completes his *Life of Saint Ursula* paintings.

1501 Giovanni Bellini paints the *Portrait of Doge Loredan*.

1502-07 Carpaccio works on the cycle of paintings for San Giorgio degli Schiavoni.

1504 Giorgione's *Castelfranco Altarpiece*.
Luca Pacioli's treatise *De Divina Proportione* is published in Venice.

1505 Giovanni Bellini's *San Zaccaria Altarpiece*.
Lotto's *Saint Christine at the Tiverone*.

1506 Albrecht Dürer in Venice; he paints the *Madonna of the Rose Garlands*.
Death of Gentile Bellini.
Giorgione's *Tempest*.

1508 Giorgione works on the frescoes for the Fondaco dei Tedeschi.

1509 Sebastiano del Piombo delivers the organ wings for the church of San Bartolomeo.

1510 Death of Giorgione.
Carpaccio's *San Giobbe Altarpiece*.

1513 Giovanni Bellini's *San Giovanni Crisostomo Altarpiece*.

1514 Giovanni Bellini's *Feast of the Gods*.

1515 Death of Pietro Lombardo.

1516 Death of Giovanni Bellini.

1520 Pordenone frescoes the Malchiostro Chapel in Treviso Cathedral.

1520-21 Pordenone paints frescoes in Cremona Cathedral.

1524 Giulio Romano settles in Mantua.
Lotto executes the frescoes in Trescore.

1525 Pietro Bembo publishes his *Prose della volgar lingua*.

1526 Death of Carpaccio.

1527 Aretino and Sansovino take refuge in Venice following the Sack of Rome.

1529 Michelangelo visits Venice.
Jacopo Sansovino made overseer of San Marco.

1534 Bassano's *Flight into Egypt*.

1535 Pordenone and Schiavone take up residence in Venice.

1538 Pordenone's paintings for the Doge's Palace.

1545 Opening session of the Council of Trent.
Doge Pietro Lando dies and is succeeded by Francesco Donà.

1547 Victory of Charles V against the Protestants at Mühlberg.

1548 Imperial Diet held at Augsburg.

1549 Pope Paul III dies and is succeeded by Julius III.

1553 Prince Philip marries Mary Tudor in London.
Doge Francesco Donà dies and is succeeded by Marcantonio Trevisan.

1554 Doge Marcantonio Trevisan dies and is succeeded by Francesco Venier.

1556 Charles V abdicates and retires to the monastery of Yuste; the Imperial crown passes to Ferdinand I and the Spanish one to Philip II.
Another serious outbreak of plague in Venice.
Francesco Venier dies and Lorenzo Priuli is elected as his successor.

1558 Death of Charles V.

1559 The Peace of Cateau-Cambrésis puts an end to the religious conflict in Europe.
Lorenzo Priuli dies and is succeeded by Girolamo Priuli.

1563 Final session of the Council of Trent.

1566 Election of Pius V to the papacy.
Selim II ascends the Ottoman throne.

1567 Doge Girolamo Priuli dies and is succeeded by Pietro Loredan.

1570 The Turks conquer a large part of the island of Cyprus.
Pietro Loredan dies.

1571 Venice allies herself with Spain and the pope against the Turks.
Victory of the Christian fleet at the Battle of Lepanto.

1573 Separate peace with Selim II as a consequence of which the Venetians cede Cyprus to the Turks.

1575 Devastating plague in Venice which lasts until half way through the following year, resulting in over 50,000 deaths.

1539 *Presentation of Mary at the Temple.* He is given back the 'Senseria'.
1540 *Crowning with Thorns* (Louvre).
1541 *Alfonso D'Avalos Addressing his Troops* (Prado).
1542 *Portrait of Ranuccio Farnese* (Washington).
1543 *Portrait of Paul III Farnese* and *Isabella of Portugal.*
1544 Completes the paintings for the ceiling of Santo Spirito in Isola.
1545 He goes to Rome on the invitation of Alessandro Farnese.
1546 He is given honorary citizenship of Rome; he returns to Venice.
1548 He meets Charles V at Augsburg. *Portrait of Charles V on Horseback; Portrait of Prince Philip.*
1549 He paints the "damned" for Mary of Hungary (Prado).
1550 Summoned by Charles V, he returns to Augsburg.
1551 He returns to Venice where he is received into the Scuola di San Rocco.
1552 He begins to correspond with Prince Philip to whom he sends a number of paintings.
1553 *Venus and Adonis* and *Danaë* (Prado).
1554 He sends Charles V the *Trinity in Glory* (Prado).
1556 Death of Pietro Aretino.
1557 He forms part of the panel of judges who are to select a painter to decorate the ceiling of the Marciana Library — the commission goes to Paolo Veronese.
1558 *Crucifixion* for the Church of San Domenico, Ancona. Death of Charles V.
1559 Death of his brother Francesco. *Diana and Actaeon* and *Diane and Callisto* (Edinburgh).
1561 Death of his daughter Lavinia.
1562 *Rape of Europa* (Boston); *Annunciation* for the church of San Salvador.
1564 Trades in timber with the Duke of Urbino. Travels to Brescia.
1566 Requests the copyright to the prints made from his work by Cornelis Cort. He meets Giorgio Vasari who visits his studio. Together with Palladio and Tintoretto, he is made a member of the Florentine 'Accademia del Disegno'.
1568 *Portrait of Jacopo Strada* (Vienna).
1569 He requests that the 'Senseria' be passed to his son Orazio.
1570 *Tarquin and Lucretia* (Cambridge).
1571 In a letter to Philip II he claims to be ninety-five years old.
1575 Sends *Spain Succouring Faith* (Prado) to Philip II.
1576 Once again he asks Philip II payment for work done. *Pietà* (Venice) and *Flaying of Marsyas* (Kroměříž).
He dies on the 27 August and his house is ransacked

1539 Francesco Salviati and Giuseppe Porta arrive in Venice.
Pordenone dies in Ferrara.

1540 Savoldo's *Nativity.*

1541 Giorgio Vasari arrives in Venice. Lotto's *Saint Anthony distributing Alms.* Vasari executes a ceiling painting for the Palazzo Corner Spinelli.

1547 Tintoretto's *Last Supper.*

1548 Tintoretto's *Miracle of the Slave.*

1549 Lorenzo Lotto leaves Venice definitively.

1550 First edition of Vasari's *Lives of the Artists.*

1551 Paolo Veronese *Giustiniani Altarpiece.*

1553-56 Paolo Veronese, Ponchino and Zelotti decorate the ceilings of the 'Sala dei Dieci' in the Doge's Palace.

1558 Scarpagnino's *Golden Stairway* (Scala d'oro) in the Doge's Palace.

1560-61 Paolo Veronese's frescoes at the Villa Barbaro at Maser.

1561-62 Bassano paints the *Crucifixion* for the church of San Teonisto, Treviso.

1563 Paolo Veronese's *Marriage at Cana.*

1564 Tintoretto begins the decoration of the Scuola di San Rocco.

1566 Jacopo Sansovino's *Mars and Neptune* for the Doge's Palace.

1567 Dominikos Theotokopulos, called El Greco, arrives in Venice.

1568 Second edition of Giorgio Vasari's *Lives.*

1570 Death of Jacopo Sansovino. Publication of Andrea Palladio's *Four Books of Architecture.*

1571 Paolo Veronese's *Last Supper.*

1574 A fire destroys the 'Sala del Collegio' and the 'Sala del Senato' of the Doge's Palace with the loss of a great many paintings.

1575 Bassano's *Entombment.*

1576 El Greco moves to Spain.

1577 A second fire in the Doge's Palace destroys paintings by Giovanni and Gentile Bellini, the Vivarini, Carpaccio, Paolo Veronese, Tintoretto and Titian.

Bibliography

The literature on Titian is vast; the most comprehensive bibliography can be found in the catalogue, edited by M. Gambier, which accompanied the Titian exhibitions in Venice and Washington in 1990.
Here the bibliography is confined to what are considered the essential publications on Titian, with reference to the most important sources and general studies of the life and work of the painter; they are listed in chronological order. For brevity's sake the numerous important studies on individual paintings are not included and neither are general books on sixteenth-century Venetian painting.

G. VASARI, *Le vite de' più eccellenti Architetti, Pittori, e Scultori. . .*, Florence 1550 (2nd ed. enlarged; Florence 1568).

L. DOLCE, *Dialogo delle pittura intitolato l'Aretino*, Venice 1557.

G.M. VERDIZZOTTI, *Breve compendio della vita del famoso Tiziano Vecellio di Cadore*, Venice 1622.

C. RIDOLFI, *Le Maraviglie dell'Arte*, Venice 1648.

M. BOSCHINI, *Le ricche minere della Pittura veneziana*, Venice 1674.

S. TICOZZI, *Vite de' Pittori Vecelli di Cadore*, Milan 1817.

G.F. WAAGEN, *Life of Titian*, London 1854 (3 vols).

J.A. CROWE and G.B. CAVALCASELLE, *Titian, his Life and Times*, London 1877 (2 vols; Italian ed. Florence 1877-78).

B. BERENSON, *The Venetian Painters of the Renaissance*, New York and London 1894.

G. GRONAU, *Titian*, London 1921.

O. FISCHEL, *Tizian*, Stuttgart 1924.

W. SUIDA, *Tiziano*, Rome 1933.

Mostra di Tiziano, Venice 1935 (exhibition catalogue edited by N. Barbantini and G. Fogolari).

H. TIETZE, *Tizian. Leben und Werk*, Vienna 1936 (2 vols).

H. TIETZE, *Tizian*, Innsbruck 1949.

F. VALCANOVER, *Tutta la pittura di Tiziano*, Milan 1960 (2 vols).

A. MORASSI, *Tiziano*, Milan 1964.

R. PALLUCCHINI, *Tiziano* Florence 1969 (2 vols).

E. PANOFSKY, *Problems in Titian, mostly iconographic*, London 1969.

F. VALCANOVER, *Tiziano. L'opera completa*, (intro. by C. Cagli), Milan 1969.

E.H. WETHEY, *The complete Paintings of Titian*, London 1969-1975 (3 vols).

R. PALLUCCHINI, *Profilo di Tiziano*, Florence 1977.

Tiziano e il Manierismo europeo (ed. by R. Pallucchini), Florence 1978.

D. ROSAND, *Titian*, New York 1978 (Italian ed. Milan 1983).

A. GENTILI, *Da Tiziano a Tiziano. Mito e allegoria nella cultura veneziana del Cinquecento*, Milan 1980.

C. HOPE, *Titian*, London 1980.

Tiziano e Venezia (Proceedings of the international conference held in Venice in 1976), Vicenza 1980.

Da Tiziano a El Greco. Per la storia del Manierismo nel Veneto (exhibition catalogue edited by R. Pallucchini), Milan 1981.

T. PIGNATTI and F. PEDROCCO, *Tiziano. Tutti i dipinti*, Milan 1981 (2vols).

D. ROSAND, *Painting in Cinquecento Venice: Titian, Veronese, Tintoretto*, New Haven and London 1982.

M.A. CHIARI MORETTO WIEL, *Tiziano. Corpus dei disegni*, Milan 1989.

Tiziano (catalogue to the Venice and Washington exhibition), ed. by F. Valcanover, Venice 1990.

A. GENTILI, *Tiziano*, in "Art Dossier" 1990.

Index of Illustrations

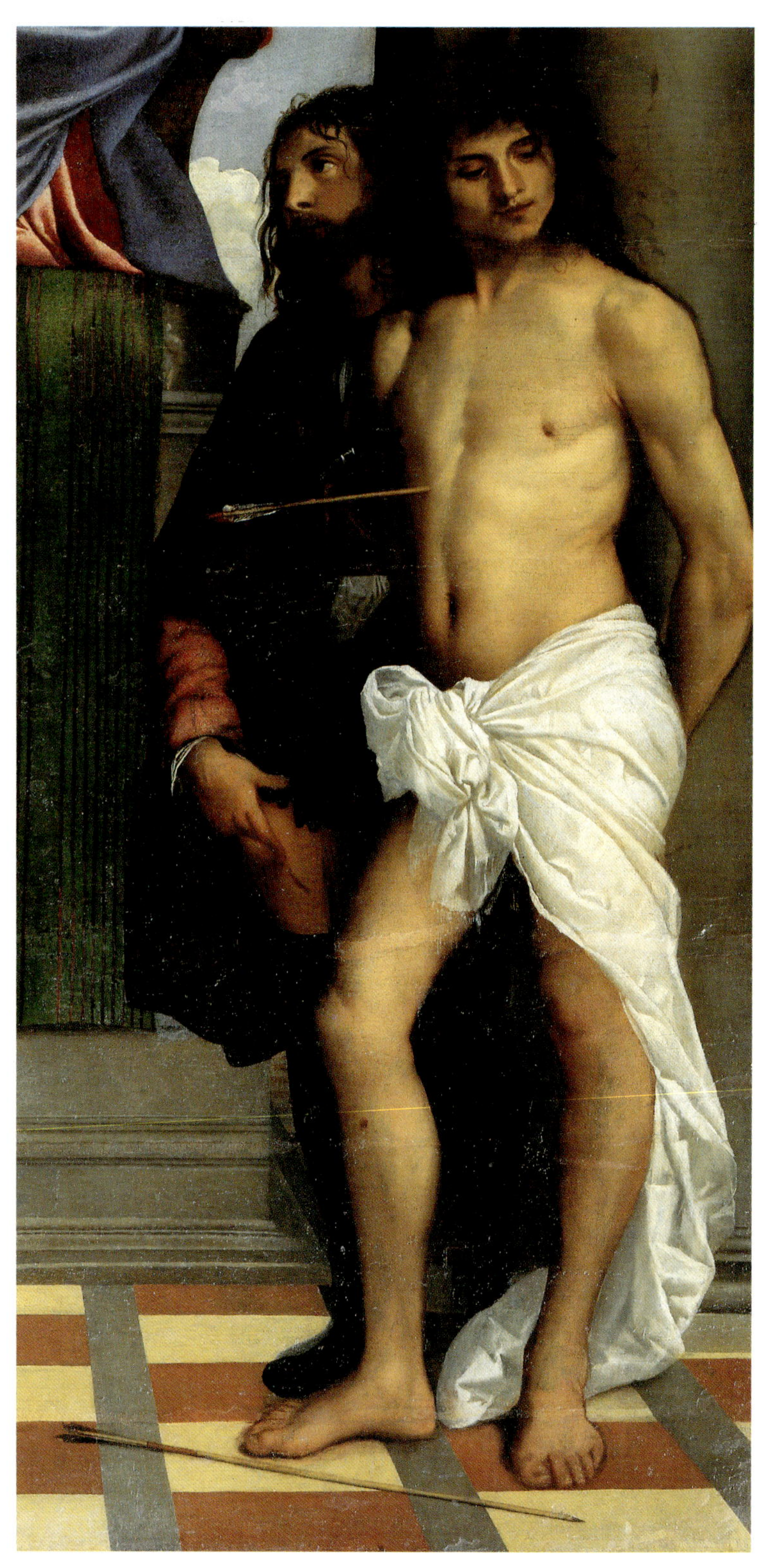